C O
P O C K

FISH
OF BRITAIN & EUROPE
PETER J MILLER • MICHAEL J LOATES

HarperCollins*Publishers*

Author's Preface

Fish are a familiar component of biodiversity in the seas and fresh waters of Europe. They are of intense economic, recreational, and natural history interest to millions of Europeans. However, at the same time, many species are under threat by over-exploitation in fisheries, water pollution and habitat destruction or obstruction. I hope that this pocket guide will serve to introduce the richness of European fish faunas, and help to strengthen concern for this resource, from the familiar inhabitants of local rivers and lakes to the less frequently encountered but equally fascinating species of offshore waters and to those straying from elsewhere. The beauty of both marine and freshwater species has been vividly and accurately depicted by Mick Loates, whose enthusiasm for fish life and close cooperation have contributed indispensably to the realization of this book.

For the past forty years, my interest in European fish has centred on the systematics and biology of the gobies, and, in these days of specialization, my thanks are due to the many experts in other groups who have given me advice, information and material over the years. I would also like to acknowledge support and encouragement from my wife Beryl during the work on this book.

Peter Miller
February 1997

Artist's Preface

Throughout the past quarter century I have studied fishes in their natural habitats from the awesome bulk of placid and inoffensive basking sharks off the South Devon coast of England, catching various members of the family Sparidae for study off Mediterranean North Africa and Aegean shores, the ostentatious livery of species from the mid-Pacific islands to the magnificent salmonids of New Zealand.

At the time of writing, when demands on world resources and recreation are taking a heavy toll on habitat, seriously depleting vulnerable species, by no means least fish stocks, it seems appropriate that a book such as this should be in the hands of anyone caring about aquatic environs.

For those identifying species from above or below water, or off the market slab, some notes on the colour plates should be observed. I have, to the best of my knowledge, portrayed typical specimens although both shape and coloration can differ considerably depending on water quality and nature and the fish's condition. Additionally, it should be noted that coloration is rapidly lost following capture; specimens in the market place are predisposed to lacklustre.

Where possible, I have obtained both live and freshly captured specimens, some of which were transferred to a home study aquarium. I found this particularly useful when studying the smaller cyprinids, postlarval and jack Pike, Stone Loach, sticklebacks, bullheads and percoids (although the latter species do not seem to adapt to the tank and should not be treated as suitable aquarium subjects). Observations of larger marine species were made at various laboratories, principally Plymouth Marine Aquarium. Some anatomical details were taken from specimens purchased in markets or off the fishmonger's slab whilst smaller species were collected from tidepools and brackish lagoons.

My thanks are due notably to the author, Peter Miller, for his invaluable assistance, Silja Swaby of Plymouth Marine Laboratory, Dr Peter Reay of the Department of Natural Sciences, Plymouth University, Bob Burridge of the Devon Birdwatching and Preservation Society for allowing access to vulnerable reedbeds for observation and collection of certain brackish species, and Myles Archibald (Head of Natural History, HarperCollins*Publishers*) for his co-operation, encouragement and patience throughout the production of this book. Finally to those friends who over the years have shared my enthusiasm by the water, the memories are indelible: Geoff Nicholls, companion of the 60s, Richard Hill, Derek 'Sedgie' Maw, Nigel de la Hay and more recently Brian Clarke and Dr Chris Cheeseman whose ethic on angling and conservation runs parallel to my own.

Mick Loates
Kingsbridge, South Devon 1997

HarperCollins*Publishers*, 77–85 Fulham Palace Road, London W6 8JB

10 9 8 7 6 5 4 3

04 03 02 01

Edited and pages made up by D & N Publishing, Lambourn Woodlands, Hungerford, Berkshire.
Colour reproduction by Colourscan, Singapore.
Printed and bound by Rotolito Lombarda, Italy.

Contents

INTRODUCING THE FISH

True fish are aquatic vertebrates that breathe by means of gills. Other animals that live in water are sometimes termed fish. However, shellfish and crayfish are not true fish because they do not possess a backbone. Whales and porpoises are vertebrates living permanently in water, but are mammals, breathing through lungs and suckling their young.

Jawless Fish

The earliest fish, from Silurian rocks, were the heavily armoured jawless ostracoderms. Today, such fish are represented by the much modified lampreys and Hagfish. These are eel-like, with a cartilaginous skeleton, and a persistent primitive body axis, the notochord. The mouth carries horny teeth unlike those of other vertebrates. There are no paired fins. Despite these and other primitive features, the feeding mechanisms are highly specialized, with a rasping suctorial mouth in the parasitic lampreys and a lateral bite in scavenging Hagfish.

Cartilaginous Fish

All the remaining fish have true jaws that are a modified front gill arch behind the original mouth.

Modern cartilaginous fish (elasmobranchs), comprising the sharks, rays and rabbit-fish, first appeared in the Devonian period. They have no bone in their cartilaginous skeleton. There is no cover (opercle) over the exposed gill slits, normally five, which are often preceded by a much smaller modified spiracle behind the eye. A prominent snout, with ventral mouth and nostrils, is also highly characteristic.

The more generalized sharks and dogfish have cylindrical bodies, gill slits on the side of the head and pectoral fins with a free leading edge. Angel sharks are true sharks, but are flattened like a ray.

The other major group of cartilaginous fish, the skates and rays, are adapted for bottom living, with their head and body flattened dorsoventrally, and greatly expanded wing-like pectoral fins. Stingrays, eagle rays and cow-nosed rays have whiplike tails, with one or more barbed spines. Devil rays, secondarily pelagic off the bottom, are the largest of the group. Sawfish and guitarfish are shark-like but true rays.

In modern seas, there are still some representatives of another group of cartilaginous fish once common in the Carboniferous period. These are the bizarre rabbit-fish, or 'King of the Herring', living offshore and in the deep sea. They have large heads, a body tapering to a long pointed tail and toothplates rather than teeth. The gills are under an opercle.

Bony Fishes

Comprising the major element of modern fish diversity, the bony fishes have their gill slits covered by an opercle, enclosing a gill chamber which opens to the rear and below. In the Devonian, the bony fish split into two branches: the sarcopts (Sarcopterygii) and actinopts (Actinopterygii). The sarcopt fish began our own lineage from the bony fish, with the modern lungfish and coelacanths as famous survivors.

Today, among actinopts, a better-known living group of early origin are the sturgeons and paddle fish. The sturgeons include the largest bony fish. After sturgeons, the stem actinopts produced another major radiation of fish, the holosteans, with gars and bowfins remaining in fresh waters of North America.

Teleosts

By far the majority of living bony fish form a group called the teleosts, with about 25,000 species. They are distinguished by the outwardly symmetrical tail fin and possession of a swimbladder, a hydrostatic (buoyancy) organ used to achieve neutral buoyancy and facilitate movement in midwater. The classification and evolutionary history of the teleosts is very complex but it is possible to recognize two major grades of form and function.

The more generalized grade has typically a fusiform (spindle-shaped) body, with low-set pectoral fins and the pelvic fins in the middle of the body, just before the anus. The median fins have jointed branched rays as the principal elements, and there is only one dorsal fin, although a tiny adipose fin, lacking rays, may be present on the tail.

The basic teleosts are the aruanas, elephant fish and allies, and the boneheads. Also relatively low on the teleost tree, herrings are marine, schooling forms, typically plankton feeding, with long gill rakers. The most important group of freshwater fish (Ostariophysi) includes the carps, as well as the characins (tetras, piranhas), loaches, and catfish. In the more generalized types, such as the Carp, the swimbladder is divided into two chambers, with the anterior one acting as a resonating chamber and linked to the inner ear by a series of tiny bones (Weberian ossicles). Hearing acuity is thereby greatly improved. The tropical tarpons are at the start of another evolutionary series which is believed to have given rise to the eels and gulpers. Although differing so markedly in appearance, tarpons and eels share a leaf-like 'leptocephalus' larva.

Salmons, migratory and freshwater, and the pikes, form a generalized starting point for the higher teleosts. Early in teleost history, the depths of the sea were colonized. Among deep-sea fish, the stomiatoids are a major group, including the flattened tiny marine Hatchet Fish and the elongate Viperfish, all with a double row of light organs along the lower edge of the body.

A somewhat higher level of the teleosts includes the cod-like fishes, within which the cods are unusual among teleosts in having three dorsal and two anal fins, and a tail fin which is internally as well as externally symmetrical, possibly derived from the tapering tail in the related rat-tails or grenadiers. Classified near the cods, stargazers and angler fish show a trend for modification of the first dorsal fin into a fishing rod, to lure fish into a capacious mouth.

The main grade of higher teleosts is the spiny-rayed form (Acanthomorphs). Typically, in these, pectoral fins are sited higher on the side, and pelvic fins are shifted forwards, to lie below the pectoral fins. The body is often deeper and flatter. All these changes enhance manoeuvrability. Spiny rays occur in the front of the dorsal and anal fins.

The first offshoot from this acanthomorph level comprises the sandsmelts and toothed carps. Opahs and flying fish are another early line, adapting to oceanic life, which also includes the ribbonfish. Sticklebacks mark another side branch, leading to the more bizarre pipefish and seahorses. The generalized oval body and spiny anterior dorsal rays are seen in the squirrel fish, John Dories and berycids. The scorpaeniforms are a large group beginning with the viviparous redfish, through gurnards and bullheads, to the seasnails and lumpsuckers.

Much more diverse, the mass of perch-like fish and their derivatives form the bulk of higher teleosts. Generalized percids, such as the horse-mackerels and groupers, grade into groups like seabreams and wrasses. These have similar body form but various dental modifications. More of this diversity includes the pelagic dolphin fish, the bottom-living red mullet, venomous weever fish, burrowing sandeels, and even the sharksuckers. Above this radiation, there are found a number of specialized suborders, including dragonets and mandarins, gobies, blennies, and the contrasting tunnies and flatfish. Finally, the plectognath fish, with triggerfish and pufferfish, culminate in the oceanic sunfish, the largest teleosts.

HOW FISH LIVE

Swimming

Fish move to find food or mates, and to migrate or flee. There are different swimming methods for different ways of life, but the basic principles of fish locomotion are the same for all.

The muscles involved in typical swimming are the axial series, forming the 'fillet' along each side of the backbone. These comprise cone-like segmental blocks (myotomes). Several such cones are seen cut through on the surface of a tuna steak. The muscle fibres of each myotome attach to sheets of connective tissue separating the faces of each myotome. Laterally, these sheets are attached to the skin, and, internally, to the vertebrae. Their outer edges form the thin white lines which delimit the myotomes on the surface of a skinned fish.

Contraction of these axial muscles begins at the front of the body and passes rearwards, alternating on each side of the fish. Because the vertebral column is flexible from side to side, but not compressible along its length, a series of waves of lateral bending pass towards the tail and, in effect, push against the water, driving the fish forward by a sculling or propeller-blade effect. Side-to-side amplitude of the wave increases towards the tail, so that the caudal fin, as the final propulsive surface, typically provides most thrust. Water hinders movement by the effect of drag. Skin slime reduces frictional drag, and scale structure is also significant. Typically, to minimize drag under moderate speeds, the fish body is fusiform (spindle-shaped). Caudal fin shape also affects drag: high 'aspect ratio' forked or sickle-shaped fins minimize this.

Stability of the moving fish may be affected by pitching (vertical dipping and rearing), yawing (swinging from side to side), and rolling (listing to each side), all of which can be controlled by the fins. The paired fins of fish are the pectoral and pelvic (ventral) fins, corresponding to the fore and hind limbs of land vertebrates. The median unpaired fins are the dorsal, one or two, even three, along the back, with a small rayless adipose dorsal fin on the tail in some teleosts. The tail fin of the cartilaginous fishes and lower bony fishes has an upturned axis, but, in teleosts, it is externally symmetrical. On the underside, there is usually a single anal fin behind the anus. In elasmobranchs, the fins have rigid cartilaginous supports, but teleost fins are flexible, the bony fin rays being separated by membrane and controlled by sets of tiny muscles. Teleost fins can thus be spread, collapsed or waved.

All the fins control rolling, median fins (dorsal, anal, caudal) yawing, and the paired fins (pectoral and pelvic) pitching. Conversely, the fins can be used to control direction of movement. In the higher teleosts, such as the perches, the deeper body, forward shift of the pelvic fins to below the pectorals, and the higher pectorals on the sides of the body, all increase manoeuvrability. A longer body, such as that of the pike, is stabilized by small, rearwardly located dorsal and anal fins, like the feathers of a dart.

In the average teleost, swimming is slow or by intermittent bursts, with propulsion based on a relatively broad, rounded or truncate caudal fin. For the sustained swimming activity of watercolumn feeders, such as the tunas and horse-mackerels, further specialization improves energy conservation in movement. Streamlining is enhanced by adaptations in the shape of the solidly muscular body and of the pectoral and caudal fins, and by narrowing of the caudal wrist, while a series of tiny accessory finlets behind the dorsal and anal fins serve to reduce drag. Lateral keels on the caudal wrist aid manoeuvrability, greatly reducing the turning circle. Without appreciable body waves, nearly all thrust in such fishes is provided by the characteristic lunate caudal fin, of high aspect ratio, operating at high frequency. For sustained swimming, the musculature contains a high proportion of red fibres, familiar in tuna meat. Swimming speeds may be high, with Blue-finned Tuna reaching up to 90 kph.

Elongate bottom-living fish, such as eels, with an increased number of myotomes and vertebrae, swim with pronounced body waves as the prime source of movement. Such eel-like wriggling is also effective on land. Another swimming technique is shown by seahorses, where the body is protected within a rigid armour of bony plates, with fewer myotomes and vertebrae. Here, swimming is achieved by vigorous movement of the short pectorals and the dorsal fins, and the tail region is typically prehensile.

Feeding

By feeding, the fish obtains energy and material to fuel and advance all its life processes. The feeding behaviour and digestive systems of fish show great variety in keeping with many different ecological niches.

Modern jawless fish have highly modified feeding habits. In lampreys, the rounded mouth is used to rasp and suck the skin and tissues of other fish. This is done by means of horny teeth around the mouth and on the tongue, and helped by an anti-coagulant 'saliva'. The semifluid intake passes into a narrow gullet and gut which bypasses the gill pouches to prevent loss of the fluid diet in respiratory water currents. Hagfish, searching on the sea bed, have developed a lateral bite, with enlarged horny teeth. Locating by scent and taste, rather than vision, Hagfish feed on invertebrates and carrion, or can bite and bore into the body of a moribund fish.

In the jawed fish, true teeth occur on the jaws, and there are no salivary glands. In the pharynx, the inner face of each gill arch is lined by gill rakers. These prevent food loss through the gill slits and in many instances are actually part of the feeding complex, retaining small food items such as plankton. A short but muscular gullet opens into a distinct stomach in most fishes. The accessory organs of pancreas, gall bladder and bile duct are of universal occurrence. The liver is large and lobulated, reddish-brown but paler in herbivores and cultivated fish.

The jaws of cartilaginous fishes are lined with parallel rows of teeth which replace one another after wear or loss. The teeth of carnivorous sharks are typically triangular and may have serrated edges, while in the rays, the teeth form a pavement which is flattened and very close-set for those species which need to crush the shells of molluscs. All cartilaginous fishes have a short intestine that contains the spiral valve, formed from a spiral fold of intestinal lining which becomes fused along its free edge. This greatly increases gut surface area.

Most teleosts use the buoyant effect of water to feed on relatively small food items, sucking these in when the mouth is opened and expanded, often by protrusion of the jaws. In extreme cases, such as the John Dory, a vast tube is created to engulf the prey. This is achieved by the mobility of upper jaw bones, which are slid forwards and swung outwards. Similar mechanisms have evolved independently in such groups as the cyprinids and the higher teleosts. Teleost teeth are usually small, in several rows, but vary between species with diet and are sometimes enlarged. They occur on the jaws, and on other bones in the roof of the mouth and on the rigid tongue in lower teleosts, as well as on upper and lower plates at the rear of the pharynx. The plectognaths, such as puffers, have tooth-plates instead of individual teeth in the jaws. In cyprinids, there are no teeth and food is crushed in the pharynx by bony processes (pharyngeal teeth) biting upwards against a horny pad on the underside of the skull.

At the start of the intestine, many teleosts have small blind tubes (pyloric caeca), from one to well over a hundred in salmonids and mackerel. The length of the gut is related to diet, being much longer in herbivores.

Fish diets range from entirely animal to plant material and detritus. Feeding behaviour differs accordingly, from placid grazing to infrequent violent acts of predation. There is also daily and seasonal rhythm in feeding activity and consumption of food, and feeding migrations of greater or lesser extent may occur. During these, much oily storage material may be deposited in the liver or elsewhere to supply energy for overwintering or reproduction.

Breathing

Fishes breathe water to obtain oxygen for use in mobilizing energy for metabolism. In fish, the gills act as through-flow organs where oxygen is absorbed from the water into the blood which circulates through the gill filaments. In a reverse direction, waste products, such as carbon dioxide and ammonia, are discharged from the gills into the same water.

Water contains relatively little dissolved oxygen, so that the gills must receive an adequate and rapid supply of water. However, the muscular work required to move water over the gills is considerable, since water is about one thousand times as heavy as air and about one hundred times more viscous. At rest, over ten per cent of the oxygen uptake of a fish might thus be needed just for the task of getting more. When oxygen is depleted in the water, the amount of oxygen needed merely for the muscular effort of pumping more water may be impossible to obtain, and the fish will asphyxiate.

The jawless and jawed fishes differ greatly in gill operation. Jawless fish have muscular gill pouches lying inwards of the supporting skeleton. In jawed fish, there are simple gill slits, and the gill filaments are attached to the outer side of the skeletal arches. There are basically six slits, but the first persists only as the spiracle in sharks and rays, so that normally there are five functional slits. In sharks and rays, these are exposed along the side of the head, and each carries on its outer free edge a skin fold acting as a valve-like cover for the gill slit behind. Teleost gill slits are covered by the gill-cover or opercle, enclosing the opercular chamber which opens behind and below, and whose rear edge is the hard anterior rim of the bony girdle carrying the pectoral fins. From the front and rear face of each gill arch, vertical lines of long flattened filaments project. These are pink because of their dense capillary blood supply.

To breathe, water is drawn into the mouth of the teleost by expansion of the jaws and lowering of the mouth floor. Resistance of the gills prevents any reverse flow from the opercular chamber on their other side. With the mouth closed, the water is then forced through the gills by alternately either raising the mouth floor (buccal pressure pump, increasing pressure before the gills) or expanding the opercular cavity (opercular suction pump, reducing pressure behind the gills). Folds of skin inside the jaws act as valves to prevent loss of water out through the mouth and a similar flap, edging the gill cover, permits only outflow to the exterior from the opercular chamber. Coordination of these pumping movements maintains a continuous flow of water over the gills. Smaller fish breathe more frequently than larger individuals; at rest, sticklebacks and minnows may pump at up to 150 times per minute, while tench respire no more than about 60. More active species like herring have rates around 120, while sedentary bottom-living fishes show much slower rates, down to 12-20 in the dragonet. Active swimmers, such as mackerel and the tunas, use a passive means for gill ventilation, which takes advantage of the fish's movement through the water. They swim with the mouth open and the gill chambers expanded, thereby saving the energy which might otherwise be needed for pumping. However, fish like these can be suffocated if prevented from swimming. Stream fish may also passively ventilate the gills with mouth and opercles held open while the fish holds station against the water current. Under stress, fish will gasp at or near the surface, but the Weather Loach actually swallows air and absorbs oxygen through modified parts of the gut wall.

Floating

The solid tissues of a fish's body, mostly bone and muscle, are somewhat denser overall than water, so that fish have a natural tendency to sink. However, to explore the water column off the bottom, and to do this with minimum effort, fish rise and maintain themselves in midwater by means of lift generated in two main ways.

The simpler source is 'dynamic', produced during forward swimming by merely angling of the paired fins to act as hydrofoils. The pectoral fins are most important for this purpose, although the broad wedge-like snout in sharks can generate significant lift. Fishes which swim actively for other purposes, such as the pelagic sharks and the tunas, employ this method. 'Static' lift conserves more energy. In various ways, the overall density of the fish may be reduced so that lift is achieved by approach to neutral buoyancy, such as by storage of low-density lipids in the body. Shark liver oil provides about five- to six-times the buoyancy of an equal weight of pure water, and may reach a quarter of adult weight.

Much greater scope for vertical activity is seen in the teleosts, which achieve neutral buoyancy by means of a gas float, so that the fish needs no mechanical energy to maintain position off the bottom. This hydrostatic organ is the swimbladder, found only in teleosts and derived from a primitive lung. The gas-filled swimbladder occupies about 5 per cent of total body volume in marine fishes, and somewhat more (about 7 per cent) in freshwater fishes. To maintain neutral buoyancy, it is necessary to alter volume (by inflation or deflation), as this changes with water pressure at different depths. Thus, descent from the surface to 10 m will reduce volume by a half, as pressure increases from about one to two atmospheres. In more generalized teleosts, gas content can be altered by swallowing or voiding air along an open duct. In the more specialized closed swimbladder, gas is secreted or absorbed through regions of the wall (the gas-gland and the oval).

The gas gland is in the anterior ventral part of the swimbladder, and may also be found in many fish with an open swimbladder duct. For inflation, gas is liberated from the blood in a network of capillaries, into the cavity of the swimbladder, sometimes against a considerable pressure differential (even up to two thousand times).

Gas is retained within the swimbladder because of the impermeability of the walls, a property enhanced by a guanine layer, a nitrogenous excretory product, which imparts a silvery appearance to the swimbladder. The actual gases are oxygen, nitrogen and carbon dioxide; in shallow water fishes, they are often in similar proportions to that of air, but a number of deep-sea fish have a much higher oxygen composition. In carps, only nitrogen is present.

The swimbladder is often reduced in bottom-living teleosts, like intertidal gobies and clingfishes. For pelagic species, which may undertake extensive vertical migrations for feeding, the relative slowness of gas adjustment to swimbladder volume may be disadvantageous, and in scombroids the swimbladder is also small or absent (as in mackerel). Many oceanic mesopelagic species, especially the abundant lanternfishes, perform vertical migrations of several hundred metres during the day, in the course of which major adjustment of swimbladder volume would not be feasible. Such species can replace swimbladder gas with low density lipid, reduce body density in other ways, or employ dynamic lift. In non-ascending species in deeper water, this drawback is less important, and swimbladders may persist in species down to the greatest depths, with little need for adjustment against enormous pressures. Under abnormal vertical movement, notably when brought to the surface in a trawl, the swimbladders of deep-sea fish expand to destructive size, protruding the stomach from the mouth or bursting.

Regulating Body Fluids

Although essential for gas exchange, gills are also liabilities. To obtain oxygen, the gills must be semipermeable. In water, a difference in concentration between solutions on either side of a semipermeable membrane generates osmotic pressure. This causes water to flow from the more dilute to the more concentrated solution. Also, an ionic component will diffuse across the membrane into the less concentrated solution. Unless the fish can control these processes, its body fluids are likely to alter in their water and ionic (salt) content beyond the limits for survival, whether the surrounding water is salt or fresh, since the internal concentration in both freshwater and marine fishes is intermediate between these two extremes. The two organs involved in relieving the problem are the gills and the kidneys. Fish kidneys are elongate, below the vertebral column. Urine is discharged at an opening behind the anus, sometimes on a urogenital papilla. In fish, the kidneys are not an important site for nitrogenous excretion. The main excretory product in fish is ammonia, and this is rapidly lost through the gills.

Marine teleosts are internally more dilute than the surrounding sea, with body fluid concentrations about one quarter to one third that of seawater. Consequently, there is loss of water from the fish by osmosis through the gills, and this is counteracted by continuous drinking of seawater. The problem is also compounded by absorption of salt from this water, and by diffusion of sodium ions into the blood stream through the gills.

However, marine fish can maintain their less concentrated body fluid by active excretion of excess salt at special salt secreting 'chloride' cells in the gills. These secrete the major ions of sodium and chloride, while the kidney eliminates merely magnesium, sulphate and other ions, only about 10 per cent of the salts in seawater.

In fresh waters, the problem is completely different. Here the fish's body fluid, similar in concentration to that of marine fish, now has a higher osmotic pressure than the surrounding fresh water, and water will move into the body across the gills and skin. Freshwater teleosts must therefore excrete large amounts of inflowing water, as a copious urine through the kidneys. Although this is very dilute, so much is discharged that it could leach valuable salts from the body. These can be made up by absorption of ions from water as it is pumped over the gills, involving the same cell type as the salt-secreting cell in marine fish.

Many fishes are euryhaline (tolerant of a wide range of salinities) or migrate from the sea to fresh water, or vice versa, during their life-history. Fishes such as eels and sticklebacks take one to two days to change from one system of water control to the other, reversing their response to the outside medium, including uptake or excretion of ions.

Sharks and rays, the cartilaginous fishes, which are almost entirely marine, employ a different technique for water regulation. Body fluid ionic concentration is held at the usual one-third of that of the surrounding sea, but water loss is prevented by raising the overall concentration to that of seawater by retaining large amounts of nitrogenous waste products, chiefly urea. Because overall blood concentration is slightly higher than seawater, elasmobranchs do not need to drink but can obtain water by osmosis through the gills.

Sensing

The sense organs of fishes are geared to the physical properties of water. The special sense organs are the eye, the inner ear (without any external trace), the system of lateral-line canals, and the olfactory sac, with nostrils on the snout. There are also taste and smell buds over the skin, as well as nerve endings in the skin and swimbladder, responding to touch, temperature, and pressure. In air, it is possible to distinguish smell from taste but in water this distinction becomes less obvious.

In the jawed fish, the olfactory sacs are paired on either side of the snout, opening to the surface of the snout. Inside there are folds or processes carrying the sensory tissue. Water passes through the sac during swimming, jaw movement or by ciliary action. Fish have great sensitivity to traces of organic chemicals, including blood, and homing salmon may distinguish their own rivers by smell. Chemicals can be secreted for communication (pheromones), including sex steroids in courtship and alarm substances from damaged skin. Taste-buds occur not only on the mouth and pharynx, but also over the surface of the head, body and fins, especially on barbels in such fish as the rocklings and on the mobile pectoral rays of gurnards. Touch is important for bottom-living fish with suckers, and for remoras on meeting the body of a shark or ray.

In water, higher frequency waves of mechanical energy travel further and more consistently than in air, and are detected by the fish's inner ear in 'hearing'. Lower frequency waves are received by the lateral-line system as 'vibrations', a 'distance-touch sense' for short-range disturbances. The fish ear is encased within the skull, and in teleosts contains sizeable ear-stones (otoliths) of calcium carbonate.

In at least a quarter of all modern teleosts, the swimbladder is used as a resonating chamber or hydrophone to enhance acuity of hearing. Various kinds of link-up to the inner ear are found. Carp and their relatives have an hour-glass shaped swimbladder, with the anterior chamber linked to the inner ear by a chain of three small bones, the Weberian ossicles. Such fishes have sharper hearing and better pitch discrimination. Conversely, many fish produce sound, for schooling, territoriality and courtship, by swimming movements, gas release from a swimbladder, friction of one hard part on another or even by snapping skull and coronet in mating seahorses. The swimbladder is drummed by muscular action in cod, gurnards, and other species.

The lateral-line system is a series of perforated tubes under the skin, which run over the head and body, notably along the lateral midline. In some teleosts, lateral-line canals may be greatly reduced with exposure of free neuromast papillae, especially in gobies. The lateral-line system of a fish detects current-like disturbances caused by other fishes, which might be prey or predators, and also those from its own movement relative to obstacles.

Electrical stimuli are conducted in water, and many fish have electroreceptors. Receptors in cartilaginous fishes are noticeable as tiny pits over the snout. These are extremely sensitive, and can even detect the small DC fields from the muscles of prey organisms. Probably for this reason, sharks sometimes mistakenly attack submarine electric cables. Electric generation in most cases is based on muscle tissue converted into disc-like electroplates, stacked like coins. Among European species, there are weakly electric fish, such as skates and rays (Thornback up to 4 V), using the tissue along the tail. In contrast, electric rays, with powerful organs in their wings, generate high potentials (up to 220 V) for stunning prey or attackers.

Vision permits the most detailed recording of surroundings and instant reception of changes, based on the intensity and wavelength (colour) of light. Colours and even the pattern of letters can be discriminated by teleosts. In water, the best shape for the lens of the eye is spherical, with a short focal length, and the lens tends to protrude through the pupil, giving fish eyes a characteristic appearance. Focus adjustment (accommodation) in fishes is done by moving the lens, not changing its shape as in man. Cartilaginous fish are long-sighted, and pull their more flattened lens forward by a small muscle inside the eye-ball in front of the lens. Teleosts are mostly short-sighted, and pull the lens backwards by a muscle from the retina.

Fishes in the deep sea, where light is filtered out or becomes entirely of biological origin, exhibit bizarre features such as tubular eyes, and may also emit light from luminescent organs (photophores). Such bioluminescence may serve to conceal the fish (against the illuminated ceiling of the sea down to about 1000 m) or form part of mating, schooling or predation strategies.

Behaviour

Behaviour is the muscular activity by which the fish explores, survives, feeds and reproduces. It results from an interaction between outside stimuli and the internal state of the fish.

The internal state produces behaviour to satisfy basic needs, like hunger. Sex hormone level in the mature fish promotes reproductive behaviour in the breeding season. Rhythmic behaviour on a daily basis is found in many species, such as the evening 'swim' of herrings and the daytime activity, with sleep at night, by wrasse. Nocturnal fish, such as morays, reverse this pattern, while activity by shore fish, such as the Shanny, is related to high tide. The vertical migration around nightfall by many deep-sea fish is another example.

Outside stimuli which elicit behaviour are both physical and biological. Simple responses include movement and orientation of the body in response to gravity, light, electrical fields, substrate contact and water current, as well as to many chemicals, sometimes as part of homing behaviour.

Reaction to individuals of other species may lead to feeding behaviour, escape or defence of territory. Other associations between species can be mutually beneficial, as in 'cleaning' of larger fish by small wrasse. The most obvious example of behavioural interaction between individuals of the same species is schooling. This may comprise enormous numbers of individuals but is leaderless yet mutually coordinated, with stereotyped behaviour and positioning between individuals. Schooling behaviour is seen in perhaps as many as five thousand teleost species and such fishes may also possess colour patterns, such as banding and spots, designed to act as 'sign stimuli' for coordination of movement with their fellows. School shape may be characteristic for a particular species and may permit identification of species from an image on fishing sonar.

Among the possible benefits of schooling behaviour are that mucus lost into the water tends to reduce frictional drag as the group moves forwards, and that the discovery of food is more likely in company than alone. Many species, such as sticklebacks, school more obviously on the approach of a predator, and being part of a school not only reduces the probability of individual capture, but also increases the chance of detecting predators, with transmission of warning through the school. A large tightly integrated school could also deter a predator by resembling a single enormous organism. In the last resort, a temporary random scatter of the school after an attack may confuse the predator.

In fishes which do not school so consistently, behaviour by members of the same species may be more combative, often seen in display, by expanding the body outline through arching, fin erection or spreading the opercles. Retreat may then be followed by submissive behaviour, denoted by changes in posture or coloration. A dominance or pecking order is often formed in a group of fish, and position in the hierarchy in turn affects success in feeding, growth and reproduction. Other interactions often relate to defence of territory within a wider home range, and, as an extension of this, to reproduction around a spawning site. Such behaviour usually involves fixed patterns of body and fin display, initiated as a response to other sign stimuli from the opposite party. Visual stimuli may be supported by the emission of sounds and pheromones.

Much fish behaviour, especially in schooling and courtship, appears instinctive. However, learning or individual modification in behaviour, largely controlled by the forebrain, can play an essential part in honing instinctive patterns. The ability of fish to learn is soon noted by the aquarist, as fish congregate for feeding when the cover of the tank is raised. After suitable training, cod can be summoned by bells and catfish can be whistled. In the sea, bass, a naturally inquisitive species, become more wary in well-dived habitats. Conditioned reflexes in fish have been used to investigate powers of sensory discrimination. On average, about 30 presentations are needed for the connection to sink home, and the reflex may survive intervals of up to several weeks. Sunfish and cichlids can learn to avoid glass partitions in feeding, and sticklebacks may remember this for some months. In the wild, the features of a territory may be learned, and it has been established that sticklebacks are able to differentiate between objects of different shape. Salmon are believed to learn the odours of their birth streams, remembering these for some years at sea prior to homing.

Breeding

Most fish species occur in two sexes but in some, such as the sea-perches, parrot fish, and wrasse, hermaphroditism is the rule, usually with females changing to males. In many teleosts, the sexes are difficult to distinguish except by coloration, body proportions, finnage, or special structures like the nuptial warts in carps. The reproductive organs (gonads or 'roe') of fish are typically paired, elongate structures, flanking or below the swimbladder when this is present. Testes are the 'soft' and ovaries the 'hard' roes respectively. Gonad maturation involves substantial increase in bulk, especially for the ovaries. Once the developing egg cells reach a certain size, they begin to accumulate yolk, enlarge greatly, and become golden yellow in colour. At ripening, the yolk-laden oöcyte becomes translucent.

In all cartilaginous fish, the female is fertilized internally via the male's claspers, tubular intromittent organs attached to each pelvic fin. Most cartilaginous fish are viviparous (livebearing), but in those which are egg-laying (oviparous) the egg is protected by a horny shell ('mermaid's purse'). In viviparous species, the embryo may feed from yolk within the egg, by ingesting unfertilized eggs or via a yolk-sac placenta within the uterus. Embryo stingrays, electric rays and eagle rays are fed by milky secretions from the uterine wall. The butterfly and devil rays have a single embryo in each oviduct nourished through long uterine processes that extend down into the gut.

By contrast, among the majority of teleosts, eggs pass to the outside before fertilization. Teleost eggs are usually very small and extremely numerous. The number of eggs produced (fecundity) is related to the body size of the female, against which number increases exponentially, so that bigger individuals of a species tend to have more eggs per unit body length than smaller ones. Marine, deep-water and many shelf species, all produce floating planktonic eggs, buoyed with an oil-globule or globules, while others lay relatively fewer, larger demersal eggs on the sea-bed. In fresh water, eggs are usually demersal. Teleost eggs may possess attachment filaments or a sticky egg-shell.

A number of different teleost groups are also viviparous, using various methods. In teleosts, the simplest form of livebearing is seen in the redfish, where the numerous young rely entirely on yolk, and are born as planktonic postlarvae. In the European fauna, there are no endemic representatives of the best-known freshwater livebearing families from the New World, but the Mosquitofish has been introduced to southern Europe. In these fish, eggs are fertilized while still within the ovary, where all gestation takes place. The male Mosquitofish has a rod-like gonopodium of modified anal fin rays, and this is used to shoot sperm clusters into the female where sperm is stored.

The time of gonad ripening and production of young must coincide with favourable conditions for the survival and feeding of the progeny. Distinct breeding seasons are therefore evident in most species. The European fishes, both marine and freshwater, comprise species from both cold-temperate (boreal) and low-Arctic faunas, as well as from warm-temperate (Lusitanian-Mediterranean) and even tropical groups. In the sea, cold-temperate/low-Arctic species, such as Plaice and cod, breed in winter or early spring, with one spawning per year. As well as a lower temperature requirement, this short breeding season correlates with the brief period of plankton richness at higher latitudes. In contrast, warm-temperate species, like sprat and whiting, breed in late spring to summer, with a long breeding season and repeat-spawning of successive egg batches by individuals. This seems related to the much longer occurrence of adequate plankton levels in warmer seas. In fresh water, in a similar relationship to the distribution of the species, the salmonids tend to spawn in colder months, while cyprinids and perches breed in the warmer spring and summer. Over a geographical range, breeding seasons will change within a species. Thus in warm-water marine species, such as the mackerel, the breeding season starts later and becomes shorter farther north.

The timing of reproduction during the year depends on the response of the fish's sensory and endocrine system to environmental cues which fluctuate seasonally. Changes in daily duration of light (photoperiod) influence hormone secretion by the pituitary and pineal glands, which in turn control the reproductive organs. A daily rhythm in sensitivity to light, first shown in sticklebacks, indicates how daylength can be measured by the fish. The seasonal temperature cycle is more variable from year to year, but has value for adjustment of reproduction to conditions in a particular year. Most species are influenced by some combination of both daylength and temperature. Some species can be brought to maturity earlier by altering daylength, especially after the winter solstice. Temperature is more important than photoperiod in cyprinids, such as Carp, Tench and Goldfish, and, within tolerance limits, an increase will extend spawning. Gonad maturation can also be affected by water quality, social factors, food supply and body stores.

Courting
Producing offspring needs energy to drive the great diversity of reproductive behaviour and techniques found among the fishes.

Even before mating, extensive journeys are undertaken by some migratory species, such as Salmon and Sea Trout returning from the sea to spawn in fresh water (anadromy), and conversely the lengthy transit of freshwater Eels back to their breeding area in the Sargasso Sea (catadromy). Many species move from feeding or overwintering habitats to breeding grounds suitable for survival and dispersal of their offspring.

In teleosts with planktonic eggs, spawning behaviour involves no preparation of a spawning site. However, in large schools of species like the cod, pair-formation, a three-dimensional territory and a formal courtship, all in the water column, have been observed. Similarly, in spawning schools of carps or perch transient pair formation and competition for mates, with butting or quivering, may occur, but the eggs in this case demersal are scattered over plants and thereafter abandoned.

In many other teleosts, a variety of nesting arrangements exist, usually involving demersal eggs and typically surrounded by a defended territory. Shore fish (gobies, blennies and clingfish) provide examples of such simple nesting, with eggs laid under a stone or shell. Nesting under natural shelters may entail some preparation. Males of the Common Goby will turn a small bivalve shell and cover this with sand by tail movements which leave characteristic radiating marks in the substrate around it.

Excavation precedes a number of spawning practices. Lampreys shift larger stones by means of the suctorial disc. In salmonids, the female 'cuts' on her side with her tail a 'redd' or trough for the eggs, which are then covered from upstream. This technique requires gravel and flowing water, to ensure not only cover but also adequate water flow around the buried eggs.

Some fishes build a nest from loose materials, with guarding and repair by one or both parents. On the shore, large nests constructed by Corkwing Wrasse may be found in rock crevices. The best researched nesting behaviour is that by the sticklebacks, which use plant fragments bound together by a glue-like secretion from the kidneys of the male. Among European fishes, perhaps the most unusual nesting technique is that of the Bitterling, in which the female uses a long tubular ovipositor to insert eggs among the gills of a freshwater mussel. The eggs are then fertilized by sperm drawn onto the gills by the feeding current of the mussel. On hatching, the young fish emerge in the exhalant water.

Courtship behaviour is closely integrated with sexual dimorphism in body form, coloration and other signals, which may include sound and scent. To ensure reproductive isolation, closely related species, such as the freshwater sticklebacks, show differences in all these aspects of courtship behaviour.

The classical analysis of courtship in fishes regards the process as consisting of a series of behavioural stages. Each of these presents a combination of special actions with display of sexual sign stimuli to the opposing partner. The red breast of the male Three-spined Stickleback and the swollen abdomen of the ripe female, are features which are displayed by courtship behaviour. The appropriate sign stimulus induces in the other fish either the next step in behaviour or a retreat from the territory by the intruder. In the Three-spined Stickleback, courtship centres on the nest constructed by the male who is in bright nuptial coloration, at the centre of his territory. When a female enters this area, the male approaches in a zig-zag fashion, to which a ripe female responds by raising her head and turning towards the male. In the absence of this response, the intruder is bitten or pricked with the dorsal spines. A responding female, however, is then led to the nest by the male, who indicates the entrance with his snout and shows jerky or rolling movements. When the female is in the nest, the male presses his snout against her tail and quivers, which induces the female to spawn and then leave the nest through the other opening. The male enters, fertilizes the eggs, and mating is completed. The next phase of reproductive behaviour is brood-care by guarding and fanning, an exclusively male preoccupation in the sticklebacks and other brood-carers, such as the gobies. After hatching, mouthing of the young sticklebacks by the male (where young are taken into his mouth) is believed to sharpen their ability to avoid predators.

Growing

Except in lampreys, most fish eggs contain a relatively large amount of yolk at fertilization. As development proceeds, dark pigment appears in the retina, and the embryo is said to have become 'eyed'. The time taken for embryonic development is most obviously influenced by temperature. Within a range of tolerance, rate of development increases with increasing temperature and hatching occurs sooner. Temperature also affects the number of serial features, such as vertebrae and fin-rays. Most species have a distinctive larval stage. Planktonic fish larvae float by means of oil globules, a high water content or elongate processes, such as fins or spines. Between hatching and metamorphosis, the larva is traditionally described as a prolarva while still possessing a yolk sac and a postlarva between complete absorption of the yolk sac and metamorphosis. Many species hatch as postlarvae. Others change from a yolk-carrying prolarva into the juvenile form without a distinct metamorphosis and, as in salmonids, these are termed alevins.

Embryonic development is the start of the overall growth pattern of the fish during its life-span. Fish length and weight are interrelated, but exponentially, so that as length increases there is a progressively greater increase in weight per unit length. Fishes show great flexibility in both growth rate and maximum size, but a maximum length can be specified for a population. Sometimes growth pattern is far from smooth. As well as seasonal influences, growth patterns over the life-span may involve successive developmental or ecological stages, each with a limiting size, such as those for salmon parr and grilse.

Important factors affecting fish growth include temperature, photoperiod, salinity and physical space, such as aquarium size. Others are more subtle, such as water quality, flow-rate and even status in a pecking-order. Rate of growth of the young fish is usually directly proportional to temperature, but the faster a fish grows initially, the smaller will be its final size. This may partly explain why fish in cooler waters of higher latitudes tend to reach a larger size than is found in related populations farther south.

The material and energy for growth is obtained ultimately from food. Factors affecting food availability and intensity of feeding, efficiency of absorption from the gut and then other requirements in the fish's metabolism, such as respiration, must all influence the 'scope' for growth from what is left over. There has to be a net energy gain before growth can occur, and the demands of basal metabolism for simple survival will take precedence. Growth rate therefore becomes markedly reduced at the highest temperatures and under stress. Fastest growth usually occurs at temperatures somewhat warmer than those at which food is processed most efficiently into body tissue. As food supply diminishes, so the growth rate will fall and also the temperature at which the optimum growth takes place. At sexual maturity, reproduction often has priority over growth for energy and material. Consequently, growth may slow at this point in life history, and may even be temporarily halted during the breeding season. However, for a particular species, much depends on whether or not continued growth could increase reproductive success. Thus, a larger size might increase fecundity or make easier the defence of territory.

The final product of a growth pattern, maximum size, differs profoundly across the fishes, extending over several orders of magnitude. The European marine teleosts range from a tiny clingfish, *Opeatogenys gracilis*, of 2 cm, to the Blue-finned Tuna, at over 300 cm, and the Ocean Sunfish, at 2,240 kg. In fresh water, the smallest European species is a goby from Lake Trichonis, in western Greece, *Economidichthys trichonis*, mature at 1.8 cm, while the Danubian Catfish or Wels has reputedly reached 4.5 m, and sturgeons considerably more. Cartilaginous fishes in European seas range from the world's smallest shark (*Squaliolus laticaudus*, 25 cm) to the Basking Shark (probably well over 10 m in length) and, occasionally, Devil Rays (5 m or more in wing span).

For fish, there are some advantages in larger size. These include less risk of predation, higher fecundity, and decreased energy cost per unit weight in body maintenance. Because larger fish have relatively less surface area, large size reduces heat loss for the somewhat warmer pelagic species, and in sharks and rays helps control of water balance by means of urea retention. At the other end of the size spectrum, a smaller body can also be advantageous for some ecological niches. It ensures that there is a net energy gain from the individual picking of small food items, which may form an enormous resource, like the tiny copepods exploited by small sand gobies. Habitats of restricted dimensions, literally ecological niches, also become available for small fish. Small size in many deep-sea pelagic fishes may be related to the general sparseness of food in the deep water column.

Living

The interaction of feeding, surviving, growing and breeding is the history of a fish's life. All is centred around a pattern of reproduction likely to yield most progeny in a certain habitat or way of life. The biologically important features of life-history are age at sexual maturity, duration of life (longevity), the frequency of spawning and the quantity of energy and material expended on reproduction in relation to the body size of the fish.

The age of a fish can be estimated by counting seasonal growth checks ('rings') on scales, bones and ear-stones (otoliths). For young fish, even daily growth layers can be distinguished in the otoliths. In the wild, longevity varies greatly between species, and natural expectation of life may be seriously curtailed by intensive fisheries. The longest-lived bony fish are probably sturgeon (over 80 years), Halibut and Danubian Catfish (both over 60 years). For 'annual' fishes, such as the European Transparent and Crystal Gobies, life lasts no more than a year.

In fish as well as humans, life-span is affected by the process of ageing (senescence), as well as by stress or accident. Predation is a widespread risk for fishes, especially for small species inhabiting an open habitat. Fish avoid attack by hiding, camouflage, schooling or active flight. After an attack, escape may be effected by simple burst swimming, violent flexing of the body (even inflation by pufferfish), and erection of spines, as in the sticklebacks. Spines, like those of the first dorsal fin and opercle of the weever fishes, are sometimes provided with poison glands. Protective bony armour ranges in coverage from the lateral shields of sticklebacks to the hard shell of dermal bones in pipefish and seahorses.

How much energy is spent on reproduction, and the age and time of year when this takes place, are life-history features which probably relate to the risk of death from outside causes. The less predictable is adult survival, the earlier is sexual maturation and the greater the expenditure of energy and body resources on all the aspects of reproduction. In species which spawn several times during a breeding season, such costs of reproduction can reach a high total. Age at maturity is another important part of reproductive strategy, since rate of reproduction is greater the sooner it commences.

In frequency of reproduction within the life-span, there is a basic contrast between species which reproduce more than once, and those which reproduce only once. Once-only reproduction, seen in many salmon and eels, requires that breeding success be assured, since an individual spawner gets only one chance. Salmon may be said to ensure a suitable environment for their offspring by dying. In Pacific salmon, where adult mortality is total after spawning, decomposition of dead adults enriches aquatic habitats (especially in phosphorus) which are subsequently exploited by the young during the freshwater parr stage.

A complete contrast in life history is shown by temperate economic species, such as Cod and Plaice. The rich but seasonal plankton of the shelf seas is a source of food for their young, which consequently need not be provided with as much yolk in the egg at fertilization. However, releasing tiny young to feed on plankton raises problems. A predictable one is predation by a host of other animals, and to meet this fecundity is high, with tens of millions of eggs per spawning liberated by fishes such as the Ling. A less predictable factor in survival of young is the variation in plankton availability from year to year. Species with planktonic young must therefore follow a reproductive strategy which involves a number of attempts at reproduction and consequently increases the chance of coinciding with a good year for plankton. In temperate waters, the frequency will be only once a year, in view of the relatively short plankton season. Consequently, adults must survive for a number of years. The emphasis is therefore on producing large numbers of eggs but with only moderate commitment of energy and material, to reduce the stress of reproduction on the adult and thereby maximize survival of the latter over a number of spawning opportunities. In the species mentioned, there is late maturation and low reproductive effort in the single spawning each year. In the potentially long adult life, growth increases fecundity. Unfortunately, for the large marine species, modern fisheries introduce a highly unpredictable adult mortality with which their reproductive strategies are not designed to cope.

WHERE FISH LIVE

European Seas

A primary difference in pattern of distribution is shown by the fishes of the continental shelf, and those of the open seas and oceans, where in turn the epipelagic surface dwellers (in the top 200 m), can be distinguished from the deep-sea fishes. Shelf and pelagic distributions are influenced primarily by water temperatures resulting from the set of superficial currents. Another factor in shallow seas is reduction in salinity by fresh water from the land, most evident in the enclosed Baltic and Black Sea basins.

In the seas, it is possible to recognize major geographical assemblages of fishes, whose boundaries usually correspond with some change in annual temperature range or other hydrographic features. Along the shelf of the eastern Atlantic, the North Atlantic drift creates a very broad belt of temperate waters, from the ice-free North Cape of northern Norway to its southernmost influence around the Canaries and along the Mauritanian coast, where upwelling also has a cooling effect. This temperate eastern Atlantic area contains two major groupings of marine life, the cold-temperate eastern Boreal, and the warm-temperate Mediterranean-Lusitanian. Many species occur in both areas. In the temperate region as a whole, species from adjoining faunas, both north and south, are also found. These include some from the Arctic fauna, which is found around north-west

Iceland and Greenland, Siberia, and Spitzbergen, as well as from the marine fish fauna of tropical West African, which occurs from Mauritania to Angola. Transitional areas are often broad, and many species can occur over adjoining regions or regularly move into adjoining areas on a seasonal basis. Also, in the eastern Atlantic, boundaries are believed to have shifted with climatic change especially connected with the Ice Ages. At this time, cold-temperate marine species inhabited at least the western Mediterranean during the glacial periods, being replaced by more tropical forms in the warm interglacials. Some northern species, such as bullheads and Wolf-fish, present in the coolest parts of the Mediterranean, may thus be glacial relicts.

Many well-known fishes occur in both boreal and Mediterranean faunas, such as the lampreys, Common Skate, Sprat, various gadoids (including Whiting and Hake), Mackerel, dragonets, Brill, Turbot, Plaice and the Common Angler. Sharks, like the Porbeagle, Basking Shark and the spurdogs, also occur in other temperate seas.

The boreal marine fauna extends from south-west Iceland and North Cape to the Celtic Sea, as well as into the Baltic. Because of a wide annual temperature range, both warm-temperate and Arctic species are found, but breed at different times of year. Species characterizing this area include the smelt, various gadoids (Norway Pout, Greater Forkbeard and Five-bearded Rockling), the Viviparous Blenny, Fifteen-spined Stickleback, Pogge, Lesser and Greater Sandeels, and some gobies, including Europe's smallest marine species, *Lebetus* spp. There are also flatfishes such as the Lemon Sole and the Dab. Other species, such as Ling, Coalfish and Pollack, occur here and in corresponding conditions of the western Atlantic cold-temperate area, from Newfoundland to Cape Hatteras.

Low-Arctic fishes also present in the boreal area are the Greenland Shark and a variety of teleosts, notably the Herring, Cod and Haddock, as well as the Capelin, Torsk, redfish, a range of bullheads and the Lumpsucker. In more offshore shelf waters, there are also the marine Wolf-fish. Flatfish in this category include the Halibut.

In the shallow Baltic Sea, salinity is low (2-8‰) and temperatures range widely from 0-2°C to 12->16°C. Consequently, the Baltic is colonized by only the more euryhaline marine species of the North Sea. There are no resident sharks or rays, and some typical freshwater fishes, like Pike, Bream and Perch, occur along the coasts. The marine species are mostly cold boreal or boreal-low-Arctic forms, such as Herring and the Viviparous Blenny, but several widespread temperate fishes, like Mackerel, Sprat and Turbot, are present in the open sea. In the more saline western Baltic, other marine species occur, including Whiting and Plaice.

The warm-temperate Mediterranean-Lusitanian fauna has a considerable spread in the eastern Atlantic, from the Celtic Sea to Cape Blanco, northern Mauritania, and also predominates around the Azores, Madeira and the Canaries. As well as the Mediterranean basin, part of this fauna also inhabits the Black Sea. The Mediterranean-Lusitanian fauna has many more endemic fishes than the boreal one. Cartilaginous forms include smoothhounds, the Maltese Ray, and even a cownose ray. Familiar teleosts are the Pilchard and the Anchovy, which extends into the southern North Sea in summer. Others include sandsmelts, various pipefish and a seahorse, scorpionfishes and gurnards, seaperches, seabreams, wrasses, flatfishes, many gobies and blennies, and several clingfish. As a subdivision within this area, a number of small teleosts are restricted to some or all of the Azores, Madeira and the Canaries in the eastern Atlantic, islands otherwise with a predominantly Lusitanian warm-temperate fauna.

The Mediterranean-Lusitanian area is also penetrated by fishes from tropical West Africa. The more bizarre cartilaginous fishes comprise monkfish, sawfish, stingrays, an eagle ray, and a devil ray. Among teleosts, there are the sardinellas and several carangids, including the Horse Mackerel, as well as a variety of seabreams, grunts, drums, seaperches, and grey mullets. Other, more obviously tropical, are Cardinal, Butterfly, Damsel and Parrot Fish, a barracuda and the bottom-living moray eels. At least eleven species of sole are Mediterranean-West African in distribution. Some teleosts in this category also occur in the western Atlantic. These include the wreckfish, various jacks, the Flying Gurnard, and trigger- and pufferfish.

Others fishes extend from West Africa through the Mediterranean region and, to a greater or lesser extent, into the boreal fauna. The Thornback Ray, Conger, Pilchard, Bass, Cuckoo Wrasse and Common Sole are all widely distributed in this respect. Several larger sharks and rays, such as the Basking Shark, Mako, Tiger Shark, Blue Shark, hammerheads, the Violet Stingray and Butterfly Ray, occur in warm-temperate Atlantic-Mediterranean waters and also into higher latitudes on a seasonal or more sporadic basis. Teleosts of similar distribution include the Bluefish, a dolphin fish, flying fishes, various tunnies, sailfish and swordfish, as well as the largest teleost, the Oceanic Sunfish.

The present narrow connection between the Black Sea and the Mediterranean (via the Aegean Sea) is postglacial. The Black Sea has a much lower salinity and greater temperature range than the Mediterranean proper. Its depths greater than 125-300 m are poisoned by hydrogen sulphide. A limited number of Mediterranean fishes have entered the Black Sea. These are mullets, seabreams, Anchovy, Mackerel and Bonito, gobies, wrasse, blennies and pipefish, with some local differentiation of species such as in the Brill. Tuna migrate seasonally. In the open waters, these Mediterranean forms mingle with Ponto-Caspian endemic fishes like sturgeon, the clupeids *Caspialosa* and *Clupeonella*, marine zander, *Percarina demidoffi*, and many gobies, including a tadpole goby. Conversely, some Ponto-Caspian fishes occur in brackish waters of the eastern Mediterranean and Adriatic, such as the abundant small gobies of the genus *Knipowitschia*.

In recent times, the Mediterranean basin has been colonized by 'lessepsian' immigrants, tropical Indo-Pacific fishes which have entered since de Lessep's Suez Canal was opened in 1869 to link the eastern Mediterranean with the Red Sea Gulf of Suez. Thanks to their euryhalinity, a northerly set to currents through the canal, and a possible competitive edge, at least 30 Indo-Pacific fish species are now established in the eastern Mediterranean. These include not only a stingray, but also representatives of tropical families otherwise absent from the Mediterranean, like the Rainbow Sardine, siganid rabbit-fish, Pony Fish, Red Soldierfish, therapon perches, goat-fish and a tongue-sole. Several lessepsian species are now of commercial value in Levant waters.

Off the continental shelf of north-western Europe, the fish fauna of the deeper Atlantic falls into two major groups, characterizing the Atlantic and Norway deep-sea basins. These are separated by the submarine North Atlantic transverse ridge between Scotland and Greenland, not deeper than 560 m, and incorporating Iceland, the Faroes and the Shetlands. The Norway basin is delimited to the north by the Nansen ridge between Greenland and Spitzbergen. The Norway basin deep water is cold, with a limited number of deep pelagic fishes, such as the Pearlsides and a few lantern fishes, but contains some endemic bottom-living eelpouts and seasnails. To the south of the Greenland-Scotland ridge, off the British Isles and southwards, the Atlantic Basin is much more extensive and warmer, with many more mesopelagic, bathypelagic and benthic species. These include numerous smoothheads, hatchet fishes, lantern fishes and anglers, as well as rattails on the continental slope. The depths of the Mediterranean, bounded by the Gibraltar sill (not deeper than 320 m), and supporting a deep outflowing current above the sill, are warmer and more saline but less oxygenated than the Atlantic. The deep-water fish fauna is accordingly an impoverished derivative of the Atlantic one.

European Fresh Waters

Inland, mostly fresh, waters form much a smaller part, in both area and volume, of the European aquatic world than the seas and experience much more climatic variation. Because of greater subdivision into separate catchments and basins, as well as isolation of stocks by past climatic changes, there is more likelihood of local diversity in the species.

European freshwater fishes can be divided into categories according to area of distribution. A number are found over a large area of Europe, as well as through Asia, and some, or a close sister-species, even occur in North America. The Pike, Burbot, Three-spined Stickleback and Perch are in this category. Cyprinids such as Carp, Goldfish, Dace and minnow, as well as Stone Loach and Ruffe, are widespread in Asia as well as through much of Europe. The catadromous Eel enters all Atlantic and Mediterranean rivers, and young are introduced by man into rivers of the Black Sea, while the migratory Trout of glacial times has left freshwater populations from North Africa to Scandinavia.

For species of more restricted distribution, the European watershed of the Ponto-Caspian (Black, Caspian and Aral Seas) basin is the centre of diversity, and from this region the north and westerly parts of Europe were recolonized in postglacial times. Following isolation of the Ponto-Caspian basin after the middle Miocene, there evolved a special freshwater and hyposaline fauna, whose endemic species characterize Black Sea and Caspian drainages of today. These fishes contribute to the diversity of eastern European fresh waters, chiefly in the Danube and the major rivers of the Ukraine. Ponto-Caspian fishes are also present in northern Aegean rivers.

Ponto-Caspian endemics include *Eudontomyzon* lampreys, and sturgeons, such as the Huso, although the latter and the Stellate Sturgeon are also reported from the Adriatic. *Umbra krameri* is the small freshwater mud-minnow, with a nearest relative in North America. The Huchen is an endemic salmon and there are a number of cyprinids (Danubian bleak, gudgeons and roach) and small perches. The latter comprise not only ruffes and a zingel, but also one of the rarest European freshwater fishes, the Rumanian Bull-perch. Several Ponto-Caspian gobies occur in fresh water, including the Tube-nosed Goby.

South of the east–west ranges of the Balkans, the Alps and the Pyrenees, the three peninsular areas of southern Europe show some degree of endemicity among their freshwater fishes, such as the barbels, although forms like the soiffe and Rhône Zingel are related to the Ponto-Caspian fauna. Among fish endemic to the peninsulas, *Barbus comiza* may be noted for Iberia. In Italy, and coastal rivers of the Adriatic, there are the Lombardy Brook Lamprey, a sturgeon, and several cyprinids (a bream, roaches and *Barbus plebejus*, which is also in western Greece, the northern Aegean and Pontic Turkey). There are also endemic gobies, an Adriatic *Padogobius martensii* and the Tyrhenian *P. nigricans*. In the Balkans, there is the greatest degree of differentiation and a west Balkanian province has been distinguished as an area of high endemicity. As well as a lamprey, there are two species of a distinct salmonid genus *Salmothymus*, the Danubian Barbel Gudgeon, minnow-like cyprinids (*Pachychilon* and *Paraphoxinus*) and two species of the goby *Economidichthys*, with *E. trichonis*, Europe's smallest freshwater fish, only in Lake Trichonis. There is also a six-whiskered form of the Danubian Wels, Aristotle's Catfish, restricted to the Achelous river.

More northerly and western areas of Europe, other than western and northern Norway, form the Baltic faunal province, a region once affected by glaciation and only repopulated by freshwater fishes in the last 20,000 years. Also including a number of salmonids, it is transitional in species towards the adjoining Arctic freshwater faunal region. During cool glacial periods, migratory stocks of salmonids occurred much farther south along the Atlantic seaboard, and left behind lake-locked populations in oligotrophic lakes in the Alps, British Isles, and Scandinavia. Spread of Ponto-Caspian species did not completely extend to the British Isles before these were isolated by rising sea-level, but species which reached the old Rhine (traversing the present North Sea basin) spread into British east coast rivers. A temporary freshwater phase of the postglacial Baltic permitted dispersal of fish species into all its tributary rivers.

In this north-western province it is possible to distinguish a Rhine district, of North Sea and Biscay drainages, and a Neva district, essentially the Baltic watershed. Presumably from the Ponto-Caspian basin, a number of familiar species extend across Europe into both parts of the Baltic province, some to the British Isles. These include Tench, Rudd, Bleak, Schneider, Barbel, Silver Bream, Nase, Common Gudgeon and Bitterling, which also occurs in the Far East. The Weather and Spined Loaches, the Bullhead, pike-perches and the Zingel are likewise in this category, the Bullhead also ranging into the White Sea watershed. Other Ponto-Caspian species extend only into the Baltic watershed. These are several cyprinids (breams, Asp, Ziege and Swamp Minnow), Golden Loach and Danubian Catfish. The Siberian Bullhead, *Cottus poecilopus*, in Siberian and Baltic drainages, also occurs in some northern Ponto-Caspian waters. Freshwater species distributed mainly in or restricted to the Baltic (Neva and Rhine) areas are species with some potential for euryhalinity, such as lampreys, whitefish, the Grayling and the Nine-spined Stickleback. In the Baltic watershed, there are other whitefish, and the relict Arctic Four-horned Sculpin, *Myoxocephalus quadricornis*.

The northern and western watersheds of Norway and the Kola Peninsula possess a freshwater fish fauna which has been classified as Circumpolar, characterized by the preponderance of migratory salmonids, especially whitefish, and the presence of the Atlantic salmon and trout species. In this area, the Arctic Charr is also anadromous.

Marine Habitats

Marine habitats are defined essentially by water depth and salt content of the water (salinity). Typical salinities, mostly sodium chloride, but also many other inorganic substances, are about 34-35‰ around the British Isles, increasing to 36-37‰ around the Canaries and to over 39‰ in the Mediterranean. Seawater becomes diluted in estuaries and also in enclosed shallow seas, such as the Baltic and Black Seas, where low salinity is an ecological barrier for many marine species. In terms of depth, there is a primary division between waters over the continental shelf, and those of the open ocean basins.

The shelf seas are shallow (to about 180-200 m), well mixed, rich in nutrients from the land, and likely to fluctuate seasonally; light can penetrate the entire watercolumn unless the water is turbid. Fringing the land, in suitable areas, there are intertidal habitats, where a vertical gradation in environment results from differences in time of exposure at low tide, with its associated extremes of temperature, light and risk from desiccation. The intertidal habitat is also affected by wave action and the shore substrate.

Estuaries where rivers enter the sea show salinity gradients and fluctuation, marked temperature change and often turbidity. They are highly productive, especially in the tiny invertebrates and algae living on or in the bottom sediments. Associated saltmarsh pools and creeks are also habitats for fish. Lagoons are more or less isolated coastal shallows, and consequently subject to extremes of salinity and temperature, as well as deoxygenation.

Shelf fishes associated with the sea bed can be divided roughly into two kinds. 'Epibenthic' forms live on the bottom but feed to a varying extent in the overlying watercolumn. These include gobies, scorpaenids, sea-poachers, dragonets and small dogfish. Living immediately above the sea bed or its associated vegetation are marine sticklebacks, pipefish, wrasse and some gadoids, while grey mullet, although schooling in midwater, are bottom feeders. The other division comprises fishes which lead more secretive 'cryptobenthic' lives, normally hiding under stones or in other structures or burrows. These include blennies, various gobies, rocklings, eels and clingfish.

Bottom-dwelling fish are more or less adapted to a two-dimensional environment in body shape and behaviour. The body tends to be flattened or elongate, with eyes more dorsolaterally positioned. Movement is sporadic and body modifications for other functions, such as concealment, may override swimming efficiency. Cryptic coloration acts against viewing from the side or from above rather than from below. Body outline may be broken up by skin filaments, as in anglers, and there is a marked ability for adaptive colour change in flatfish. Internal adaptations can include a reduced swimbladder, burst swimming musculature aided by large pectoral fins, and smaller gill surface area. In some fish which move over the bottom, the paired fins are employed as levers; blennies use long pelvics and the gurnards 'walk' on their stout free lower pectoral rays. Other modifications for crawling, burrowing, hiding or clinging to the substrate often require sensory structures such as barbels or fin rays. Suctorial attachment organs, based on the fused pelvic fins, have evolved independently in gobies, seasnails and clingfish.

In the most specialized bottom dwellers, there is extreme flattening of the body either dorsoventrally as in skates, or from side to side as in the teleost Plaice and Sole. These latter show the postural modification of lying on one side and, during development, one eye shifts to join the other on what will become the upper surface of the head. The opposite trend is elongation of the body to insert into crevices, like the Conger Eel, or to fit between seagrass stems in the manner of pipefish and seahorses.

The fish found between the tidemarks may be residents, some exclusively intertidal, such as the Shanny, or of temporary occurrence, for breeding, like lumpsuckers. Others enter at high water to feed and are occasionally stranded on ebb tide. Residents under rocks include blennies, gobies, clingfish, rocklings and the worm pipefish, while wrasse, Fifteen-spined Sticklebacks and Bullheads occur in weedy pools. On sandy shores, in pools, there may be Common Gobies, young of flatfish, grey mullet and sandsmelts.

Fishes which live in the shelf watercolumn and the surface layers of the ocean are more active, and adapted for efficient swimming, by body streamlining and modifications of fins, skin, muscle and physiology. Gill surface area is relatively much greater than in sedentary species. Fast swimming also permits, as in the mackerel and tunnies, gill ventilation through the open mouth rather than by muscular pumping. The pelagic lamnid sharks, such as Porbeagle and makos, and scombroid teleosts, like tunnies and mackerel, show similarities in body and tail shape for swimming efficiency and stamina. Both sharks and scombroids also have body temperatures up to 10°C above that of the surrounding water, facilitating muscle activity. Coloration in fishes which live above the sea-bed normally incorporates countershading, with the upper surface dark and the sides and belly silvery. This helps concealment when viewed from above against the darker background of the sea, and from below against the illuminated surface ceiling. Such fishes may feed on both benthic and other watercolumn animals, but plankton is a rich resource obtained by sieving the inhalant water of gill ventilation by means of numerous fine gill-rakers, as seen in herrings, mackerel and scad. Schooling is common among fishes in the three-dimensional habitat of the water mass.

Off the continental shelf, oceanic waters can also be divided into watercolumn and bottom habitats. These are (i) epipelagic, (ii) deep pelagic (mesopelagic and benthopelagic) and (iii) benthic, either bathyal (slope) or abyssal (deep-sea floor).

The uppermost or epipelagic zone, from the surface to about 200 m, is well lit but affected by seasonal variation. Its lower boundary is formed by the thermocline, a layer of steep temperature gradient. In the epipelagic zone, the bulk of ocean photosynthesis occurs and promotes animal plankton. However, the epipelagic loses nutrients to the depths below, and is normally less productive than shelf waters. In warmer regions, the epipelagic zone houses large predators, such as tunnies, marlin and swordfish, as well as oceanic sharks (Blue Shark, Great White, makos). There are also large plankton feeders, such as Basking Sharks and Devil Rays. Pilot Fish and remoras accompany the bigger species. Smaller fishes include dolphins and flying fish. Drifters, such as the sunfish, ribbonfish and oarfish, move with ocean currents, and in the case of the sargassum fish with floating weed.

In the deep sea, major environmental constraints are light, which becomes unidirectional or absent as sunlight, diminished temperature, increasing pressure and very limited productivity in the watercolumn. Nevertheless, there are many more species of deep-sea fishes than there are in the surface layers of warm-temperate or tropical oceans. They show many bizarre modifications for life in a dark environment, in eye-structure (tubularity, extra lenses and retinas) and in the production of light from light organs (photophores), either by their own cellular processes or by symbiotic bacteria. This bioluminescence may serve for protection, prey detection by 'searchlight' or 'lure', or mate-recognition. Many deep-sea fish are black, thereby reflecting little of the blue from attenuated sunlight or bioluminescence. Only whale fish are red, although this is the normal colour for deep-sea prawns and other invertebrates.

Mesopelagic waters are those below the thermocline, from about 200 m until around 1,000 m, at which sunlight is finally extinguished. Because of selective wavelength scattering, the twilight becomes bluish with a distant surface glow. Mesopelagic fish tend to have large eyes adapted for light at the blue end of the spectrum. Light organs are often concentrated along the ventral part of the body, probably to conceal against light from above. With diminishing light, photosynthesis and plankton is greatly reduced. In this part of the ocean watercolumn, lantern fishes and stomiatoids are the most numerous and abundant fishes. There are also deep-sea salmonoids, lancetfish, javelinfish, barracudinas, gulpers, ridgeheads and cutlassfishes. Mesopelagic plankton feeders, especially lanternfish and small stomiatoids, and their predators migrate upwards into the richer epipelagic waters at night. During the day, lantern fishes occur at about 250-700 m, but begin to move upwards by an hour before sunset. They reach the surface shortly after dark, and start to descend before sunrise. These migratory planktivores tend to have well-developed swimbladders.

The bathypelagic habitat lies deeper than 1,000 m, where only bioluminescence, from both fishes and invertebrates, is seen. Bathypelagic waters, which may extend some miles in depth, are cold (1-5°C) even at the equator and are the least fertile of the entire watercolumn. Deep-sea angler fishes are the most important group (over 100 species), with gulpers, whalefish and giganturoids. Although there are few stomiatoid species, the black bristle-mouths (*Cyclothone*) are most numerous as individuals. Bathypelagic fishes do not follow a daily vertical migration and have either rudimentary or no swimbladders. They prey on the deep-sea fauna of squid, prawns, copepods and also fish. Some can perform prodigious feats of swallowing, probably related to the infrequency of meeting prey, which in the anglers may be attracted to luminous lures. Most species are small, with reduced body mass and structural delicacy.

From the edge of the continental shelf, at about 180-200 m, the sea bed falls to about 1,000 m as the steep continental slope, often dissected by submarine canyons and with scattered sea-mounts, and thence to the more gentle continental rise before an abyssal plain. These bottom habitats differ in substrate according to depth, but may be rich in fallen organic material and support a greater biomass than waters above, especially on the slope nearer to the land. A component of the fish fauna, living immediately above the sea bed but feeding on benthic animals, has been distinguished as benthopelagic. Such fishes include chiefly grenadiers and ophidiids; there are also deep-sea cods (Moridae), notacanths, alepocephalids and tripod fishes, as well as deep-sea sharks and rabbit-fish. On the sea-bed, with a benthic life-style, there are green-eyes, eelpouts, seasnails and rays. The benthic species in general tend to be larger and more substantial than those of the deep watercolumn. Rattails and notacanths have a pointed snout and ventral mouth, for rooting in ooze. Tripod fish are raised on elongate pelvic and caudal rays and feed on benthopelagic plankton; they may also use their elevation for surveillance.

Freshwater Habitats

Inland water habitats have typically 'fresh' water, with relatively limited salt content, in transit to the sea. Freshwater habitats are of much smaller volume than marine ones and consequently more susceptible to change in temperature and water quality. The two main kinds of freshwater habitat are distinguished by degree of water movement, obviously flowing (lotic) in a stream or river or static (lentic) in a pond or lake.

The course of a river can be divided into four major parts (reaches): mountain, submontane, lowland and estuarine, although these are more evident in long continental rivers than in most British ones. Criteria include temperature and stream velocity (depending on altitude, gradient and depth) which in turn affect oxygenation, substrate and vegetation. Tides introduce salinity at the estuary. Boundaries between these reaches are not sharp, and many species spread widely along rivers, although their centres of abundance may be restricted to a particular zone.

The mountain reach commences as a spring, transforming into a mountain brook. Initially, the spring is shallow, very fast flowing over a stony bottom in a steep-profiled bed, often with waterfalls, and lacks higher plants and many invertebrates. The water is clear, cold in summer, and highly oxygenated. Fishes of mountain brooks are bullheads and Brown Trout, supplemented lower down by minnows, Stone and Spined Loach, and Brook Lampreys, with more rarely gudgeon and bleak. Introduced Rainbow and Brook Trout may also occur.

The submontane region has a more gradual descent, but, in the upper parts, current is still relatively fast and the water clear, albeit somewhat less well oxygenated than upstream. The river bed is wider and deeper, with pools, bays and smaller tributaries and also marginal plants. Under these conditions, Grayling can replace trout as the dominant fish species, in company with other salmonids (salmon, and the Huchen in eastern Europe). Several cyprinids are also found, including Chub, Burbot, Dace, gudgeon and minnows, and sometimes the predatory Asp and Pike.

The lower submontane river is larger, and the current rapid to moderate down a gentle gradient. In summer, the water becomes warmer and is often turbid, with oxygen possibly depleted near the bottom. The river bed has both sandy and pebble reaches, with thick marginal vegetation. Barbels and many other cyprinids, such as Roach, Rudd, Bleak, Nase, Chub, Dace and Asp, are typical of this zone, together with Perch and pike-perch. In the Danubian watershed, other perches, the Schraetzer, Zingel and Streber, occur. Salmon and Eel pass through on migration.

In the lowland reach, the river is wider and deeper with shallows and backwaters, of very gentle gradient and moderate to slow current. The water tends to be cloudy with suspended material, and becomes very warm in summer. At the river bottom, of mostly sand and organic detritus, deoxygenation may result. There is much aquatic vegetation, and a rich invertebrate fauna. This is essentially the zone for cyprinids, in particular the Bream, Carp and Tench. Continental species include White Bream, Ide, Vimba and Crucian Carp, and sometimes the rarer Zope, Ziege and Zobel. Perch and pike-perch thrive here, and also the Danubian Catfish attains its largest size in lowland rivers. Eels are common, and migratory species, such as Shad, Houting, Smelt, flounders and even sturgeon, may be encountered.

In the estuary, there is virtually no gradient. The water, under tidal influence, is more or less saline, turbid with much detritus, very warm in summer and sometimes depleted in oxygen at the bottom. The estuarine reach is very productive, but lacks many freshwater fishes. Instead, there are migratory anadromous and catadromous species, and towards the mouth marine fishes, especially juveniles. These may comprise Common and Sand Gobies, eels, sticklebacks, Viviparous Blennies, flounders, bass, and grey mullet.

Static water habitats for freshwater fishes vary greatly in size, from Alpine lake to small pool. Larger water bodies are divisible according to basin shape and fertility. Two extremes have been recognized at each end of a series of intermediate conditions and combinations. Typical of high Alpine lakes in valleys heavily gouged during the glacial periods, the oligotrophic type has a deep rocky basin and sufficient depth of water to become temperature-stratified like the open sea. The warmer surface layer (epilimnion) and the much more extensive and cold deeper part (hypolimnion) are separated by a thermocline (which may lie from 10-20 m). Lake stratification is usual in later spring to autumn, but can last from only a few hours to most of the year, depending on depth, wind action, atmospheric temperature and other factors. In the depths, there may be deoxygenation near the bottom under winter ice. Oligotrophic lakes receive little nutrient inflow and their clear cold waters have limited fertility and plant growth. The fish fauna is essentially salmonid, with lake trout, and, in many cases, glacial relict charr and whitefish which retire to deeper water in summer. The narrow shallows with vegetation house a number of other species, especially minnows, and both Perch and Pike occur in deeper basins. In some continental lakes, the Danubian Bleak also inhabits greater depths but moves into the shallows for spawning, while other cyprinids, such as Roach, like lake trout, ascend tributaries to spawn.

The opposite environment is that of eutrophic lakes. These are shallow basins, typically lowland, with much silt and nutrient inflow. Fertility is high, and organic material sinking to the bottom may cause deoxygenation of a hypolimnion if thermal stratification occurs in summer. There is extensive marginal and other vegetation. The fish fauna of eutrophic lakes is typically cyprinid, of which a variety of these and other species, such as Ruffe, inhabit the shallows. Only if deeper water remains cool and oxygenated in summer do these lakes support whitefish, such as Vendace. On a smaller scale, ponds are shallow with vegetation which may colonize the entire bottom. Their reduced volume of water suffers wider tempera- ture extremes with season, and there is the possibility of drying-out. Crucian Carp, Tench and Weather Loach are the most tolerant of such conditions, and Carp, Rudd, Bitterling, Bleak, sticklebacks and minnows may also be found in smaller water bodies. The freshwater dogfish mud-minnow also lives in pools.

Freshwater fishes show adaptations parallelling those of marine watercolumn and benthic species. Midwater forms are streamlined, with high aspect ratio forked tails, neutral buoyancy and the countershading of dark back and silvery underside. Faster swimming species, able to hold position in a strong current, such as salmonids, have more cylindrical bodies than the deeper bodied, compressed, midwater dwellers in quieter reaches, like Bream. Darting predators, such as Pike, are torpedo-shaped, with rear-set fins. Even among the cyprinids, Dace and Chub have slimmer bodies than the more sedate Roach and Carp. Behavioural adapta- tion for energy saving in running water involves fast burst swimming to rest behind rocks, with more territoriality under these conditions. Fish may also turn upstream to use the water flow for passive gill-ventilation. There is also visual position- holding in midwater species, and substrate hugging by the benthic fishes.

Bottom living species such as bullheads, catfish, and Burbot have large flat heads, with lateral gill openings, reduced swimbladders, larger pelvics, flattened bellies, and cryptic coloration. Loach and Eels are more elongate, moving by body undulation against the substrate. The most characteristic sensory adaptation in freshwater fishes is the enhancement of hearing in the carps and their relatives by transmission of vibrations from swimbladder to inner ear. In the bottom-living loach, where neutral buoyancy is not necessary, the anterior part of the swim- bladder still persists in a bony capsule for this purpose.

USING THIS BOOK

Coverage
This book deals essentially with the marine fishes found on the continental shelf of European seas from Iceland and North Cape, Norway, to Morocco and adjoining islands, including the Baltic, Mediterranean and Black Sea basins. A number of species from the upper continental slope or open oceanic waters have also been incorporated, and reference made to Indo-Pacific species which have entered the eastern Mediterranean via the Suez Canal. The freshwater species covered are those found on the continent of Europe but it has not been possible to treat in detail or to mention every one of the local species and subspecies of southern and eastern areas.

Classification
Nomenclature is taken from the works noted under Further Reading; a few common names have had to be coined. Overall classification follows the general arrange- ment of Nelson (1994), but has been simplified and tends to be conservative.

Presentation
Higher systematic categories, families and above, are given separate paragraphs when (i) high in the scheme of classification or (ii) more than one species is con- sidered in detail. In general, family definitions and information refer to features in European species. Otherwise, the name of a family represented by only one species follows in parentheses after the species name, whose description defines the family as it occurs in European waters. Features noted for the species are those most useful in identification, and are ones which vary between species within a family or a series of related families. For each species, a full sequence of data com- prises, in order, common name, scientific name, body form and external features, coloration, size, habitat, diet, reproduction, life-history and any other significant information, such as economic importance or distribution beyond Europe. Geo- graphical distribution within Europe is shown on the adjoining map.

Technical terms are explained in the Glossary, and the main features of a teleost are shown in the illustration overleaf. Fins are referred to in the text by merely the initial letter. Thus, D: dorsal fin, numbered when more than one present, for example D1 and D2 when spinous and soft parts are separate; A: anal fin, numbered in gadoids; P: pectoral fin; V: pelvic (= ventral) fin; and C: caudal fin. Counts of spinous fin-rays are given in Roman numerals, soft (segmented, branched) rays in Arabic numerals. In some cases, extreme values are shown in parentheses. Lateral scales (LL) are counted along the lateral-line or the lateral midline of the body to the origin of the caudal fin. Gill rakers are counted along the anterior face of the first gill arch.

Body size, total length and often weight is the maximum on record, and most individuals of a species will not reach these limits. Sexual dimorphism in size is denoted by m (male) and f (female). World all-tackle angling record weights (as a:) are given in parentheses, as published by the International Game Fish Association. For marine species, the usual depth range may be followed by extremes in parentheses. Breeding seasons are for the British Isles unless otherwise stated; months in parentheses are less usual for breeding. Fecundity values indicate an approximate range. Any reference to geographical distribution in the text is from south to north for predominantly southern and boreal species, north to south in polar fish; freshwater distributions from west to east, south to north.

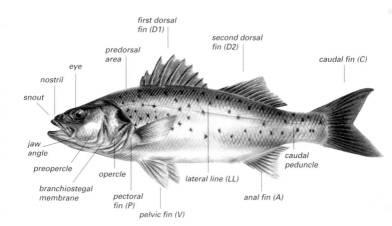

Identification

Many readers will already be able to identify a fish at least to its family. Any further problems will probably be solved in most cases merely by glancing through the illustrated keys, which cover most of the groups and species in the book. To use the key text, compare the fish with the successive lists of features until a name is reached, which may be a general group, such as sharks and dogfish, a family like the blennies or a particular species such as the Opah. Work down each listing, from 1 onwards, until the features mentioned after a numbered letter agree with those of the specimen. Then proceed to the next list of characters under the following number. For example, a cod would be identified by the sequence 1b → 2b → 3c → 4f → 5d → 6n, and then finally 7b 'Cods'.

Key to Marine and Estuarine Fishes

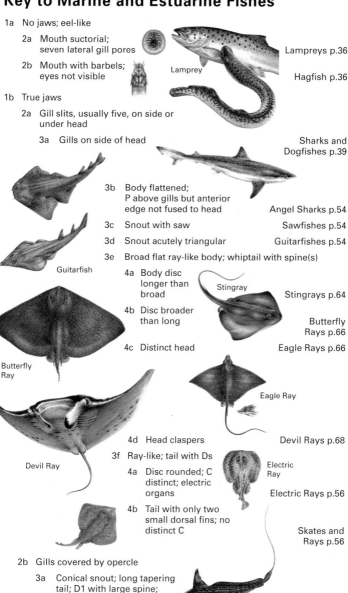

1a No jaws; eel-like

    2a Mouth suctorial; seven lateral gill pores   Lampreys p.36

    2b Mouth with barbels; eyes not visible   Hagfish p.36

Lamprey

1b True jaws

    2a Gill slits, usually five, on side or under head

        3a Gills on side of head   Sharks and Dogfishes p.39

        3b Body flattened; P above gills but anterior edge not fused to head   Angel Sharks p.54

        3c Snout with saw   Sawfishes p.54

        3d Snout acutely triangular   Guitarfishes p.54

Guitarfish

        3e Broad flat ray-like body; whiptail with spine(s)

            4a Body disc longer than broad   Stingrays p.64

Stingray

            4b Disc broader than long   Butterfly Rays p.66

            4c Distinct head   Eagle Rays p.66

Butterfly Ray

Eagle Ray

            4d Head claspers   Devil Rays p.68

Devil Ray

        3f Ray-like; tail with Ds

            4a Disc rounded; C distinct; electric organs   Electric Rays p.56

Electric Ray

            4b Tail with only two small dorsal fins; no distinct C   Skates and Rays p.56

    2b Gills covered by opercle

        3a Conical snout; long tapering tail; D1 with large spine; tooth plates   Rabbit-fish p.68

3b Upturned tail axis; body with lateral
   bony plates; small ventral mouth
   with transverse row of barbels

                                        Sturgeons p.70

3c C symmetrical or absent   [Teleosts] p.74

   4a Eyes on one side of head; swims on side   [Flatfishes] p.260

      5a Left side up   Turbots p.260

      5b Right side up   Plaices p.266

      5c Right side up; mouth inferior, curved   Soles p.270

      5d Left side up; no C   Tongue-soles p.273

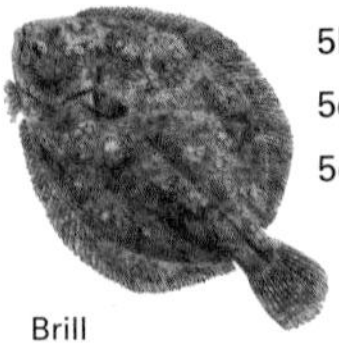

Brill    Dab

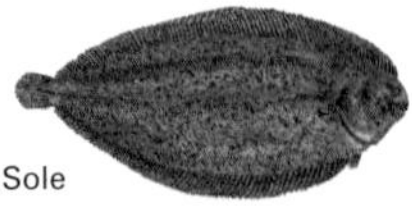

              Sole

   4b Sucker present on belly or head

      5a Sucker on head   Sharksuckers p.184

      5b Vs forming elliptical sucker;
         two Ds   Gobies p.232

      5c Vs as simple round
         sucker; one D   Seasnails and
                                           Lumpsucker p.168

      5d Vs as complex sucker;
         one rear D   Clingfishes p.248

   4c Light organs, sometimes
      large mouths   [Deepsea fishes] p.122

   4d Long body   encased in bony rings; tubular
                       snout with tiny mouth

                                           Pipefishes and
                                           Seahorses p.152

   4e No C; body elongate

      5a Large head, prominent lips,
         notch in rear part of D in
         Viviparous Blenny   Eelpouts p.136

      5b Vs under chin; anus well
         behind vertical of P   Cuskeels p.136

      5c Vs absent; anus
         below P   Pearlfishes p.136

      5d Vs absent; anus behind P or well
         behind gill opening if P is absent

                                           Eels p.74

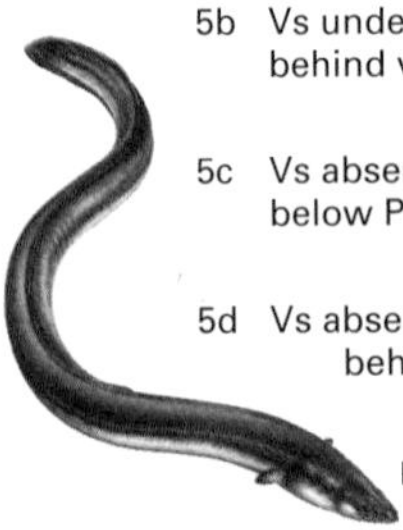

              European Eel

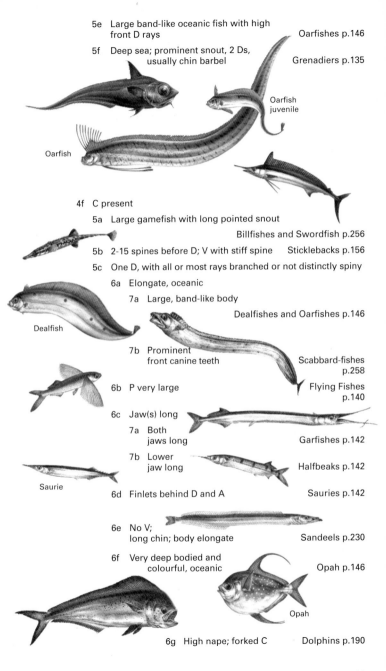

5e   Large band-like oceanic fish with high front D rays   Oarfishes p.146

5f   Deep sea; prominent snout, 2 Ds, usually chin barbel   Grenadiers p.135

Oarfish juvenile

Oarfish

4f   C present

5a   Large gamefish with long pointed snout

Billfishes and Swordfish p.256

5b   2-15 spines before D; V with stiff spine   Sticklebacks p.156

5c   One D, with all or most rays branched or not distinctly spiny

6a   Elongate, oceanic

7a   Large, band-like body

Dealfishes and Oarfishes p.146

Dealfish

7b   Prominent front canine teeth   Scabbard-fishes p.258

6b   P very large   Flying Fishes p.140

6c   Jaw(s) long

7a   Both jaws long   Garfishes p.142

7b   Lower jaw long   Halfbeaks p.142

Saurie

6d   Finlets behind D and A   Sauries p.142

6e   No V; long chin; body elongate   Sandeels p.230

6f   Very deep bodied and colourful, oceanic   Opah p.146

Opah

6g   High nape; forked C   Dolphins p.190

29

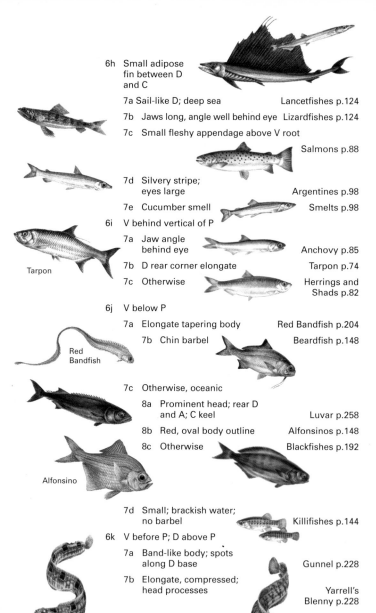

6h   Small adipose fin between D and C

7a   Sail-like D; deep sea   Lancetfishes p.124

7b   Jaws long, angle well behind eye   Lizardfishes p.124

7c   Small fleshy appendage above V root   Salmons p.88

7d   Silvery stripe; eyes large   Argentines p.98

7e   Cucumber smell   Smelts p.98

6i   V behind vertical of P

7a   Jaw angle behind eye   Anchovy p.85

7b   D rear corner elongate   Tarpon p.74

Tarpon

7c   Otherwise   Herrings and Shads p.82

6j   V below P

7a   Elongate tapering body   Red Bandfish p.204

7b   Chin barbel   Beardfish p.148

Red Bandfish

7c   Otherwise, oceanic

8a   Prominent head; rear D and A; C keel   Luvar p.258

8b   Red, oval body outline   Alfonsinos p.148

8c   Otherwise   Blackfishes p.192

Alfonsino

7d   Small; brackish water; no barbel   Killifishes p.144

6k   V before P; D above P

7a   Band-like body; spots along D base   Gunnel p.228

7b   Elongate, compressed; head processes   Yarrell's Blenny p.228

Gunnel

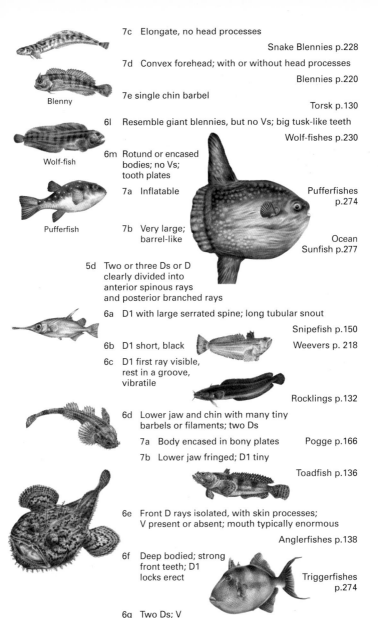

7c Elongate, no head processes

Snake Blennies p.228

7d Convex forehead; with or without head processes

Blennies p.220

Blenny

7e single chin barbel

Torsk p.130

6l Resemble giant blennies, but no Vs; big tusk-like teeth

Wolf-fishes p.230

Wolf-fish

6m Rotund or encased bodies; no Vs; tooth plates

7a Inflatable

Pufferfishes p.274

Pufferfish

7b Very large; barrel-like

Ocean Sunfish p.277

5d Two or three Ds or D clearly divided into anterior spinous rays and posterior branched rays

6a D1 with large serrated spine; long tubular snout

Snipefish p.150

6b D1 short, black

Weevers p.218

6c D1 first ray visible, rest in a groove, vibratile

Rocklings p.132

6d Lower jaw and chin with many tiny barbels or filaments; two Ds

7a Body encased in bony plates   Pogge p.166

7b Lower jaw fringed; D1 tiny

Toadfish p.136

6e Front D rays isolated, with skin processes; V present or absent; mouth typically enormous

Anglerfishes p.138

6f Deep bodied; strong front teeth; D1 locks erect

Triggerfishes p.274

6g Two Ds; V below P tip or behind

7a Flattened snouts; broad lips

Grey Mullets p.206

31

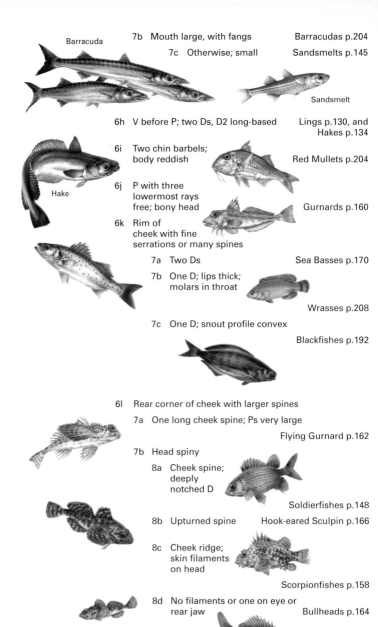

Barracuda

7b Mouth large, with fangs — Barracudas p.204

7c Otherwise; small — Sandsmelts p.145

Sandsmelt

6h V before P; two Ds, D2 long-based — Lings p.130, and Hakes p.134

6i Two chin barbels; body reddish — Red Mullets p.204

Hake

6j P with three lowermost rays free; bony head — Gurnards p.160

6k Rim of cheek with fine serrations or many spines

7a Two Ds — Sea Basses p.170

7b One D; lips thick; molars in throat

Wrasses p.208

7c One D; snout profile convex

Blackfishes p.192

6l Rear corner of cheek with larger spines

7a One long cheek spine; Ps very large

Flying Gurnard p.162

7b Head spiny

8a Cheek spine; deeply notched D

Soldierfishes p.148

8b Upturned spine — Hook-eared Sculpin p.166

8c Cheek ridge; skin filaments on head

Scorpionfishes p.158

8d No filaments or one on eye or rear jaw — Bullheads p.164

8e Otherwise — Roughfishes p.148

7c Head not spiny, other than 2 or more
   spines in cluster on cheek edge;
   prominent snout; head flattened

Dragonets p.246

Triggerfish

6m D spiny and branched rays in continuous fin

7a V reduced to spine; Mouth
   with tooth plates

Triggerfishes p.274

7b Front part of
   D high

Ray's Bream p.190

7c Jaw teeth of more or less
   different types

Seabreams p.194

7d Throat teeth
   molar-like

Wrasses p.208

7e Mouth with tooth plates

Parrot Fish p.216

7f Reddish;
   head spiny;
   offshore

Redfishes p.158

Parrot Fish

7g Otherwise

Seaperches p.171, Menolas, Drums, etc. p.200

6n Ds separate

7a Three Ds, one A;
   small

Triplefins p.220

7b Three Ds, two As

Cods p.126

7c Two Ds,
   two As; deep sea

Morids p.134

7d A spines separate; often lateral bony
   plates or enlarged scales

Jacks and Scad p.184

7e Streamlined; D and A finlets

Tunas and
Mackerels p.250

7f Deep flat
   body

Dories p.150

Mackerel

Key to Freshwater Fishes

1a No jaws, mouth suctorial; seven lateral gill-pores; eel-like

Lampreys p.38

1b True jaws; gills covered by opercle

2a Upturned tail axis; body with lateral bony plates; small ventral mouth with traverse row of barbels

Sturgeons p.72

2b Eyes on one side of head; swims on left side

Flounder p.267

2c C symmetrical or absent; eye on each side of head

3a Long body encased in bony rings; tubular snout with tiny mouth

Pipefishes p.154

3b Vs as elliptical sucker

Gobies p.238

3c Elongate; no Vs

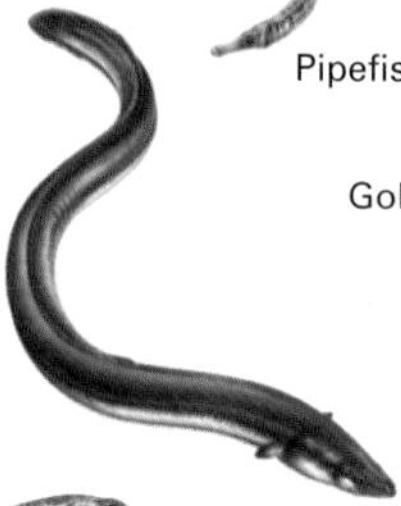

Eel p.74

3d One D; V behind vertical of P tip

4a D behind centre of body; large jaws and teeth

Pike p.86

4b D base behind centre of body; mouth small; small size

Mud-minnows p.87

4c D over middle of body; belly keeled; no lateral line; barbels absent

Shads p.84

4d Abdomen mostly rounded; LL present; never > 2 pairs of barbels

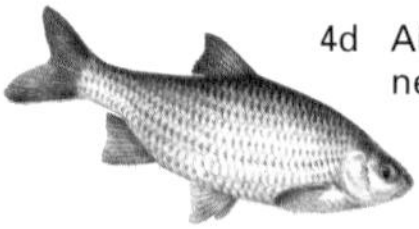

Carps p.100

4e 3-5 pairs barbels; body elongate

Loaches p.118

3e One D; V below
P tip

Killifishes and Mosquitofish p.144

3f Adipose fin between
single D and C

4a Barbels on
head

Catfishes p.120

4b Small fleshy process above V root

Salmons p.88

4c Cucumber smell; D not enlarged

Smelts p.98

3g Two to ten spines before D;
V spine large

Sticklebacks p.156

3h Two Ds, separate or contiguous

4a Chin barbel; D2 long

Burbot p.130

4b V under at least front
half of P

5a Body scaled;
A with two
spines

Perches p. 178

5c Body scaled;
A with 3 or
more spines

Sunfishes p.182

5b Body without scales;
head flattened Bullheads p.164

4c V beneath rear
or tip of P; Ds
well separated

Grey Mullets p.206

3i One long-based D;
V narrow, before
vertical of P

Blennies p.224

JAWLESS FISHES (SUPERCLASS AGNATHA)

Today's lampreys and Hagfish are eel-like survivors of the first fishes, which did not have true jaws. These modern representatives show a mixture of primitive and highly specialized features. They have a cartilaginous skeleton; horny teeth; slimy, scaleless skin; no paired fins or distinct caudal fin; muscular gill pouches that are supported by gill arches to the outside of the gill membranes; and a large nasohypophyseal sac opening from a single median nostril pore on upper surface of snout. Lampreys and Hagfish are placed in different classes (Cephalaspidomorphi and Myxini), depending respectively on possession of 2 or only 1 semicircular canal in the inner ear; jawed vertebrates (ranging from other fish up to man) have 3.

HAGFISH *Myxine glutinosa* (**Myxinidae**). A species which might be found very much alive inside the body of another fish. As such, it can be a nuisance in long-line fisheries, but it is more a predatory scavenger than a parasite. Body very slimy, with row of prominent mucous pores; no functional eyes; only low ridge as D and A and no C; 6 pairs of gill pouches, but only 1 opening on each side; teeth on tongue and palate; a barbel flanking the slit-like mouth, and 2 barbels on each side of nostril; body greyish, suffused pink. 45 cm (eastern Atlantic). Cooler waters of shelf and upper slope, 20-600 m, burrowing in mud; feeds on invertebrates and moribund or dead fish, eating into tissues and organs of body cavity. Formerly believed to be hermaphrodite, but functionally sexes separate; breeds all year but chiefly June-August in 100-300 m; eggs relatively few (19-30), large (17-25 mm), with filaments at each end, and laid in clusters. Also western Atlantic.

SEA LAMPREY *Petromyzon marinus* (**Petromyzonidae**). Lampreys are frequently parasitic on other fishes, and, in North America, landlocked populations in the Great Lakes have extensively damaged fisheries. They feed chiefly on blood and body fluids, obtained by rasping through the skin of the host by means of teeth on a suctorial disc around the mouth and on the tongue, with buccal glands secreting an anticoagulant and tissue solvent. Eel-like, but with 2 D and low C. Suctorial disc large, with teeth numerous, close-set in radiating rows; front edge of mouth has 2 large teeth; dorsal fins more or less contiguous; breeding males have ridge along back, and females have an anal fin; olive-brown with darker mottling, below whitish to pale fawn or yellow, brighter during breeding season; young are dark bluish or leaden, white below. 120 cm, 2.5 kg, probably to 11 yrs. Bottom-living, inshore and estuarine, but may go down to upper slope. After 1-2 yrs in sea, adults at 60-80 cm ascend rivers March-June (British Isles) to faster reaches, where male uses sucker to clear depression in gravel for perhaps up to 300,000 small (0.8-1.25 mm) fawn eggs spawned May-June; adults die after spawning. Freshwater juvenile stage (*ammocoete*, or 'pride') lacks suctorial disc, and filter-feeds on microorganisms; ammocoete spends 4-5.5 yrs in mud, before metamorphosis at 13-20 cm and descent to sea in late autumn or early winter. Also western Atlantic.

SUCTORIAL DISCS

Brook Lamprey

Sea Lamprey   River Lamprey

head of Hagfish

Hagfish

Sea Lamprey

RIVER LAMPREY *Lampetra fluviatilis.* Lampreys are a delicacy, a surfeit of which proved lethal for Henry I. There are local fisheries, especially in Baltic. Teeth yellowish, well spaced on suctorial disc, with 3 groups on each side of mouth; front edge of mouth has curved plate; dorsal fins separate, except during breeding season; leaden-grey above, creamy-white below, with golden tint during migration. 50 cm, 150 g, 7 yrs. Inshore shelf and estuaries, ascending rivers to overwinter and spawn; parasitize fish in sea. Adults ascend rivers September-October, and after nest preparation spawn in pebbly reaches in following April-June, 1 female with several males; adults die after spawning; fecundity to 40,000; eggs elliptical, about 1 mm long; ammocoetes in rivers for about 5 yrs, with metamorphosis completed by spring of sixth at 9-15 cm, when downstream migration occurs.

BROOK LAMPREY *Lampetra planeri.* Smallest form of lamprey and exclusively freshwater; teeth feebly developed, white and blunt, but arrangement as in River Lamprey; dorsal fins confluent; dark bluish-grey to brownish above, white or yellow below. 20 cm, 7 yrs. Breeds late March-April (British Isles), spawning sometimes in groups; fecundity to about 2,100 eggs; ammocoetes metamorphose after 6 yrs at 14-17 cm; adults do not feed and die after breeding in the same spring. **Po Brook Lamprey** *Lentheron zanandreai*, 20 cm, has 2 cusps on middle side tooth of disc rather than 3.

A ▪
B ▨
C ▪

CARPATHIAN LAMPREY *Eudontomyzon danfordi.* Ⓐ Body somewhat broader in middle; suctorial disc with lateral teeth arrangement similar to River Lamprey but with more small teeth, additional teeth plates behind mouth, and plate on tongue with 9-13 well-developed cusps, central cusps largest; body coloration brownish. 30 cm, 7 yrs. Freshwater in smaller rivers, parasitizes fishes and may also scavenge organic waste. Breeds April-May after upstream migration to fast headwaters; ammocoete 4-5 yrs before metamorphosis. Related freshwater forms, both with body thicker anteriorly, are: **Ukrainian Lamprey** *E. mariae,* Ⓑ 22 cm; and smaller **Greek Lamprey** *E. hellenicus,* Ⓒ 16 cm, but neither species is parasitic.

JAWED FISHES
(SUPERCLASS GNATHOSTOMATA)

All the remaining fishes and the higher vertebrates, including man, possess jaws, evolved from a modified anterior gill arch and with a vertical bite, and a distinct stomach. The gill arches of jawed fishes lie median to the gill filaments, and respiration involves pumping across the gills, not by muscular gill pouches. The inner ear has 3 semicircular canals. There are paired pectoral and pelvic fins, equivalent to fore- and hindlimbs. The jawed fishes may be divided into Cartilaginous and Bony forms.

CARTILAGINOUS FISHES
(CLASS CHONDRICHTHYES)

The cartilaginous fishes include sharks and rays, these being immediately recognizable from a range of external features: mouth and nostrils usually below prominent snout; fins supported by horny rays and not foldable; teeth not fused to jaws and serially replaced; and skin usually having numerous denticle-like placoid scales. Males have paired intromittent organs (pelvic claspers) for internal fertilization of female. The skeleton is cartilaginous, sometimes calcified but never

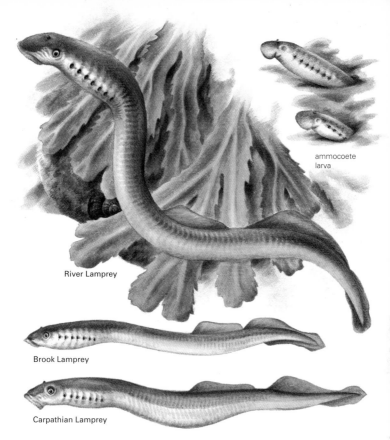

ammocoete larva

River Lamprey

Brook Lamprey

Carpathian Lamprey

ossified with bone. The intestine is short and contains a so-called spiral valve. Cartilaginous fishes are usually viviparous, or, if oviparous, produce large eggs in horny cases. They are almost exclusively marine, osmoregulating by maintaining high levels of urea and other nitrogenous compounds in the blood, which can give the flesh an ammoniacal taint. Today, sharks and rays (Elasmobranchs) predominate, although the class also contains a smaller number of rabbitfishes (Holocephali). Sharks and rays have separate gill slits, usually 5, but 6 or 7 in a few sharks, on side of head or on underside of flattened body; teeth are numerous, in rows. Rabbitfishes have an operculum (gill cover), large tooth-plates and a tapering tail.

SHARKS AND RAYS (Subclass Elasmobranchii)

SHARKS (SELACHIMORPHS)
Essentially adapted for efficient swimming in midwater. Body streamlined, cylindrical, usually with 5 gill slits on side of head; even in flattened forms, anterior edge of pectoral fin is never fused to side of head; teeth large or small, and cutting types may have more than 1 cusp.

FRILLED SHARK *Chlamydoselache anguineus* (**Chlamydoselachidae**). Sometimes taken in commercial trawling from deeper water. Body elongated; 6 gill slits, with frilled rear edges, those of first pair meeting like a collar around throat and others close to ventral midline; mouth large, terminal; D on tail, spineless; C with long lower lobe, not upturned; teeth with 3 main cusps; body dark brown or greyish-brown, lighter below, with lateral dark band. 200 cm (m), 150 cm (f). Midwater or benthic, offshore shelf and slope (120-1,100 m). Ovoviviparous, 4-12 young, born at about 60 cm after 1-2 yrs gestation. Probably worldwide in temperate waters.

SIX-GILLED SHARK *Hexanchus griseus* (**Hexanchidae**). Slender offshore sharks with 6 gill slits; 1 spineless D, set far back above A origin; upper jaw teeth with large median cusp and a few smaller ones more or less evident, lower jaw teeth comblike, cusps larger towards median end; dark brown or grey, paler below, and eyes glow green. 500 cm (a: 485 kg). Temperate seas, offshore shelf and slope to 2,000 m; benthic, reputedly sluggish, but may occur in water column especially at higher latitudes; feeds on fish such as hake, and crustaceans. Ovoviviparous, 47-108 young, 40-65 cm at birth (October-May). Probably worldwide in temperate and subtropical waters. **Seven-gilled Shark**, *Heptranchias perlo*, 100 cm (m), 140 cm (f), is slimmer and has an additional pair of gill slits.

SAND SHARKS (Odontaspidae)

Large sharks of tropical continental waters. 2 D, both spineless; nostrils not connected by grooves to corners of mouth; spiracle present; no nictitating membrane over eye; teeth large, with large middle cusp flanked by minute lateral cusp on each side; median teeth of upper jaw separated by gap from other large teeth of row. Ovoviviparous.

SAND TIGER *Eugomphodus taurus*. A somewhat unpredictable shark which bites vigorously when netted, but otherwise unlikely to attack swimmers. Median tooth of upper jaw similar in size to next tooth; V origin below rear corner of D1; light grey-brown, darker along back, to greyish-white below, with many yellowish-brown to ochre spots on sides and fins. 320 cm (a: 158.81 kg). Shelf, usually inshore, benthic; more active at night, sometimes in schools. 1-2 young, feed in uterus on unfertilized eggs during gestation of about 1 yr, born at 76 cm or more.

SMALL-TOOTHED SAND TIGER *Odontaspis ferox*. Median tooth of upper jaw much smaller than next tooth; V origin behind rear corner of D1; pale grey, whitish below, with or without dark blotches on upper parts, and fin edged dark. 360 cm. Shelf to upper slope (to 420 m).

THRESHER SHARKS (Alopiidae)
THRESHER SHARK

Alopias vulpinus. Identified by very long upper C lobe; snout conical, nostrils not linked to corners of mouth; spiracle small; gill slits fairly small, last 2 above P root; D1 opposite P/V, D2 and A minute; teeth have central erect cusp and lack lateral cusps; body brown, bluish-grey to almost black, white below. 609 cm. Epipelagic and shelf, mostly near surface but to 360 m; usually feeds on fish schools (mackerel, pilchards, garpike, etc.), circled and concentrated by splashing of long C (also used to stun prey). Ovoviviparous, 2-4 young, 120-150 cm at birth. Worldwide in tropical and temperate waters. **Big-eyed Thresher** *A. superciliosus*, 460 cm (a: 363.8 kg), has lateral groove on head, and V origin below rear corner of D1.

Frilled Shark

Six-gilled Shark

Sand Tiger

Small-toothed
Sand Tiger

Thresher Shark

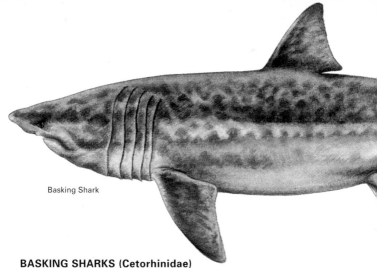

Basking Shark

BASKING SHARKS (Cetorhinidae)

BASKING SHARK *Cetorhinus maximus*. Second-largest shark, but entirely harmless. Its skeleton has several times been identified as that of a 'sea-serpent' when cast ashore. 5 very long gill slits, from near dorsal midline of head to underside; gill rakers long, like bristles; snout proboscis-like in smaller fish; nostrils not connected by groove to corners of mouth; spiracle minute; D1 opposite P/V, D2 small, on tail slightly before small A; C lunate, upper lobe longer, about one-quarter of total length, and wrist with lateral keel; teeth very small and numerous, each with a single cusp; above grey-brown to black, below similar, patchy or white. 1,350 cm (eastern Atlantic). Epipelagic, moving over shelf in summer, but retiring to deeper water for 'hibernation' when gill rakers are renewed; sluggish, usually near surface, with D1 and C protruding above water, feeds on plankton, filtered by gill rakers as shark swims slowly with mouth wide open and gills expanded (at 2 knots, an average individual may filter well over 1,000 tonnes of water per hour). Viviparous, pairing in late spring-early summer; young may be 150-180 cm at birth following a gestation perhaps as long as 3.5 yrs. Probably worldwide.

MACKEREL SHARKS (Lamnidae)

Voracious and notorious stoutly built predators with large teeth; tail wrist with lateral keel; fifth gill slit before, rather than above, anterior edge of P root; spiracle lacking in some species; 2 Ds, D1 much larger than tiny D2 above similar A on tail. Migrate into northern waters during summer months.

PORBEAGLE *Lamna nasus*. Active sportfish, often caught near surface. D1 origin over rear corner of P; secondary keel below lateral midline keel on tail wrist; teeth slender, straight, with smooth main cusp flanked on each side by small lateral cusp; the most median 2 teeth similar to rest, but third upper tooth smaller than adjacent teeth; body dark blue-grey above, sharply demarcated from white below; P dusky near tip; A white or greyish. 305 cm (a: 230 kg). Epipelagic, mostly 200-700 m, and shelf in warmer months; feed on fishes. Ovoviviparous, with embryos absorbing yolk sac at small size and then ingesting unfertilized eggs, thereby acquiring greatly distended 'yolk stomach'; 1-4 born at 45-60 cm, probably in summer. Worldwide in temperate waters.

Basking Shark
at surface

embryo of
Porbeagle

Porbeagle

SHORT-FINNED MAKO *Isurus oxyrinchus*. Larger surface species, often leaping, and the fastest swimmer among sharks (to 35 km/h). D1 origin behind rear corner of P; P shorter than head; only 1 lateral keel on tail wrist; teeth slender, straight, smooth, without lateral cusps; most median 2 teeth larger, curved, third upper tooth somewhat smaller than adjacent teeth; deep blue-grey above, sharply delimited from snow-white below. 390 cm (a: 505.76 kg). Epipelagic, surface to 400 m, and shelf; very active, feeding on fishes. Reproduction as Porbeagle, with possibly up to 10 young, born at 60-70 cm. Worldwide in tropical and temperate waters, and some commercial fishing as well as angling. **Long-finned Mako** *I. paucus*, 290 cm, has pectoral fin as long as head.

GREAT WHITE SHARK *Carcharodon carcharias*. This is 'Jaws': the largest predatory fish, and reputedly the most dangerous to man. D1 origin over rear corner of P; only 1 well-developed lateral keel on tail wrist; teeth large, triangular, with serrated edges and no obvious lateral cusps; broader in upper jaw, whose third tooth is hardly smaller than adjacent teeth; above slatey-brown, leaden-blue, to almost black; whitish below, with dark spot at inner root of P; larger individuals may be whitish above, without P spot. 450 cm (m), 600 cm (f), records to 1,100 cm now discredited (a: 1,208.38 kg). Epipelagic, surface to 1,300 m, and shelf; feeds on fishes, turtles, seals and squid. Worldwide in temperate and warmer seas but fortunately never abundant; a breeding population is believed to occur off Sicily.

Short-finned Mako

teeth of Mako

Great White Shark

teeth of Great White Shark

CATSHARKS (Scyliorhinidae)

Small elongated dogfishes, with Ds low, D1 not before V origin; tail axis subhorizontal; groove under eye; last 1 or 2 gill slits over P origin; teeth small, multicuspid. Bottom-living; oviparous, horny egg cases.

LESSER SPOTTED DOGFISH *Scyliorhinus canicula*. Commonest dogfish along southern and western British Isles. Nostril flaps almost or completely joined to each other in front of mouth; sandy to brownish above, with numerous small (pupil-sized) dark spots, uniform pale cream below. 105 cm. Shelf, on sandy or muddy grounds, but deeper in Mediterranean (to 400 m); nocturnal, resting during day. Mate in deeper water in late summer, lay eggs (about 20) inshore chiefly November-July; egg case pale brown, oblong (3-4 × 2.2-2.5 cm), with curly tendril at each corner for attachment to sea-bed; young hatch after 8-9 months, measuring about 10 cm.

GREATER SPOTTED DOGFISH *Scyliorhinus stellaris*. Similar to preceding, but larger, having nostril flaps well separated from each other, and larger less-numerous dark spots. 162 cm. Usually on more offshore coarse grounds, to about 65 m or deeper. Ripe females April-September; egg case dark brown, 11 × 4 cm, young hatch at 16 cm. Also known as Nursehound. To West Africa.

BLACK-MOUTHED DOGFISH *Galeus melastomus*. Longer snout and nostrils well separated, with flap little developed; crest of enlarged denticles along upper edge of anterior tail; above with close-set dark brown more or less oblong blotches, paler below; inside of mouth black. 61 cm (m), 90 cm (f) (a: 1.37 kg). Offshore shelf but chiefly upper slope, 55-1,200 m. Spawn July (SW Ireland), all year (chiefly spring and summer) in Mediterranean; egg cases 6 × 2 cm, corners of one end in short points, rounded at the other. To Senegal.

FALSE CATSHARK *Pseudotriakis microdon* (**Pseudotriakidae**). A very elongated small shark, with low, long-based D1 opposite most of gap between P and V; teeth tiny and numerous; dark brown, fins edged darker. 295 cm. Slope, sometimes onto offshore shelf. Ovoviviparous, 2 young, 90 cm when born. Worldwide in warmer seas.

SMOOTH DOGFISHES (Triakidae)

Chiefly small and less active, but shark-like; nictitating membrane, subocular ridge, and spiracle present; last 2 gill slits over P base; D1 over P to V gap; no precaudal pit; notch on lower edge of C near tip.

TOPE *Galeorhinus galeus*. Largest of our smooth dogfishes, and often caught by anglers. D2 much smaller than D1; teeth mostly oblique, with main cusp flanked laterally by series of small cusps; grey to light brown above, paler below. 210 cm (a: 33 kg). Inshore, on gravel or sand, but in deeper water (to 282 m) in winter; feeds chiefly on fish, especially gadoids such as whiting. Ovoviviparous, 20-50 young, born at 37.5-40 cm June-September, close inshore.

SMOOTH HOUND *Mustelus mustelus*. D2 slightly smaller than D1; teeth low, rounded, in close-set pavement; uniform brown or grey above, white below. 150 cm. Coastal, bottom-living, feeding on invertebrates and small fish. Viviparous, 4-10 young, 35 cm at birth. Also West Africa.

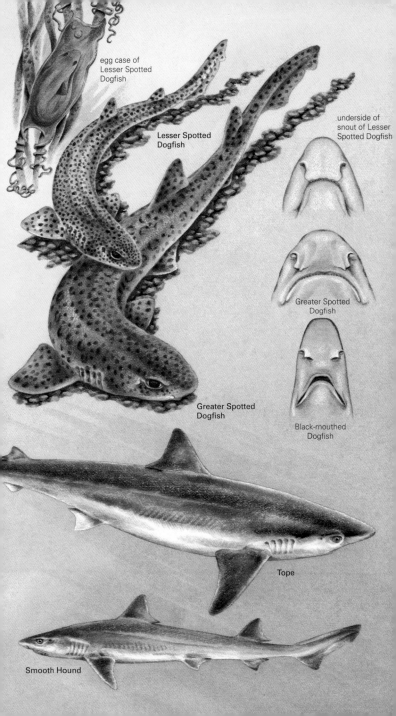

egg case of
Lesser Spotted
Dogfish

Lesser Spotted
Dogfish

underside of
snout of Lesser
Spotted Dogfish

Greater Spotted
Dogfish

Greater Spotted
Dogfish

Black-mouthed
Dogfish

Tope

Smooth Hound

STARRY SMOOTH HOUND *Mustelus asterias*. As preceding, but with many white spots over greyish or brown back. 140 cm (a: 4.76 kg). Feeds especially on swimming crabs. Ovoviviparous, about 20 young, 30 cm at birth. **Black-spotted Smooth Hound** *Mustelus punctulatus*, also warm-temperate, has small dark spots over grey or brown nape and back, and Ds with dark rear edges. Over 60 cm. Possibly viviparous, young 30 cm at birth.

REQUIEM SHARKS (Carcharinidae)

The most numerous and significant group of sharks in marine ecology, of variable reputation but some very dangerous; most species worldwide in warm seas, along temperate coasts in summer and even known in Venetian canals. Nictitating membrane present; teeth with a single main blade-like cusp, typically serrated; spiracle usually absent; last 2 gill slits over P base; precaudal pit present; D1 much larger than D2.

SPINNER SHARK *Carcharinus brevipinna*. Snout long, conical; D1 origin just behind rear corner of P; D2 opposite A; teeth narrow, only upper teeth serrated; greyish to coppery above, with narrow greyish stripe along upper side of body; below white; fins with black tips (except young <80-130 cm). 278 cm (a: 86.18 kg). Shelf and epipelagic, active, may leap at surface, spin and fall backwards into sea. Viviparous, breeding every other year; young 6-15, born at 60-75 cm.

BLACK-TIPPED SHARK *Carcharinus limbatus*. As preceding, but D1 origin over rear corner of P; fins with black tips, except A. 250 cm (a: 122.75 kg). Habitat and behaviour also as Spinner Shark. Viviparous, breeding every other year; 4-10 young born at 50-60 cm. Eastern Atlantic.

SANDBAR SHARK *Carcharinus plumbeus*. Body deeper; snout short; D1 origin well over rear corner of P; upper teeth broad, triangular, lower teeth narrow; greyish to bronze above without greyish stripe, and white below; fins lacking conspicuous black tips, except P. 250 cm (a: 117.93 kg). Shelf, near bottom, especially over sand. Viviparous, breeding every 2-3 yrs; 6-14 young, born at 50-60 cm. Other sharks of this genus which may occur within present area include: **Silky Shark** *C. falciformis*, 350 cm, with ridge between D1 and D2, D1 origin just behind rear angle of P; **Oceanic White-tipped Shark** *C. longimanus*, 350 cm (a: 66.45 kg), dangerous species with large rounded D1, white-tipped P and lower C; **Black-tipped Reef Shark** *C. melanopterus*, 180 cm, lemon-brown back, all fins distinctly tipped black; and **Dusky Shark** *C. obscurus*, 365 cm (a: 346.54 kg), ridge between D1 and D2, D1 origin over P rear angle. The related **Milk Shark** *Rhizoprionodon acutus*, 105 cm, has a long snout, smooth teeth, and D2 origin behind middle of A base.

BLUE SHARK *Prionace glauca*. Bright blue with white underside, and very long, falciform P; snout long; D1 origin well behind rear angle of P; gill slits short. 383 cm (a: 198.22 kg). Highly voracious, oceanic, often cruising at surface, and also more inshore. Viviparous, with yolk-sac placenta; 28-80 young, born at 38-46 cm after 9-12 months gestation. Sport-fishery in western Channel catches mostly gravid females, but numbers are declining, probably through overfishing; cold seasons and a dinoflagellate 'bloom' have also been implicated.

Starry Smooth Hound

Spinner Shark

Black-tipped Shark

Sandbar Shark

Blue Shark

TIGER SHARK *Galeocerdo cuvieri.* One of the most dangerous sharks, with many attacks on humans; it is otherwise a very indiscriminate feeder (turtles and dolphins to jellyfish; a car licence plate is on record). Blunt, flattened head; body robust, but tail slender; spiracle present; D1 origin above rear corner of P; C wrist with lateral keels; greyish-green or brown, with dark spots or bars, becoming indistinct in fish over about 300 cm. At least 550 cm; estimated 45-50 yrs (a: 807.4 kg). Shelf and epipelagic, bottom to surface cruising. Ovoviviparous, 10-82 young, up to 76 cm at birth. Worldwide in tropical waters, straying northwards.

HAMMERHEADS (Sphyrnidae)

SMOOTH HAMMERHEAD *Sphyrna zygaena.* Unmistakable from hammer-like plan of flattened head, whose sides are extended laterally, with eyes and nostrils on outer edges, supposedly to aid detection of prey by sight, smell or electrical stimuli. Despite bizarre appearance, none the less liable to attack man. Snout lacks midline notch; teeth with 1 smooth or feebly serrated cusp; olive to grey-brown, whitish below. 408 cm (a: 148.1 kg). Shelf, often at surface and may occur in schools; feeds on fish, especially stingrays. Viviparous, up to 37 young, born at 50-60 cm, with hammers folded. More southerly **Scalloped Hammerhead** *S. lewini*, 420 cm (a: 120 kg), has median notch on front edge of head and D2 base shorter than A base; and **Great Hammerhead** *S. mokarran*, 610 cm (a: 449.5 kg), has strongly serrated teeth, and D2 rear edge deeply concave.

DOGFISH SHARKS (Squalidae)

Many species, mostly offshore and deep-water, but spurdogs are abundant in coastal waters on both sides of the temperate Atlantic. Dorsal fins each usually with an anterior spine; anal fin absent; nostrils not connected to corners of mouth; deep preoral cleft above corners of mouth usually present; ovoviviparous.

SPURDOG *Squalus acanthias.* The common dogfish of more northerly waters around the British Isles, with commercial landings (sold as Rock Salmon or Flake); sharp D spines without lateral grooves; D1 spine origin opposite (young) or behind (adult) rear corner of P; C upper lobe not notched on ventral edge; teeth with single cusp, very oblique, with median side forming cutting edge and lateral side deeply notched, similar in upper and lower jaws; slate-grey above, usually with white spots, whitish below. 90 cm (m), 120 cm (f); 20 kg (a: 7.14 kg). Shelf, often in schools, with seasonal migration between inshore and deeper waters to 200 m or more; feeds on fish and invertebrates. Gestation 18-24 months, producing young all year (Mediterranean) or late spring-summer (North Sea); 2-15 young (usually about 6), born at 22-33 cm; not sexually mature until 11-12 yrs (m), 19-20 yrs (f). Worldwide in temperate seas, and often a nuisance to commercial and sportfisheries; D spines cause painful, slow-healing wounds. More offshore **Long-nosed Spurdog** *S. blainvillei*, 96 cm, has D1 spine origin opposite end of P base (young) or rear corner of P (adult), and grey to greyish-brown above, lacking white spots.

Tiger Shark

Smooth
Hammerhead

snout of
Hammerhead

Spurdog

Long-nosed
Spurdog

GREENLAND SHARK
Somniosus microcephalus. A large shark, and the only one to live normally in Arctic seas. 0.6 to 10-12°C. D1 and D2 small, without spines, bases similar in length; D2 height about half base length; C upper lobe with notch on rear edge; teeth with single cusp, upper teeth narrow, slightly oblique, lower teeth broader, very oblique, with cutting edges (median side of cusp) smooth; dermal denticles conical or thorn-like, recurved; coffee-brown to slate-grey or black, sometimes indistinctly banded or with pale spots. 650 cm (a: 775 kg). Mostly benthic in summer, 180-600 m or more, but near surface in winter; sluggish, feeding on fishes, birds, seals, invertebrates and carrion, reputedly luring fast-swimming fish to white (possibly luminous) parasitic copepods attached to its eyes. Reproduction may be oviparous, although ovoviviparity of up to 10 young, at least 38 cm at birth, also reported. Local fisheries (main by-product liver oil) but flesh toxic when fresh. The similar but much smaller **Little Sleeper Shark** *S. rostratus*, 100 cm, with D2 height less than base length and luminous lateral-line pores, is an upper-slope species.

DWARF SHARK *Squaliolus laticaudus.* At a maximum size of only 25 cm, the world's smallest cartilaginous fish, mature from 15-16 cm. Eyes large; gill openings very small; D1 and D2 low, D2 long-based and without spine; D2 height much less than half base length; C lobes broad, without notch on rear edge; teeth with single cusp, upper teeth narrow, lower teeth broader, oblique, with cutting edges (median side of cusp) smooth; dark brown or black. Epipelagic, offshore and over slope, 200-1,200 m. Probably ovoviviparous. Also Indo-Pacific.

A
B
C

A variety of deep-water squaloid sharks may be encountered in commercial fisheries. These include: **Velvet Belly** *Etmopterus spinax*, Ⓐ 45 cm, brown, with pale spot between eyes and lateral dark band, whose upper teeth have 3 cusps, and lower teeth cusps form an almost continuous cutting edge along jaw; **Gulper Shark** *Centrophorus* spp., 90-150 cm, with inner corner of P elongated, and single-cusped upper teeth; **Velvet Dogfish** *Centroscymnus* spp., 70-120 cm, and *Scymnodon* spp., 50-110 cm, whose tiny D1 and D2 spines may not be exposed; **Darkie Charlie** *Dalatias licha*, Ⓑ 180 cm, short-snouted, Ds spineless, lower teeth with triangular serrated cusp, and lip surface much folded and ridged; **Shovelnosed Shark** *Deania calceus*, 111 cm, with long, flattened snout, appreciably narrowed before nostrils; and the aptly named **Bramble Shark** *Echinorhinus brucus*, Ⓒ 250 cm, with large dermal spines scattered over head and body, and close-set, spineless Ds above A.

A
B

ANGULAR ROUGHSHARK *Oxynotus centrina.* Ⓐ Small but stout-bodied, triangular in section and ridged between P and V bases; gill openings very small; D1 and D2 large, with strong spines penetrating anterior edge of fin from origin well along base, D1 spine pointing obliquely forwards; C upper lobe without rear notch; teeth with single cusp; dark brown, with darker blotches, or black. 150 cm. Bottom-living on shelf and upper slope, 60-660 m. Ovoviviparous, with 22-23 offspring. To Senegal. The black **Sail-fin Roughshark** *O. paradoxus*, Ⓑ 118 cm, has a backwardly directed D1 spine.

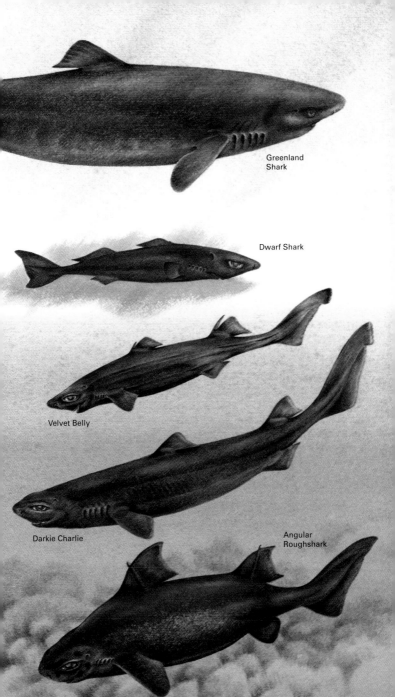

Greenland
Shark

Dwarf Shark

Velvet Belly

Darkie Charlie

Angular
Roughshark

ANGEL SHARKS (Squatinidae)

ANGEL SHARK *Squatina squatina*. Also known as Monkfish. Flattened, intermediate in shape between shark and ray, but definitely shark because anterior edges of wing-like Ps are not fused to side of head, although concealing gill slits; mouth terminal; Ds small, on tail; C with larger lower lobe; A absent; teeth similar in both jaws, each with slender, erect, smooth-edged cusp on expanded base; above brownish-green, with darker markings (often whitish reticulate pattern in smaller fish). 250 cm (a: 24 kg). Shelf, bottom-living, inshore from about 5 m to more offshore (70-90 m) in winter; nocturnal, feeding on fish, especially flatfish, whelks and crabs. Ovoviviparous, 7-25 young, born at 20-30 cm after gestation of about 10 months in December-February (Mediterranean), June-July (northern part of range). Two tropical eastern Atlantic species extending into Mediterranean are: **Saw-backed Angel Shark** *S. aculeata*, 130 cm, with series of large dermal denticles along dorsal midline, but lower surface rough only along anterior edges of fins and on tail; and **Smooth-backed Angel Shark** *S. oculata*, 150 cm, with several large white spots on upper surface and rear tip of V not quite reaching to opposite D1 origin.

RAYS (RAJIFORMS)

Cartilaginous fishes with flat, typically rounded or diamond-shaped bodies, with front border of pectoral fins fused to side of head, forming the 'wings' of a 'disc'. The spiracle remains on the upper surface behind the eye, and the gill slits are displaced below the wings on underside of disc. Teeth are small, in several rows which may form a close-set flattened pavement.

SAWFISHES and GUITARFISHES

More shark-like than rays, but are rays nevertheless because Ps are fused to head above gill slits.

COMMON SAWFISH *Pristis pristis* (**Pristidae**). Snout elongated into flat blade edged with 15-20 spaced teeth along each side; dark grey or brownish above, white below; 5 m (with saw). Bottom-living, inshore, estuaries, entering fresh water; eats fish and benthic invertebrates; saw is used in defence or for attacking fish schools. Ovoviviparous. To West Africa. **Small-toothed Sawfish** *P. pectinata*, has 24-32 teeth on each side.

COMMON GUITARFISH *Rhinobatos rhinobatos* (**Rhinobatidae**). Snout more or less pointed, with ridges widely spaced, somewhat nearer dorsal midline anteriorly; head and wings shorter than rest of body, and breadth less than half total length; eye length not less than one-fifth snout length; brownish above, white below. 100 cm. Mostly sluggish, bottom-living on sand or mud, inshore to 100 m; eats fish and invertebrates. Ovoviviparous, with 1-2 litters per year of 4-10 young. To West Africa. **Black-chinned Guitarfish** *R. cemiculus* 180 cm (a: 39.5 kg), has snout ridges close together and smaller eyes; grey with dark blotch on snout.

Angel Shark

Common Sawfish

Common
Guitarfish

Black-chinned
Guitarfish

ELECTRIC RAYS (Torpedinidae)

Round thick-bodied rays, with a powerful electric organ on each side of disc, generating up to 220 V; smooth disc has straight anterior edge lacking distinct snout; tail thick and caudal fin well developed. Electric organs used to stun prey (usually small fish, also invertebrates), in defence, and for electrolocation. Ovoviviparous, gestation lasting several months to 1 yr. Bottom-living, slow-swimming and may bury themselves. Tropical and southern Africa, into temperate areas.

MARBLED ELECTRIC RAY *Torpedo marmorata*. Typically fine brown markings over pale to brownish upper surface, white or creamy below; edges of spiracle with long processes, almost meeting across aperture. 60 cm. Inshore to 40 m, or even 100 m, on fine and coarse grounds.

EYED ELECTRIC RAY *Torpedo torpedo*. 5 (rarely fewer) large dark-edged blue spots on brownish upper surface; spiracle with small processes on edge. 60 cm. Soft grounds to 70 m or more. Females gravid March-September (Mediterranean), up to 21 young reaching 10 cm at birth.

ELECTRIC RAY *Torpedo nobiliana*. The largest of European electric rays. Upper surface more or less uniformly brownish, lacking large spots and dense pale mottling; spiracle edges smooth. 180 cm (a: 16.01 kg). Soft grounds, 10-150 m, sometimes much deeper; adults may swim off sea-bed. Young born offshore, up to 60 cm.

SKATES AND RAYS (Rajidae)

Familiar fishes in temperate seas, at least a dozen of the present species contributing to commercial fisheries. Disc rhomboidal, snout blunt ('rays') to very pointed ('skates'), but intermediate forms may be given either name; tail slender, with 2 small dorsal fins near tip and reduced caudal fin; large spines and thorns may be present, especially on upper surface in patches or rows. Bottom-living. Oviparous, with eggs in horny capsule ('mermaid's purse'). Identification can be difficult, and the following guide is based chiefly on coloration, sometimes variable, and omits distribution of spines also employed in ray systematics.

Species with a single conspicuous spot ('ocellus' or eye spot) on each wing; temperate seas:

MALTESE RAY *Raja melitensis*. Snout tip pronounced; brown with large spot (yellow vermiculations and dots on dark background) at about middle of wing base, and a few less-distinct smaller spots of similar composition on wing; under surface white. 50 cm. Shelf and beyond, 60-600 m. **African Ray** *R. africana*, 70 cm, rare, has a single small dark-edged brown spot on wing base nearer pelvics.

Marbled
Electric Ray

Eyed
Electric Ray

Electric Ray

Maltese Ray

CUCKOO RAY *Raja naevus.* Yellowish to pale drab brown, with a single large round spot (yellow vermiculation on dark background) at middle of each wing base; white below. 70 cm. Inshore to edge of shelf. Breeds all year, producing as many as 100 eggs.

BROWN RAY *Raja miraletus.* Yellowish to reddish-brown, with spot (pale blue, ringed by concentric darker blue and yellowish-orange) on middle of wing base; white below. 60 cm. Mostly more offshore shelf, but from inshore to uppermost slope, also fished.

SPOTTED RAY *Raja montagui.* Pale brownish with many small dark spots that do not extend to edge of wings, and often a larger pale spot with broken dark circumference on each wing; white below. 80 cm. Inshore and coastal shelf. **Speckled Ray** *R. polystigma.* 60 cm, usually occurring deeper (100-400 m), has conspicuous wing spot with thicker dark periphery and dark centre.

ROUGH RAY *Raja radula.* Greyish-brown, with irregular dark streaks and spots, as well as small but conspicuous spot (yellow, with dark periphery and dark centre) at middle of wing base; mostly white below, but wing margins greyish. 70 cm. Inshore to uppermost slope. Breeds throughout year, mostly late spring-summer; eggs hatch after 4 months.

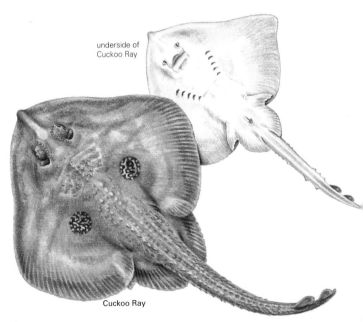

underside of
Cuckoo Ray

Cuckoo Ray

Brown Ray

Spotted Ray

Rough Ray

Species with other patterns, such as more numerous spots and streaks:

STARRY SKATE *Raja radiata*. Greyish-brown with many small clusters of dark spots; white below sometimes blotched. 60-90 cm (a: 4.25 kg). Inshore, 50-100 m, but even to 1000 m. Mature at 40-80 cm.

SANDY RAY *Raja circularis*. Brown, more or less tinged red, with about 4-6 small dark-edged white spots on wings and pelvics, in similar pattern on each side; white below. 120 cm. Offshore shelf, but to 275 m on upper slope.

SHAGREEN RAY *Raja fullonica*. Pointed snout; upper jaw with median notch; uniform ash-grey above, white below. 100 cm. Chiefly offshore shelf, especially coarser grounds, but overall range 30-550 m in cooler, deeper waters off southern Europe. **Round Ray** *R. fyllae*, 55 cm, wing tips very rounded, grey to dark brown above, variously blotched, white below with greyish or brownish wing margins and tail. Occurs offshore from the outer shelf down the continental slope to over 2,000 m.

STARRY RAY *Raja asterias*. Pale brown with scattered light spots on a background of dark, coarse stipple; white below. 70 cm. Inshore and coastal shelf. Breeds chiefly summer-early autumn, large females producing more than 100 eggs that hatch after 5-6 months (Mediterranean).

BLONDE RAY *Raja brachyura*. Yellowish-brown, with many small dark dots to edge of disc, sometimes ringing a few pale spots; white below. 120 cm (a: 14.28 kg). Inshore sandy grounds. Breeds February-August; young hatch at about 7 months.

THORNBACK RAY *Raja clavata*. Coloration variable but never has few large distinct spots; white below, often greyish towards edge of disc; upper surface of disc with numerous spines. 90 cm (a: 7.59 kg). Inshore to uppermost slope. Breeds winter-spring (Mediterranean), or spring (boreal Atlantic); eggs hatch after about 5 months. Also tropical and southern Africa. **Madeira Ray** *R. maderensis*, 80 cm, also with large spines from nape to D1, is brown with numerous pale spots except on uniform transverse streaks from base to apex of wings, pale below, except greyish snout and wing edges.

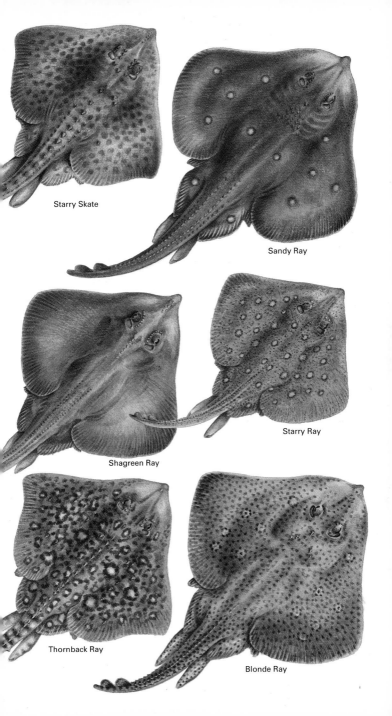

Starry Skate

Sandy Ray

Shagreen Ray

Starry Ray

Thornback Ray

Blonde Ray

SMALL-EYED RAY *Raja microocellata*. Greyish, olive or pale brown, with thin light streaks flanking edges of wings; white below. 80 cm (a: 4.5 kg). Inshore and coastal sandy grounds. Breeds summer (English Channel).

UNDULATE RAY *Raja undulata*. Yellowish to grey-brown, with dark streaks, roughly aligned with wing edges and margined by series of small white dots; white below. 100 cm. Shelf, on finer deposits. Breeds March-September.

WHITE SKATE *Raja alba*. Reddish brown in smaller fish, darkening to grey-blue in larger sizes, with many pale spots; white below with wing and pelvic fin edges more or less dark. 200 cm. Coastal to upper slope, 40-400 m. Eggs hatch after about 15 months. Also southern and West Africa.

The following species, the true 'skates', all have very elongated snouts, so that typically a line from snout tip to wing tip does not cross the intervening edge of the disc, and distance between nostrils is less than 70 per cent of snout length (nostril to tip):

COMMON SKATE *Raja batis*. Drab olive to brownish, with variable markings; dark grey below; many small black dots and lines on both surfaces. 250 cm (a: 97.07 kg). Mostly in shelf waters (less than 200 m), rarely to 600 m; feeds on fishes, crabs and octopuses. **Black Skate** *R. nidarosiensis*, 200 cm, similar to Common Skate but coloration typically concealed by durable covering of black mucus; on shelf edge, upper continental slope and in fiords, 200-1,000 m.

LONG-NOSED SKATE *Raja oxyrinchus*. Sides of disc deeply concave; brownish, darker in larger fish; below dark brown to bluish-grey, with dark dots and lines especially frequent on undersurface of anterior disc. 150 cm. Mostly offshore shelf, but to 900 m.

A
B
C

Three long-nosed species from the cold basin of the North Atlantic are: **Spine-tailed Ray** *Bathyraja spinicauda*, Ⓐ grey above, white below with rear margins greyish, 170 cm, 140-800 m; **Arctic Skate** *R. hyperborea*, Ⓑ dark greyish or brownish, underside becoming mostly dark in adults, 85 cm, 300-1,500 (2,500) m; and **Sail Ray** *R. lintea*, Ⓒ 110 cm (a: 10.85 kg), uniform grey, white below with broad dark band along rear edge of wing and blotches flanking cloaca; outer shelf to upper slope.

Long-nosed Skate

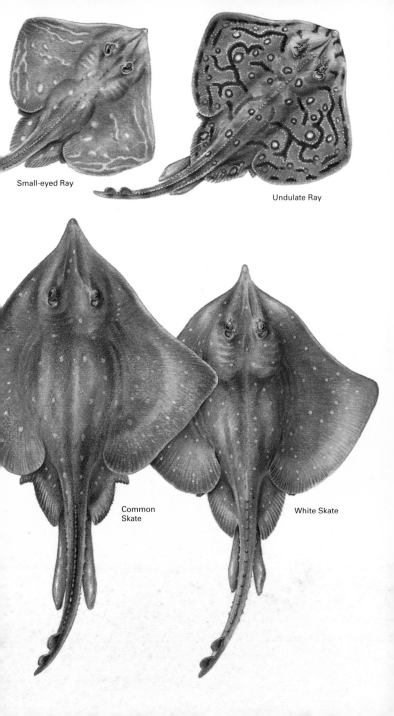

Small-eyed Ray

Undulate Ray

Common
Skate

White Skate

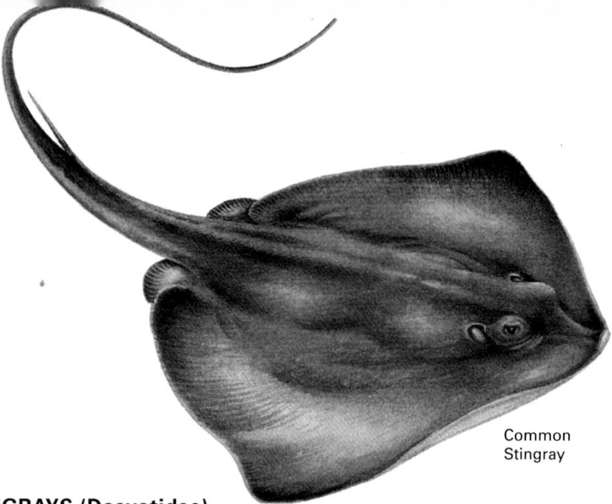

Common Stingray

STINGRAYS (Dasyatidae)

Warm-water rays of rhomboidal to pear-shaped outline, with tail typically whip-like, lacking dorsal fins or distinct caudal fins; 1 or more long serrated spines on upper side of tail near root equipped with poison glands, which can cause painful injuries. Usually sluggish swimmers or lie partially buried in substrate; feed on fish and invertebrates. Ovoviviparous, with small number of young (2-9) and gestation from 4 months to about 1 yr.

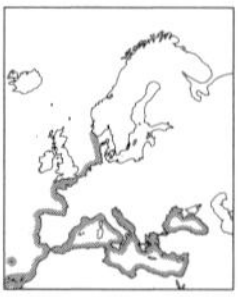

COMMON STINGRAY *Dasyatis pastinaca*. Tail lacking fold along underside to tip; no large thorns or tubercles on disc or tail in larger fish; grey to brownish, white below with disc broadly edged in dark brown or black. 60 cm wide. Shelf, on sand and muddy grounds. **Tortonese's Stingray** *D. tortonesei*, 80 cm wide, similar coloration, has definite ridge along upper midline of tail behind spine, 3 rather fine papillae or processes on floor of mouth, and fifth gill slits more widely spaced than half their distance behind mouth.

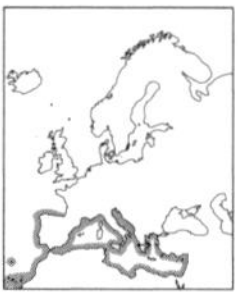

ROUGH-TAILED STINGRAY *Dasyatis centroura*. Tubercles along middle of back and thorns along dorsal midline and sides of tail; snout with obtuse tip; brownish-olive above, white below. 210 cm wide (a: 133.35 kg). Shelf. Breeds autumn-early winter, producing 2-4 young after about 4 months' gestation.

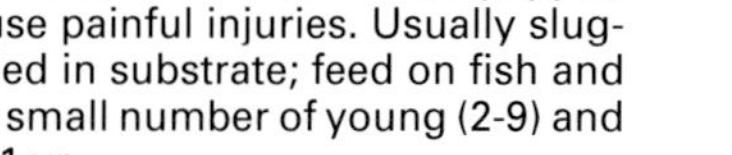

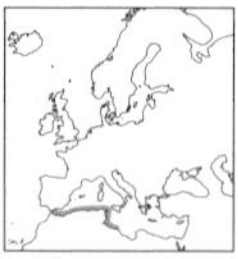

VIOLET STINGRAY *Dasyatis violacea*. Tail as Common Stingray but anterior edge of disc rounded, and both upper and lower surfaces dark, purplish to greenish-blue. 80 cm wide. Pelagic, usually down to 100 m, feeding on jellyfish, squid, fish, etc. Circumtropical.

A
B

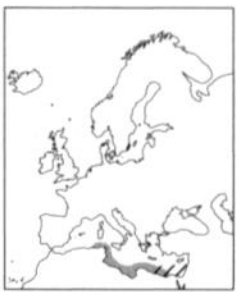

Two less-common stingrays in the Mediterranean are: the **Round Stingray** *Taeniura grabata*, A 100 cm wide, with a much shorter tail, compressed and bearing ventral fin fold towards end; and **Forsskal's Stingray** *Himantura uarnak*, B 125 cm wide, with whitish to yellow markings over dark disc, creamy-white below, and with whip-like tail, an Indo-Pacific migrant through Suez Canal along Levant coast.

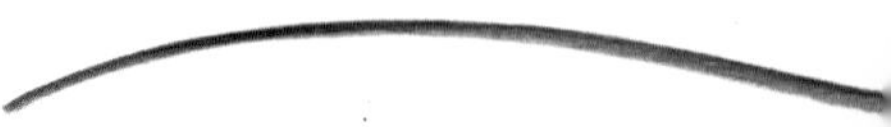

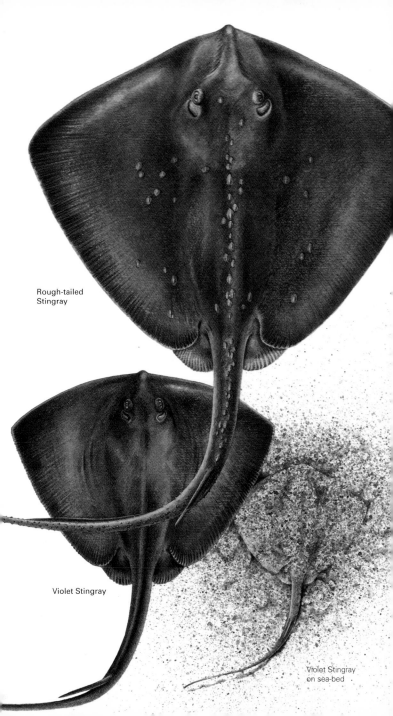

Rough-tailed
Stingray

Violet Stingray

Violet Stingray
on sea-bed

BUTTERFLY RAYS (Gymnuridae)

SPINY BUTTERFLY RAY *Gymnura altavela*. Large ray, with disc much wider than long across wings, and tail much shorter than disc length, armed with 1 or more serrated spines; brownish, variously marked with dark spots and light blotches. 400 cm wide (a: 60 kg). Inshore, sluggish, on bottom but may be seen swimming slowly in shallows; feeds on fish and invertebrates. Ovoviviparous, with several young. Also tropical Atlantic.

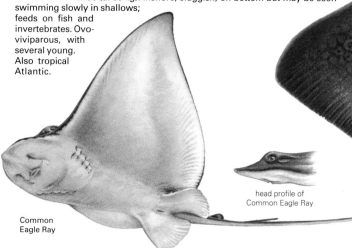

head profile of
Common Eagle Ray

Common
Eagle Ray

EAGLE RAYS (Myliobatidae)

Also large, with disc more wide than long, wing tips acutely angled, and wings anteriorly extending under snout; head raised from disc, eyes and spiracles on each side; tail whip-like, with 1 or more serrated spines, and small dorsal fin; teeth form grinding plates in a close-set pavement. Midwater to surface in coastal waters of warmer seas, sometimes in large schools, but feed on benthic molluscs and crustaceans so may be harmful to commercial shellfish beds. Ovoviviparous.

COMMON EAGLE RAY *Myliobatis aquila*. Wing anterior edge joining a median transverse lobe under snout; dorsal fin origin at rear of pelvic fin tips; disc bronze, whitish below. 83 cm wide across disc.

BULL RAY *Pteromylaeus bovinus*. Wing anterior edge not fusing with median lobe under snout; dorsal fin over pelvic fins; brown above, streaked in smaller fish; white below, P tips red-brown. 150 cm wide (a: 36.5 kg). 4-6 young, about 45 cm across wings.

COW-NOSED RAY *Rhinoptera marginata*. (**Rhinopteridae**) Median lobe under snout divided into 2 parts; no obvious papillae on floor of mouth; greenish-brown to more bronze, white below. 200 cm wide. 2-6 young, gestation up to 1 yr.

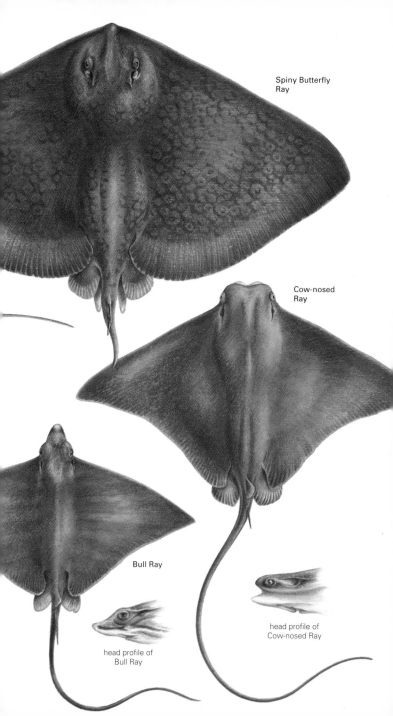

Spiny Butterfly Ray

Cow-nosed Ray

Bull Ray

head profile of Bull Ray

head profile of Cow-nosed Ray

Devil Ray

DEVIL RAYS (Mobulidae)

DEVIL RAY *Mobula mobular*. Largest of rays, with broad disc and acutely pointed wing tips, spanning up to 520 cm; anterior edge of wing forms a separate lobe ('horn') on each side of mouth; tail whip-like, with serrated spine or spines and small dorsal fin; minute teeth in bands, and gills modified for sieving; dark brown to black, white below. Coastal, in tropical and warmer waters, often in pairs at surface, sometimes leaping; feeds on small nektonic fish and crustaceans, funnelled into mouth by horns. Ovoviviparous, but only 1-2 young.

RABBIT-FISHES (SUBCLASS HOLOCEPHALI)

A very distinct group of cartilaginous fishes, with opercle covering gill slits, tooth-plates, and elongated tail; chiefly from deep water.

RABBIT-FISH *Chimaera monstrosa* (**Chimaeridae**). Large head with conical snout, and long body tapering into whip-like tail; mouth with tooth-plates (recalling front teeth of rabbit); lateral-line canals and pores prominent; D1 large, with strong spine; D2 long-based, low; both D2 and A separated from low C fins along upper and lower edges of tail; males with median appendage on forehead and paired structures before Vs, believed to function as claspers; greenish or bluish, with silvery sheen and mottling, creamy below; Ds, A and C edged black. 100 cm (including C filament). Bottom-living, upper slope (300-500 m, even to 1,000 m), with summer movement (especially by larger females) onto shelf (to 40-100 m) in more northern areas (traditionally known as 'king of the herrings'); feeds mostly on benthic invertebrates. Oviparous, spawning April-May (Norway), egg case elongated, 18 × 2.5 cm, tapering to filament at pointed end.

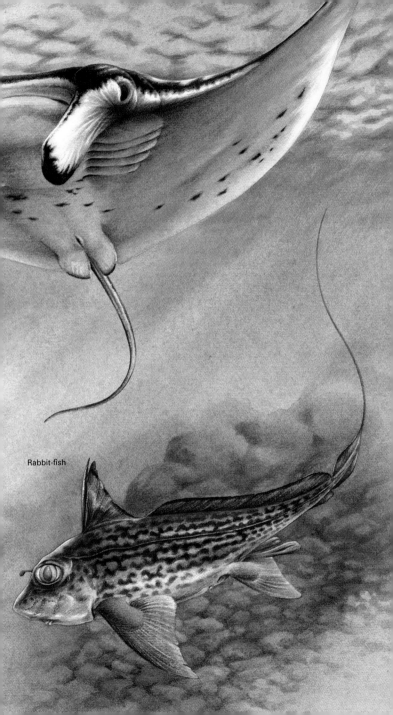

Rabbit-fish

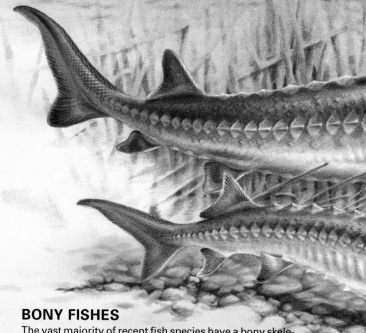

BONY FISHES

The vast majority of recent fish species have a bony skeleton, gill slits covered by an opercle, segmented bony fin rays supporting a connecting fin membrane, and a lung or swimbladder derived from the embryonic foregut. The bony fishes are divisible into 2 major classes. The **Sarcopts** (Sarcopterygii), whose paired fins have a median axis, include the present-day lungfishes and the Coelacanth, as well as extinct groups among which the ancestry of all the terrestrial vertebrates must lie. The second group, the **Actinopts** (Actinopterygii), with broad-based paired fins, consists mostly of the dominant Teleost fishes (infraclass **Teleostei**) of today, with about 20,000 recent species worldwide and comprising most of the fishes treated in this book. The Actinopts also contain various representatives of earlier stages in their evolution, including, in the European fauna, the sturgeons, which represent the order Acipenseriformes in a distinct infraclass **Chondrostei**.

STURGEONS (Acipenseridae)

Best known as the source of real caviare (golden to black ovarian eggs). Important commercial fisheries in the Black and Caspian seas, where stocks of some species are maintained by captive breeding and release of young (at about 6 cm) from rearing farms. Natural populations are increasingly depleted by overfishing, river pollution, and prevention of breeding, through obstruction of migration ways and destruction of spawning areas. Mostly large, ponderous fishes with 5 rows (median dorsal, lateral, and ventrolateral) of bony shields along somewhat elongated body; head encased in bony plates, with flattened snout, and small ventral toothless protrusible mouth, preceded by a transverse row of 4 barbels on underside of snout; one D, posterior, Vs abdominal, and C with upturned axis. Normally bottom-living, freshwater or anadromous; oviparous.

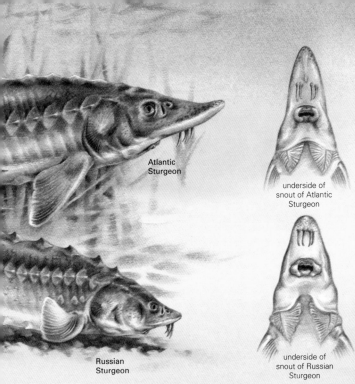

Atlantic Sturgeon

underside of snout of Atlantic Sturgeon

Russian Sturgeon

underside of snout of Russian Sturgeon

ATLANTIC STURGEON *Acipenser sturio.* A 'royal fish', now rare over most of range. Gill membranes united with isthmus, not as continuous median fold; snout length not more than three-fifths that of head; mouth small; lower lip divided in midline; barbels about half-way between mouth and tip of snout; barbels not fringed and not reaching back to mouth; P spine strong; lateral bony plates 24-39; olive, with gold or silvery tints; pale below. 350 cm, 320 kg; 48 yrs. Marine, inshore (20-50 m), feeding on invertebrates and small fish. Ascends rivers in spring and early summer (February-March in Gironde, south-west France), to spawn in February-June over gravel beds in deeper (2-8 m) swift-flowing reaches, then returns to sea; 800,000-2.4 million eggs, demersal, adherent, dark grey to brownish, 2.1-2.6 (3.0) mm, hatching at 9-11 mm in 3-7 days at 14-19°C; young remain in river or estuary for up to 3 yrs before migrating to sea; in sea, males mature at 105-150 cm (7-9 yrs), females at 120-180 cm (8-14 yrs). Today, breeding populations only in Gironde, Danube and Rioni (USSR) rivers, and now regarded as an endangered species.

RUSSIAN STURGEON *Acipenser gueldenstaedti.* Ⓐ Most important sturgeon of Russian fisheries. As preceding, but barbels nearer to tip of snout, which has blunter tip; lateral plates 24-50, anterior larger and deeper than succeeding ones; rows of smaller bony plates between dorsal and lateral plates. 211 cm, 48 yrs. Inshore, over softer grounds. Ascends rivers March-June, spawning May-June. Black Sea stocks maintained by release of young from rearing farms. Also Caspian Sea. **Siberian Sturgeon** *A. baeri*, Ⓑ 210 kg, also with small plates between dorsal and lateral rows, but barbels extending back to mouth and lateral plates 32-62, has been introduced to Baltic region.

71

ADRIATIC STURGEON *Acipenser naccarii*. As previous species, but anterior plates smaller than succeeding ones, and no additional rows of smaller bony plates between dorsal and lateral plates (latter 32-44). 180 cm. Ascends rivers from January, spawning April-May, but now very rare.

 STARRY STURGEON *Acipenser stellatus*. Gill membranes separately attached to isthmus; mouth small; snout long, at least six-tenths of head length; lower lip interrupted in midline; barbels smooth, short, nearer to mouth than tip of snout but not reaching back to mouth; small plates and ossicles between dorsal and lateral plates (latter 26-43); back dark grey to almost black, white below. 190 cm; 35 yrs. Benthic at night, but in midwater to surface during day, 10-40 m, deeper in autumn. Ascends rivers March-May and August-October, spawning May-June (Danube). Black Sea stocks maintained by release of young from rearing farms. Also Caspian Sea. Hybridizes with other sturgeons.

A ▉
B ▨

 STERLET *Acipenser ruthenus*. Ⓐ Smallest sturgeon (92 cm) and shortest lived (27 yrs), but important for fisheries and farming. Gill membranes separately attached to isthmus; mouth small; snout variable; lower lip interrupted in midline; barbels fringed, nearer mouth than tip of snout; lateral plates small, numerous, 56-71. Chiefly fresh water, feeding on invertebrates, notably insect larvae and also fish eggs, but may occur in brackish areas. After spring movement upstream, spawns in fast-flowing shallows over gravel; fecundity 7,000-108,000; eggs oval, 2.0-2.9 × 1.8-2.8 mm, hatching in 4-5 days at 13°C. Sexually mature at 40 cm; 3-5 yrs (m), 4-7 yrs (f) (Danube). The larger migratory **Ship Sturgeon** *A. nudiventris*, Ⓑ 200 cm, also has fringed barbels and many lateral plates (usually 49-74) but continuous upper lip. Also in Caspian Sea.

 BELUGA *Huso huso*. The largest European sturgeon, recorded to 490 cm (1,004 kg, reputedly 90-100 yrs) (a: 102 kg). Gill membranes continuous in fold across midline of isthmus; mouth large; snout fairly long; lower lip interrupted in midline; barbels long, smooth, nearer mouth than snout, and almost reaching former; lateral plates 37-53, anterior smaller than preceding; back dark grey to greenish, white below. Midwater, 70-180 m, feeding on fish and also invertebrates. Ascends rivers in spring (January-April) or autumn (August-November, with overwintering in fresh water), and usually spawning in April-May; fecundity usually 500,000. Sexually mature at 10-13 yrs (m), 13-15 yrs (f) (Black Sea). Maintained in Black Sea by release of young from rearing farms. Hybridizes with other sturgeons.

Beluga

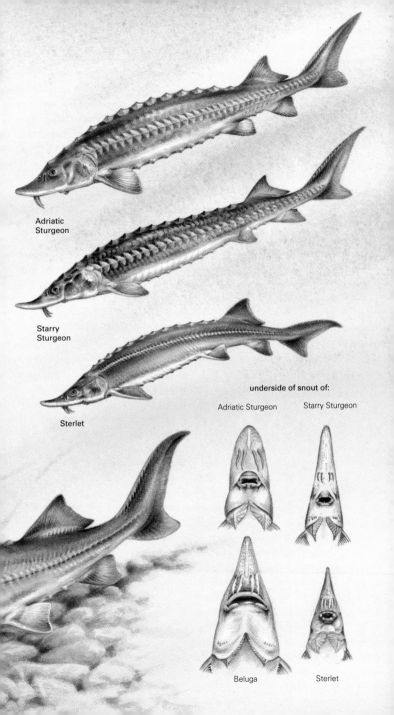

Adriatic
Sturgeon

Starry
Sturgeon

Sterlet

underside of snout of:

Adriatic Sturgeon   Starry Sturgeon

Beluga   Sterlet

TELEOSTS (Infraclass Teleostei)

The teleosts are the dominant fish group in terms of diversity and number of species. Their basic characteristics are the possession of a swimbladder, an externally symmetrical tail (not obviously upturned like that of sharks), and a distinct planktonic larval phase in many species.

TARPONS TO EELS (SUPERORDER ELOPOMORPHA)

A very diverse group, brought together by common possession of a transparent 'leptocephalus' larva.

TARPON *Tarpon atlanticus* (**Order Elopiformes: Megalopidae**). Memorable tropical game-fish, fighting regardless of size. Body compressed; mouth large, jaws curved; V abdominal; D origin behind level of V; D 13-15, last ray elongated as filament; lateral-line tubes branching over surface of scale; back bluish, silvery, brighter below. 250 cm (a: 128.5 kg). Inshore and estuarine, sometimes into fresh water, and may use lung-like swimbladder to respire air; feeds on schooling fishes. Spawns late April-August, very fecund (12 million eggs at 200 cm); leptocephalus moves into estuaries. Both sides of tropical Atlantic.

EELS (ORDER ANGUILLIFORMES)

Body elongated, archetypal 'eel-like'; pelvic fins absent. Mostly deep-water forms, but some familiar inshore and freshwater representatives.

EUROPEAN EEL *Anguilla anguilla* (**Anguillidae**). The best-known eel, widely distributed and the only European kind to live in fresh water for part of its incredible life history; commercial fisheries in fresh water and for elvers, used for stocking or as delicacy; also grown but not yet propagated in fish culture. Jaws subequal, lower slightly longer, and angle of jaws under eye; opercular opening small, lateral and vertical; D origin before A origin, but well behind P; tip of tail enclosed by continuous D and A; teeth small; scales, minute, embedded in skin; vertebrae 111-118; in fresh water back brownish, yellow below ('yellow eels'); migrating adults black above, silvery below ('silver eels', with more pointed snout). 51 cm (m), 142 cm (f) (a: 3.60 kg). Catadromous; juveniles and yellow eels in fresh water, estuaries, and intertidal; nocturnal, and may be found out of water under damp conditions; in sea, adults demersal on continental shelf, becoming bathypelagic; larvae planktonic; feed on invertebrates and small fish in fresh water and estuaries. After growth in fresh water as yellow eels, males (at 24-51 cm, 7-14 yrs) and females (33-80 cm, 9-19 yrs) cease to feed and become silver eels, descending to sea September-December, with greatly enlarged eyes, atrophied gut and occluded anus; silver eels with ripening gonads are taken on continental shelf but unknown to westward, presumably becoming bathypelagic, and after about 5 months reaching Sargasso Sea area of south-western North Atlantic, where spawning occurs probably between 100-450 m in February-May and adults die. Fecundity is high (about 10 million), and eggs, presumably bathypelagic, hatch to small larvae which become flattened, transparent leptocephali carried by Gulf Stream and North Atlantic Drift to continental waters of eastern Atlantic over about 1 yr (not 3 yrs) and reaching 7.5 cm. Metamorphosis, with development of pigmentation and cylindrical body but loss in length and weight, begins over shelf (August-November) and young enter coastal waters as 'glass eels', becoming more pigmented 'elvers' October-December (northern Spain) to March-April (North Sea and Kattegat). Elvers swim actively at night, ascending rivers, and grow into yellow eels, which in Baltic may be 20-50 cm (5-12 yrs) before entering rivers. Great commercial importance, netted, trapped and farmed, but elver runs diminishing in European waters. **American Eel** *A. rostrata*, very similar but vertebrae 103-110, reported from Denmark.

Tarpon

Eel elvers

'Silver' Eel (freshwater)

European Eel ('yellow' phase)

'Silver' Eel (sea)

Eel leptocephali

MEDITERRANEAN MORAY *Muraena helena* (**Muraenidae**). An aggressive eel, ready to attack and may inflict potentially septic wounds. Body somewhat compressed, head large and mouth with prominent conical teeth; D and A evident as ridges, including tail, D origin before pore-like opercular opening; P absent; reddish-brown to almost black, with yellow to white spots, mottling and banding on sides. 130 cm. Inshore, in crevices and other cover, even amphoras; feeds at night on fish and invertebrates such as squid. Breeds July-September (Mediterranean), with large eggs (5-5.5 mm).

BROWN MORAY *Gymnothorax unicolor*. As preceding, but rear nostril pore-like rather than tubular, head profile concave over eye, and rear teeth in upper jaw in 2 rows; reddish to dark brown, with snout, lips and opercular pore dark, and pale band behind eyes and jaw angle. 100 cm. Shelf, on coarse ground, among rocks and crevices. Breeds in warmer months, eggs 2.3-3.4 mm. Two other southern morays are: **Fang-toothed Moray** *Enchelycore anatina*, 100 cm, brown with pale blotches filled with dark dots, and prominent jaws about half head length, bearing long teeth; and *Anarchias euryurus*, 25 cm, elongated slender body, D and A evident only on tail.

Mediterranean Moray

Brown Moray

FALSE MORAY *Chlopsis bicolor* (**Xenocongridae**). Body very long and slender; rear nostril above upper lip, pore-like; opercular opening lateral, small, rounded, with flap; P very rudimentary or absent; vomerine teeth in 2 rows; back dark brown, creamy-white below. 42 cm. Burrowing in soft substrates of shelf and upper slope, to 350 m.

FIERCE CONGER *Cynoponticus ferox* (**Muraenesocidae**). Elongated; snout prominent; eye large; mouth large, angle behind eye; rear nostril pore-like, with raised rim; opercular opening large, ventrolateral; P well developed; D origin over P origin; vomer with main single row of large teeth; no scales; brown, with fins dark-edged. 150 cm. Shelf, on sand and mud, 10-100 m. Also West Africa. Related *Muraenesox cinereus* has entered eastern Mediterranean via Suez Canal.

FACCIOLA'S SORCERER *Facciolella oxyrhyncha* (**Nettastomatidae**). Body very elongated; jaws long, upper jaw longer than lower and with prominent tip; anterior nostril collared, rear nostril under fold; opercular opening curved, ventral; P absent; vomerine teeth numerous; no scales; silvery, fins dark-edged. 65 cm. Edge of shelf and slope, to 750 m. Probably breeds throughout year.

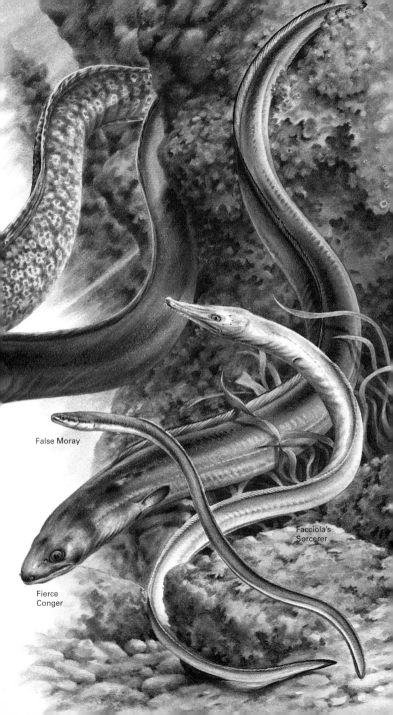

False Moray

Fierce
Conger

Facciola's
Sorcerer

CONGER EEL *Conger conger* (**Congridae**). Large, muscular eels of great strength and resistance; mouth large, subhorizontal, with outer teeth large, incisor-like, close-set as cutting edge; D origin just behind tip of P; D and A rays segmented; grey or brown above, golden to white below, with D and A edged black. 305 cm; 55.84 kg (a: 60.44 kg). Bottom-living on rocky or coarse grounds of shelf, from intertidal pools or under stones on muddy shores, to 180 m. Adults migrate from shelf to breed during summer in Atlantic between Azores and Gibraltar and in Sargasso area; very fecund, to more than 12 million eggs; leptocephalus metamorphoses over shelf. The **Black-spotted Conger** *Paraconger macrops*, 50 cm, with black spot on front part of D, burrows in soft ground, 30-100 m.

BALEARIC CONGER *Ariosoma balearicum*. Mouth moderate, subhorizontal, angle below front of eye; outer teeth in bands, conical; D origin above anterior part of P; D and A rays unsegmented; yellowish with yellowish-red blotches, D and A edged black. 50 cm. Burrowing in sand and mud, 20-100 m. Breeds in warmer months; leptocephalus metamorphoses at 20 cm. Also tropical Atlantic.

BLACK-TAILED CONGER *Gnathophis mystax*. Snout prominent, mouth large, subterminal, horizontal, angle below middle of eye; outer teeth in bands, conical; D origin over middle of P; D and A rays segmented; brown, paler below, with rear parts of D and A edged black; 60 cm. Bottom-living on muddy grounds of shelf and upper slope, 80-800 m. Breeds August-October (Mediterranean).

GARDEN EEL *Taenioconger longissimus*. A conger which forms 'meadows', with dense colonies on inshore sandy ground (15-17 m), each eel extending upwards about one-third out of burrow into which it withdraws when alarmed. Body very elongated; mouth small; outer teeth in bands anteriorly, conical; D and A very low, rays segmented, with D origin over minute P; grey-brown. 60 cm. Also tropical eastern Atlantic.

A ▪
B ▪

SLENDER FINLESS EEL *Apterichthus anguiformis* (**Ophichthidae**). Ⓐ Snake-like; eyes vestigial; all fins absent; reddish or brown, dark snout and sometimes with many small dark blotches, pale below. 60 cm. Burrowing in sand or mud, 10-40 m. The **European Finless Eel** *A. caecus*, 60 cm, with rear nostril on edge of upper lip, has similar distribution. Another eel with minute eyes and D and A only distinct near tail is **Fowler's Short-faced Eel** *Panturichthys fowleri* (**Heterenchelyidae**), Ⓑ 70 cm, dark brown mottling above, white below, from muddy ground in 30-60 m.

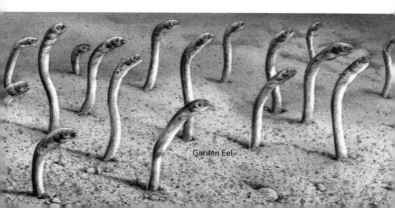

Garden Eel

Conger Eel

Balearic Conger

Black-tailed Conger

Slender Finless Eel

ARMLESS SNAKE EEL *Dalophis imberbis*. As preceding, but D and A present, low, in grooves; P vestigial or absent; tip of tail stiffened; violet-grey above, yellowish below. 150 cm. Burrowing, 20-80 m. Breeds August-September (Mediterranean).

BLUNT-SNOUTED SNAKE EEL *Echelus myrus*. Eye large; D, A and P well developed; teeth conical, in rows; grey-brown, paler below, with D and A dark posteriorly.
100 cm. Burrowing on shelf.
Breeds August-September (Mediterranean). Also tropical West Africa.

RUFUS SNAKE EEL *Ophichthus rufus*.
Body very long; D, A and P developed; anterior nostril tube directed downwards, rear nostril on upper lip; D and A not confluent around stiff tip of tail; teeth conical, in 1 or 2 rows on jaws; pale brown to yellowish, darker posteriorly, white below. 60 cm. Bottom-living, on mud of shelf. **Spotted Snake Eel** *O. ophis*, 100 cm, with distinctive but variously sized brown blotches. Tropical West Africa; may occur in Mediterranean.

LONG-JAWED SNAKE EEL *Ophisurus serpens*. Similar to preceding, but snout very elongated and jaws long, with anterior nostril short; teeth pointed, 1-3 rows; reddish-brown above, yellowish below, with D, A and lateral-line canal pores dark-edged. 240 cm. Burrowing in sand and mud of shelf and upper slope, to 300 m. Breeding June-September (Mediterranean).

SADDLED SNAKE EEL *Pisodonophis semicinctus*. Similar to preceding but body more robust, and longer, downturned anterior nostril; D and A not confluent, and short tip of tail very stiff; teeth multiserial, molariform; yellowish, with many broad dark saddles. 80 cm. Sandy shelf, 10-30 m. Also West Africa.

A ▮
B ▨
C ▥
D ▤

SNUBNOSED EEL *Simenchelys parasitica* (**Synaphobranchidae**). Ⓐ A deep-water eel which may be parasitic on other fishes. Body relatively deep, snout blunt, and mouth circular, with uniserial cutting-edged teeth; D and A confluent around narrow tail region of body; P present; scales vestigial; dark brown, D and A white-edged, belly dark in smaller individuals. 61 cm. Edge of shelf to abyssal depths, 100-3,000 m. Other deep-sea eels might be occasionally encountered, even in the stomachs of other fish: **Bean's Sawtoothed Eel** *Serrivomer beani* (**Serrivomeridae**), Ⓑ 70 cm, with very long jaws, armed with long teeth, and common opercular opening ventrally, vomer with serrated toothed ridge, D origin behind A origin, grey, head dark; pelagic, surface to 3,000 m; and **Snipe Eel** *Nemichthys scolopaceus* (**Nemichthyidae**), Ⓒ 130 cm, extremely elongated body, with beak-like jaws, but vomer not ridged and D origin before A origin, surface to 2,000 m. An **Avocet Snipe Eel** *Avocettina infans* (**Nemichthyidae**), 75 cm, similar to Avocet Snipe Eel but anus well behind, not below P, normally oceanic, surface to 2,000 m, was once found after a storm on the shore at Borth, Cardigan Bay. The **Pelican Eel** *Eurypharynx pelecanoides*, Ⓓ 10 cm, is a Gulper (**Eurypharyngidae**, related to the eels), with enormous mouth, tiny eyes at tip of snout, highly distensible stomach, and long tapering body.

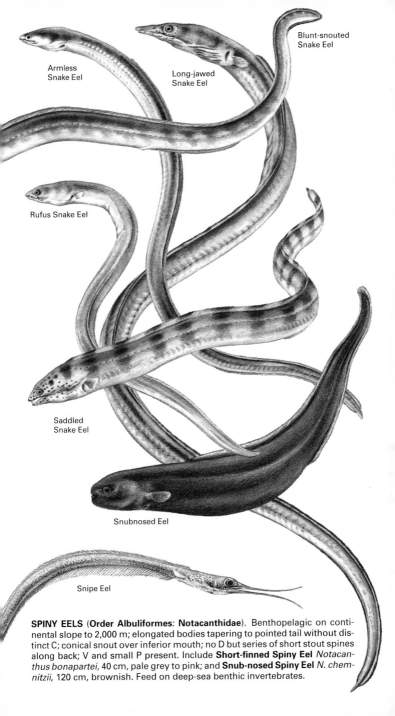

Armless
Snake Eel

Long-jawed
Snake Eel

Blunt-snouted
Snake Eel

Rufus Snake Eel

Saddled
Snake Eel

Snubnosed Eel

Snipe Eel

SPINY EELS (Order Albuliformes: Notacanthidae). Benthopelagic on continental slope to 2,000 m; elongated bodies tapering to pointed tail without distinct C; conical snout over inferior mouth; no D but series of short stout spines
along back; V and small P present. Include **Short-finned Spiny Eel** *Notacan-
thus bonapartei*, 40 cm, pale grey to pink; and **Snub-nosed Spiny Eel** *N. chem-
nitzii*, 120 cm, brownish. Feed on deep-sea benthic invertebrates.

HERRING-LIKE FISHES
(SUPERORDER CLUPEOMORPHA)

Of great economic importance worldwide, the herrings and anchovies are lower teleosts with the basic 'fish' shape: fusiform, somewhat compressed body; 1 D, V abdominal, P near lower margin of body; and silvery coloration, although a lateral-line is often lacking. Internally, they have a forward extension of the swimbladder into the side wall of the braincase, with which part of the head lateral-line canal system is also closely associated. Abundant schooling fish, feeding on plankton and small nekton over the continental shelf.

 ATLANTIC HERRING *Clupea harengus* (**Clupeidae**). Traditionally caught in the most important European pelagic fishery; once fought over, stocks are now depleted. Abdomen with weak keel of enlarged scales; upper jaw with complete edge; opercle smooth, and rear border of opercular chamber without small flaps; V usually 9, its origin below or immediately behind origin of D; dark blue above, sides and below silvery. 40 cm (a: 0.48 kg).

Shelf, juveniles inshore; neritic, in large schools, near sea-bed during day but moving towards surface at night with some dispersion for feeding (on zooplankton, especially crustaceans and postlarval fish, and also arrow worms and oikopleurans). Breeding season as below, on grounds reached by migration; fecundity varies with stock, 20,000-80,000 at same length (28 cm); eggs demersal, on stones, gravel, etc., 0.92-1.5 mm (British Isles); very elongate larvae hatch at 5.5-9.0 mm, in 49-7 days at 3.5-12.3°C; metamorphose by 50 mm. Both sides of cold Atlantic. Racial structure, migrations and breeding seasonality complex; around British Isles, 2 main groups, distinguished by population mean values of vertebral count, breeding season, egg size and fecundity, features of growth rate and in biochemical genetics. These groups of populations are: (i) 'oceanic' (Atlantic), 34-35.6 cm (12-23 yrs), mature at 26.7-30.0 cm (3-9 yrs), breeding in spring at 5-7°C, Celtic Sea to Iceland, Norway and White Sea; and (ii) 'shelf', 30 cm (12-16 yrs), mature at 22.9-26.7 cm (3-5 yrs), breeding in autumn at 11-12°C, Irish Sea to North Sea and Baltic Sea. As well as Shelf Herring, there are also related inshore spring spawning populations along the North Sea coast of Britain.

 SPRAT *Sprattus sprattus*. More local fisheries, and less important as food source because of smaller size, but great industrial usage. Abdomen with sharp keel; gill rakers 30-41; opercle smooth; rear border of opercular chamber without small flaps; V 7-8, its origin below or immediately behind origin of D; above blue or bluish-green, sides and below silvery. 18 cm, 5 yrs.

Schools, feeding chiefly on planktonic copepods, in coastal and estuarine waters during late autumn and winter. Migrates to open sea for breeding in December-April (Mediterranean), January-July (western Channel), March-August (North Sea), at depths of 18-45 m, spawning several times during season; fecundity to over 30,000; eggs planktonic, 0.8-1.3 mm, with segmented yolk but no oil globule; hatch at 3.0-3.6 mm in 3-4 days, metamorphozing at 30-40 mm; sexually mature at 1 yr, 10 cm. Morocco to North Sea (*S. s. sprattus*, mean keel scales behind V more than 11.5); Baltic Sea (*S. s. balticus*, keel scales behind V less than 11.5); and Mediterranean and Black Sea (*S. s. phalericus*, keel scales behind V not more than 11.3).

Sprat

Atlantic Herring

 PILCHARD *Sardina pilchardus.* Young pilchards are the 'sardines' found in tins. Abdominal keel blunt; gill-rakers 44-106; opercle with radiating bony lines; rear border of opercular chamber without small flaps; D origin slightly before middle of body; V origin behind that of D; last two rays of A enlarged; greenish to olive above, sides golden, silvery white below. 28 cm. Inshore shelf, schools from near surface at night to 55 m during day; young may enter estuaries; spawning April-July (March-October)(Channel), November-June (African Mediterranean); eggs planktonic, 1.3-1.9 mm, yolk segmented, with oil-globule and large space; hatch at 3.3-4.0 mm, mature usually by 4 yrs. Subspecies are *S. p. sardina* (African Atlantic and Mediterranean) and *S. p. pilchardus* (from Gibraltar northwards).

Pilchard

83

ROUND SARDINELLA *Sardinella aurita*. Tropical and warm-temperate fisheries. As Sprat, but gill rakers numerous, over 100 on lower arch; rear border of opercular chamber with 2 small flaps; D origin before middle of body; V origin behind origin of D, V rays 9; A last 2 rays enlarged; above blue-green, sides silvery, with indistinct golden lateral band; opercle with dark spot on upper rear corner. 33 cm; 7 yrs. Shelf, schools near surface at night. Breeds July-September, especially August (Mediterranean); fecundity to 65,000; eggs 1.2-1.4 mm, with wide space between yolk and capsule and small yellow oil-globule; sexually mature 12-16 cm, from 1 yr. Mediterranean fisheries employ lights to attract fish.

MADEIRAN SARDINELLA *Sardinella maderensis*. As preceding, but dark blotch behind opercle, not on rear corner, dark mark at D origin, and V 8. 30 cm. Inshore shelf and estuaries. Also West Africa and into Suez Canal. Conversely, the following have all entered the Mediterranean: Red Sea **Spotted Herring** *Herklotsichthys punctatus*, 8.5 cm, like young Round Sardinella but back having many dark dots; **Delicate Round Herring** *Spratelloides delicatulus*, 7 cm, D origin well before V, 7 branchiostegals; **Rainbow Sardine** *Dussumieria acuta*, 20 cm, 13-15 branchiostegals; and another **Round Herring**, *Etrumeus teres*.

TYULKA SPRAT *Clupeonella cultiventris*. Endemic to Black Sea and Caspian basins, with important fisheries. Abdomen with keel; upper jaw with regular margin; gill rakers 41-62; opercle smooth; rear border of opercular chamber without small flaps; D origin before middle of body; V origin behind that of D, V 7; A last 2 rays enlarged; blue-green above, otherwise silvery. 14.5 cm. Euryhaline, inshore and in fresh waters, between which some populations migrate. Spawns early summer (Sea of Azov).

ALLIS SHAD *Alosa alosa*. Shads are herring-like, but somewhat deeper-bodied and with a bluish cast; abdominal keel sharp; upper jaw notched in midline; gill rakers long, 85-130; opercle smooth; no opercular flaps; D origin slightly before middle of body; V origin below that of D; last 2 A rays not enlarged; metallic-blue above, sides silvery with large dark spot behind upper rear corner of opercle, sometimes absent or followed by additional spots. 76 cm. Inshore shelf, feeding on zooplankton, shrimps and young fish. Ascend rivers in spring (as 'may fish') for nocturnal spawning in schools over gravel beds April-May, and then return to sea by end of summer; eggs demersal, 4.5 mm, hatch at 8-12 mm in 4-8 days, young descending to sea in late spring-summer at 1-2 yrs. Mature at 30-40 cm, 3-4 yrs. A landlocked freshwater population in Lake Besikia, Greece. Allis Shad have greatly declined in abundance and no longer breed in former main spawning rivers of British Isles, where species is now protected. The **Pontic Shad** *A. pontica*, 30 cm, is similar.

A
B

TWAITE SHAD *Alosa fallax*. A Relatively more common than Allis Shad; short gill rakers, 30-80, and several dark spots along side. 55 cm. Inshore shelf and estuarine. Enters rivers in April-June to spawn in fresh water, but near tidal limit; young descend to sea by 14 cm, about 1 yr, in autumn; in British Isles, anadromous breeding still occurs in several rivers. Landlocked freshwater populations, as in Lough Leane, SW Ireland (**Goureen** *A. f. killarnensis*), and in Mediterranean as *A. f. nilotica* (a: 0.76 kg), and other stocks including *A. f. lacustris* of Italian lakes. The **Caspian Shad** *A. caspia*, B 20 cm, Black and Caspian seas, is related.

Anchovy

Round
Sardinella

Madeiran
Sardinella

Tyulka Sprat

Allis Shad

Twaite Shad

ANCHOVY *Engraulis encrasicholus* (**Engraulidae**). Distinguished from all herrings and shads by prominent snout and long jaws, with angle well behind eye; abdomen rounded; D origin at middle of body; V origin below that of D; A last 2 rays not enlarged; green or bluish-green above, demarcated from silvery sides and below. 20 cm; 2-4 yrs. Inshore shelf, entering estuaries, but to deeper water in winter (150 m in Mediterranean); feeds on plankton and small fish. Spawns April-November (Bay of Biscay), end of May-August (southern North Sea); fecundity to 40,000; eggs planktonic, ovoid, 1.2-1.9 × 0.5-1.2 mm, with reticulated yolk but no oil globule; hatch at 3-4 mm, with very long yolk-sac, metamorphosing at 3.5-4.0 cm; mature at 1 yr. Around British Isles, retires to Celtic Sea in winter after warmer months in southern North Sea.

PIKES (ORDER ESOCIFORMES)

The pikes and the related salmons are thought to exemplify a level in teleost evolution (**Superorder Protacanthopterygii**) from which all higher sorts have sprung. Pikes have subcylindrical bodies with D and A set towards tail, and lack adipose fin; V abdominal; the gape of the mouth includes the maxilla but this is toothless; internally, no pyloric caeca on the gut. All fresh water, in cooler northern hemisphere.

PIKE *Esox lucius* (**Esocidae**). A large torpedo-like predator, waiting motionless and cryptic to pounce, usually on fish (including pike) but even water voles and ducklings may be at risk. Snout and jaws long, with powerful teeth; body lateral line complete, LL 110-130; olive-green above, sides with pale spots and bars (pattern unique to larger individuals), and white or yellowish below. 90 cm (m), 150 cm (f); 15 yrs (a: 25 kg). Lakes, slower reaches of rivers, and brackish areas of Baltic; usually solitary, among vegetation, alert for prey; juveniles less than 4-5 cm may feed on invertebrates but staple adult food is fish. Spawn in weedy shallows or water meadows February-May, usually each female attended by a few males; eggs, to at least 500,000, 2.3-3.0 mm, yellowish-brown, with clusters of tiny oil globules, on vegetation; hatch in 10-15 days at 6-9 mm. Mature by 2-4 yrs, at 18-30 cm.

juvenile Pike

EUROPEAN MUD-MINNOW *Umbra krameri* (**Umbridae**). Small, shy relative of Pike, but snout blunt and jaws short; LL only 32-36; C rounded; brown with dark spots, sides and below tinged bluish. 13 cm; 4 yrs. Bottom-living, on muddy substrate of stagnant or slow, well-vegetated waters and can use swimbladder for air-breathing; feeds on invertebrates. Spawns February-April, fecundity 1,580-2,710 at 8.2-10.4 cm; about 100-400 eggs on vegetation and guarded by female; young hang on substrate until yolk sac is absorbed at 7-8 mm; mature at 1 yr. Greatly reduced by drainage of habitats and spread of alien species such as Sun-bass. The **Eastern Mud-minnow** *U. pygmaea*, 10 cm, from eastern USA, with a dark lower jaw, dark spot on C base, and lateral pale stripes, has been introduced to some European localities.

European
Mud-minnow

Eastern
Mud-minnow

Pike

SALMONS (ORDER SALMONIFORMES)

Best known of the group, species of the salmon family (**Salmonidae**) have a more fusiform body with D in middle and small adipose fin near tail; V abdominal; C more or less forked; V with small fleshy process above base. Internally, gut usually with numerous pyloric caeca. Cold-temperate and Arctic waters of northern hemisphere; spawn in fresh water, but may be anadromous. Much differentiation of local populations, especially in charr and whitefish - postglacial isolation in lakes has generated a complex nomenclature. Great commercial value, in fisheries and angling; some species intensively farmed.

 ATLANTIC SALMON *Salmo salar.* Traditionally 'the king of freshwater fish', in terms of sport, commerce and edibility. Important to marine and estuarine net fisheries, freshwater game angling and sea-loch farming, the last industry now restoring salmon to its ancient status as a regular, as opposed to luxury food item. Upper jaw to rear edge of eye, lower jaw slightly longer; teeth prominent; vomer with teeth on head and shaft (but latter few or lost in adult); preopercle anterior edge not reaching to suborbital bones; gill rakers 17-24; A III-IV/7-9 (10); LL 114-130, with 11-15 from adipose fin to lateral line; in sea, silvery blue-green above, sides silvery, white below, with x-shaped or rounded dark spots, mostly above lateral line; in fresh water, greenish or reddish-brown mottled with red or orange (especially in male) and large dark spots edged in white but C without spots; kelts dark; parr with 11-12 dark lateral bars, rarely more than 3 dark spots on opercle, D weakly spotted, adipose fin not usually edged in red, and P and V typically greyish; smolts silvery. 153 cm (a: 35.89 kg). Anadromous; silvery adults enter estuaries from spring onwards, ceasing to feed thereafter, and ascend unpolluted rivers to spawn November-December, penetrating to shallow gravel reaches (sometimes after leaping waterfalls as high as 3.7 m); before spawning, males become reddish, with hooked jaws (kype), females darker, and teeth change; over 1-2 weeks, female, using C, cuts depressions in gravel (forming redd) in which eggs are deposited, immediately fertilized by attendant male, and then covered with gravel; only minority of adults survive first breeding season, regaining sea as emaciated kelts to recover (as mended kelts) on marine feeding grounds, and spawn again (mostly females; around British Isles, proportion of repeat spawners 0.5-34.0 per cent, very rarely in up to 4 seasons). Eggs large (6-8 mm), yellowish, hatch in 90 days at about 7°C, 191 days at 0°C; larvae with yolk sac (alevins) 15-20 mm, among stones of stream bed for some weeks, and appear on surface of bed in May as fry, about 5 cm; larger juveniles (parr), to 11-15 cm, spend 1-4 yrs in fresh water (precociously mature males may participate in spawning of adults), and then descend to sea as smolts (12.5-25 cm) in late March-May; in sea for 1-5 yrs, with great increase in size, e.g. in 1 yr, from 12.5-16.0 cm (50-60 g) to 45-50 cm (1.3-1.4 kg); smaller fish (less than 2.7 kg), returning to rivers after just over 1 yr in sea, are called grilse. In cooler rivers on both sides of Atlantic, with major marine feeding concentration of North Atlantic Salmon off south-western Greenland. Numbers greatly affected by river pollution and fisheries at sea; farming in cages in sea lochs now produces about 20 times yield from fisheries, but raises problems of environmental effects and genetic change in wild stock by escapes of farm fish. Hybridizes with Brown/Sea Trout.

fresh run Atlantic Salmon

female in breeding season

alevin

parr

smolt

spawning in redd

male kelt

BROWN/SEA TROUT *Salmo trutta*. Important sportfish and also farmed; introduced in temperate waters worldwide. Resembling Salmon but usually easily recognized. Upper and lower jaws to behind rear edge of eye; teeth numerous on shaft of vomer; gill rakers 13-18; A II-III/8-9; LL 118-130, with 13-16 from adipose fin to lateral line; in sea and migrating, bright silvery to more bronze, with black and red spots on opercle, and black spots on body somewhat heavier than in salmon; in rivers and lakes variable, usually olive-brown above, more silvery on sides, and yellowish below, with few to many black and red dots, often pale-bordered, usually on sides and always on opercle; parr with 9-10 dark lateral bars, more than 3 dark spots on opercle, D distinctly spotted, adipose fin edged red, and P and V orange-yellow; smolts silvery. 140 cm (migratory **Sea Trout** form); 40 cm (freshwater **Brown Trout** form) (a: 18.25 kg). Anadromous, on inshore shelf or entirely freshwater, especially in swifter, upper reaches of rivers and in colder lakes; feed on invertebrates (surface, midwater or benthic) and fish. Sea Trout parr descend to sea in spring as smolts at 14-29 cm after 2-4 (1-6) yrs in fresh water; in sea, grow rapidly (as whitling, finnock or herling) and about 40 per cent may revisit rivers in same autumn although few then spawn; in autumn of that or a later year, Sea Trout ascend rivers to spawn in September-December, resembling Salmon in male kype, spawning habitat and behaviour, but without heavy mortality after spawning, so that individuals may spawn in up to 9-10 seasons; after return to sea, some movement along coast into estuaries and across shelf waters (such as North Sea). Trout eggs are yellowish to pink but smaller (4.5-5.5 mm) than those of Salmon. Sea Trout also in Black Sea and rivers (*S. t. labrax*, 18 (18-19) gill rakers) and occurs in western Atlantic after trout introduced to eastern Canada. Brown Trout also North Africa; many local and regional variants, with evidence for reproductively isolated populations in the same lake system, such as **Ferox** (large size), **Gillaroo** (red spots) and **Sonaghen** (black spots) of Lough Melvin, Ireland; another variety is **Loch Leven Trout** *S. t. levenensis*, with more pyloric caeca. Mediterranean land-locked 'species' include **Carpione** *S. carpio*, 50 cm, of Lake Garda, and central Italian *S. fibreni*, 23 cm, with persistent parr markings. Hybridizes with Atlantic Salmon.

Brown Trout

90

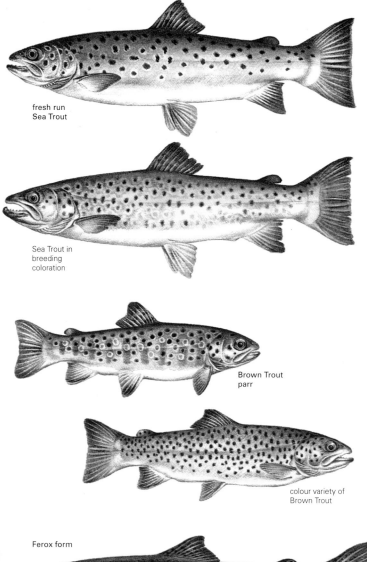

fresh run
Sea Trout

Sea Trout in
breeding
coloration

Brown Trout
parr

colour variety of
Brown Trout

Ferox form

RAINBOW TROUT *Oncorhynchus mykiss*. A New World species that is now the most commonly farmed trout, also stocked for angling; until recently, more widely known scientifically as *Salmo gairdneri*. As preceding, but vomerine teeth poorly developed; A jointed rays 9-12; LL 147-202, with 15-16 from adipose fin to lateral line; body and fins, including C, with many black spots but no red spots on body, which has iridescent reddish lateral band; adipose fin often edged black. 50 cm (Europe) (a: 19.1 kg, Alaska). Freshwater or anadromous (Steelhead), remaining inshore; feeding more on benthic invertebrates than Brown Trout. Spawn in spring; eggs 4.5-6.0 mm, pink. Originally west coast of North America, but introduced to east coast and to Europe (where rarely migratory).

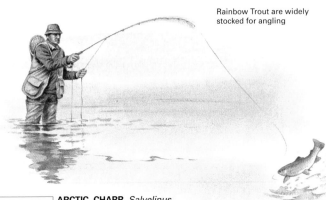

Rainbow Trout are widely stocked for angling

ARCTIC CHARR *Salvelinus alpinus*. Similar to trout, but no black or brown spots, and with vivid reddish breeding coloration; upper and lower jaws to behind rear edge of eye; vomer with teeth on head but not on shaft (which has oblong concavity); preopercle anterior edge not meeting suborbital bones; gill rakers 18-30; A III-IV/7-9; LL 190-240; P pointed; C distinctly concave; in sea, back steel-blue, sides silvery with reddish-pink and cream spots; in lakes, silvery with light spots; at spawning, lower body and fins orange or red, and red spots intensified, especially in males, with white-edged P, V and A; D and C never spotted, and red spots never edged blue; young with 11-13 parr marks. 88 cm (migratory), 41 cm (freshwater) (a: 14.77 kg). Anadromous, on inshore shelf of Arctic seas, ascending rivers (probably as the most northerly freshwater fish) to spawn on gravel beds in lakes or deeper rivers September-March; southern populations (even to Alps) non-migratory, in cool, deep lakes of glacial origin and also shallower waters; feed chiefly on planktonic and other invertebrates, also small fish. Many nominal subspecies, but some populations lost. Within one lake, and even between basins, autumn and spring spawners may be distinguished. Increasingly quarry for angling and gill-netting, and, as it adapts well to captivity, possibly sea-loch farming. Hybridizes with Brook Charr.

BROOK CHARR *Salvelinus fontinalis*. A North American charr, known there as Brook Trout. Similar to Arctic Charr, but head larger, C only slightly concave, and P rounded; in sea, silvery; in fresh water, above olive with dark marbling, and lower sides with many pale yellowish spots and fewer vermilion dots typically edged blue; below grey-blue to orange or fleshy, becoming red when breeding; parr markings 7-11; D and C always with dark spots. 66 cm (a: 6.57 kg). Anadromous, spawning October-December. Introduced to northern Europe. The **American Lake Trout** *S. namaycush*, 126 cm, with numerous yellowish spots, is a large charr, introduced to Scandinavia and Switzerland. Hybridizes with Arctic Charr.

Rainbow Trout male in spawning colouration

Rainbow Trout female

Arctic Charr male

Arctic Charr female

Brook Charr

PINK SALMON *Oncorhynchus gorbuscha*. Pacific Salmon (several *Oncorhynchus* species) are the 'salmon' found in tins. Upper and lower jaws to rear edge of eye or beyond; teeth prominent; vomer with teeth on head and shaft (but latter easily lost in adult); preopercle anterior edge meeting suborbital bones; gill rakers 26-32; A II-IV/12-16; LL 143-207; breeding male with very pronounced hump before D; in sea, silvery with few dark spots except on C, but darker, brownish-olive, with spots above lateral midline, to almost black prior to spawning. 68 cm (a: 5.94 kg). Anadromous, forming large schools; young descend to estuaries soon after hatching, moving to open sea at 3.8-10 cm, and return after 1 yr to spawn August-October, with complete mortality. Originally temperate North Pacific (Sea of Japan to California), but introduced from Sakhalin to rivers of White and Barents seas, and also of Bay of Riga; now spread to Norway and straying to Iceland and British Isles.

COHO SALMON *Oncorhynchus kisutch*. As Pink Salmon, but gill rakers 19-25, LL 127-141, breeding males less hump-backed, black spots above lateral midline and on base of D and upper C. 88 cm (a: 15.08 kg). Anadromous; spawns September-January; young descend to sea after 1 yr, and remain there for 1-2 yrs. Introduced to northern France, with records from rivers and Channel, and to Lake Garda in northern Italy; a vigorous surface fighter when hooked. **Chum Salmon** *O. keta*, 100 cm (a: 14.51 kg), similar but lacking distinct black spots on sides and C, has been introduced to White and Barents Sea rivers, and subsequently recorded off Norway.

HUCHEN *Hucho hucho*. The world's largest salmon, endemic in its typical form to the Danube (and Prut), with unsuccessful attempts at introduction to England (Thames) and western Europe. Body relatively slender; head laterally compressed; upper and lower jaws to behind rear edge of eye; teeth well developed; vomer with teeth on head but not on shaft; preopercle anterior edge not meeting suborbital bones; gill-rakers 16; A IV-V/7-9; LL 180-200; C distinctly concave; back blue-grey, sides silvery with numerous small X-shaped dark markings; males reddish. 180 cm, 70 kg (a: 34.8 kg). Entirely fresh water, feeding on fish, especially Nase. Breeds March-May (Danube), in mountain streams, digging extensive redds; eggs 5.0 mm, yellow, hatch in 20 days at 12°C; mature at 3-4 yrs (m), 4-5 yrs (f). Now under

Huchen

Nase

threat from overfishing, pollution and river works, present range is chiefly in submontane areas of Danube basin. The larger **Taimen** *H. h. taimen*, 200 cm, 105 kg, occurs from Volga to Far East.

ADRIATIC SALMON *Salmothymus obtusirostris*. A small non-migratory salmon of interest because of its restricted distribution as a component of the West Balkan endemic fish fauna. Head short, mouth inferior; upper and lower jaws not beyond rear edge of eye; teeth weak; vomer with double row of teeth along shaft; preopercle anterior edge not meeting suborbital bones; A 11-12; LL 101-103; C more or less concave; coloration as Brown Trout. 50 cm. Fresh water. Spawns October-December. Range and numbers now greatly diminished, and extinction predicted. In Lake Ochrid, *S. o. ochridanus* may be a distinct species.

Pink Salmon female

Pink Salmon male

Coho Salmon

Adriatic Salmon

WHITEFISH are silvery, usually small-mouthed salmonids associated in temperate Europe with glacial-lake basins, but migratory further north; systematics complex.

A
B

COMMON WHITEFISH *Coregonus lavaretus*. Ⓐ Snout prominent, mouth inferior; gill rakers 30-34 (25-39); LL 84-100; teeth rudimentary; above bluish to olive, sides silvery. 70 cm, 8 kg; 9 yrs (a: 5.39 kg). Anadromous in Baltic, inshore shelf to rivers and lakes; otherwise lacustrine; in schools, feeding on planktonic crustaceans or benthic invertebrates. Spawns early January (December-March) on gravel beds in shallows; eggs 2-3 mm, yellowish. In British Isles as **Powan** *C. l. clupeoides* (lochs Lomond and Eck); **Gwyniad** *C. l. pennantii* (Lyn Tegid); and **Skelly** *C. l. stigmaticus* (Haweswater, Ullswater, Red Tarn). Other lake populations in Alps, northern Europe and Scandinavia. **Houting** *C. l. oxyrinchus*, Ⓑ 50 cm, similar to Powan but snout at least twice eye diameter, and gill rakers 35-44, is anadromous in estuarine waters, ascending rivers chiefly in autumn; now increasingly rare in North Sea and regarded as an endangered species. **Humpbacked Whitefish** *C. l. pidschian*, 50 cm, gill rakers about 20 (17-25), occurs in colder, deeper parts of lakes.

VENDACE *Coregonus albula*. Whitefish with mouth superior, upper jaw to below pupil, gill rakers 36-52, and LL 75-88. 35 cm, 500 g. Anadromous in Baltic (gulfs of Finland and Bothnia) and Arctic basin, otherwise lacustrine. Breeds November-January, spawning inshore over hard substrate. In British Isles as **Vendace** *C. a. vandesius* (two Lochmaben lochs, now extinct in one) and **Cumberland Vendace** *C. a. gracilior* (Derwentwater, Bassenthwaite, introduced to some Scottish lochs). Other nominal subspecies.

ARCTIC CISCO *Coregonus autumnalis*. An otherwise Arctic species, with terminal mouth, is represented in the Irish loughs Neagh, Erne, Derg and Ree by the **Pollan** *C. a. pollan*, 35 cm, 450 g, with LL 74-86, and still netted commercially. **Peled** *Coregonus peled*. Also with mouth terminal, jaws equal; 49-68 gill rakers. 50 cm. Lakes and rivers of Baltic and Arctic basins, with fisheries in Russia.

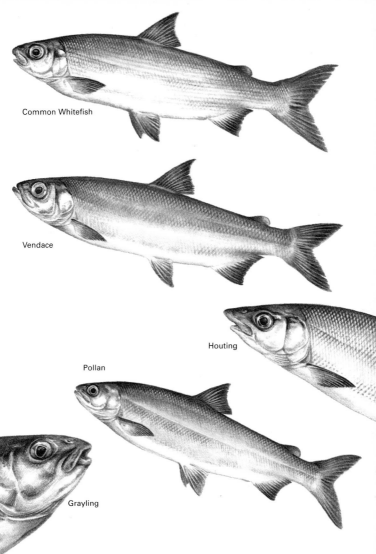

Common Whitefish

Vendace

Houting

Pollan

Grayling

GRAYLING *Thymallus thymallus*. Colourful salmonid, smelling slightly of thyme, with a 'coarse' breeding season. Body compressed; mouth small, jaws to below anterior edge of eye; teeth small; vomer with teeth anteriorly; gill rakers 20-29; D long-based, IV-VII/13-17; A II-IV/8-11; LL 74-96; C distinctly concave; back dark, sides silvery with many longitudinal violet lines; D with dark bands. 60 cm, 2.3 kg; 10 yrs. Fresh water, typically near bottom in cooler, fast-flowing streams, but sometimes in lakes and may enter brackish water in Baltic; feeds on benthic invertebrates and also drift organisms. Spawns March-May on gravel beds; eggs 3-4 mm, brown. Mature by 3-6 yrs (m), 4-7 yrs (f).

SMELT *Osmerus eperlanus* (**Osmeridae**). Small, elongated silvery fishes, with distinct odour of cucumber; mouth relatively large; adipose fin present; V base without small fleshy process above it as seen in salmons; pyloric caeca not more than 8; D II/8-10, origin somewhat behind V origin; A III/12-14; P 11-13; LL 59-69, lateral line incomplete, with only 4-14 pores, not to below D; VC 57-62 (54-62); breeding male with numerous small tubercles over scales; back yellowish-olive to green, broad lateral silvery band, white below. 46 cm, 12-15 yrs. Anadromous, inshore shelf to lower reaches of rivers (where their presence indicates good water quality), feeding on plankton, crustaceans and small fish. Ascend rivers in schools for spawning late February-May over pebbly beds, and return to sea after a few weeks or months in fresh water; some relict freshwater stocks in Scandinavia, but that in Rostherne Mere, Cheshire, is long extinct; fecundity to 100,000; eggs yellow, 0.6-1.3 mm, yolk unsegmented and several oil globules later merging into one; eggs adhere to substrate by 'stalk' of everted egg membrane, but may later detach and float in current; hatch at 5.5-6.0 mm, young drifting down to estuaries; sexually mature usually at 2-3 yrs, 16-18 cm. Local fisheries may exploit spawning runs.

CAPELIN *Mallotus villosus*. Like the famous Californian Grunion (a silverside, not a smelt), some Capelin stocks spawn dangerously at the edge of the tide; elongated, with pointed head; D II-III/10-12, origin above V origin; A III-IV/14-21; P 16-21, broad-based; LL 170-220, lateral line complete, to C; VC 64-70; breeding male with enlarged P and V, attenuated scales above lateral line to produce a broad band of 'pile' along body, and small warts along fin rays and on lower head; back olive to greenish, yellowish-olive to green, broad lateral silvery band with upper edge dark, white below. 23 cm, 5 yrs. Marine, on shelf, to 300 m, in schools, feeding on planktonic crustaceans. Spawns late April-June (Norway), or August (north-eastern Iceland), at edge of sea (western Atlantic, some Norwegian fiords) or on offshore banks to 35-55 m (eastern Atlantic; Newfoundland Grand Banks); for shore spawning, at night or in overcast weather, a pair, or a female between 2 males, runs up beach to spawn, separating to return to water (but heavy mortality); fertilized eggs, buried in gravel by wave action, are 1.0 mm, reddish or yellowish, very adherent, and hatch in 55-15 days at 0-10°C. Also Arctic basin and northern Pacific, as well as western Atlantic, where they are an important food source for cod.

ARGENTINE *Argentina sphyraena* (**Argentinidae**). Elongated small offshore relative of the salmons; eyes large; mouth small, teeth on tongue well developed anteriorly and laterally; maxillary bones of upper jaw separated in midline; LL 50-54; gill rakers 7-10 on lower arch; above translucent olive-green, lateral silvery stripe, white below. 32 cm. Shelf to upper slope, 35-450 m, rarely in as little as 10 m, probably schooling above bottom. Breeds March-July, eggs planktonic, 1.7-1.85 mm, with segmented yolk and 1 oil globule; hatch at 7.0-7.5 mm.

GREATER ARGENTINE *Argentina silus*. As Argentine, but LL 64-69, and gill rakers 11-17 on lower arch. 60 cm. Offshore shelf and slope, usually 150-900 m (55-1,400 m), probably in large schools. Breeds May-September (eastern Atlantic), eggs planktonic, bathypelagic at 300-400 m, 3.0-3.5 mm.

A ▮
B ▮
C ▨

Related deeper-water species include the **Small-Toothed Argentine**, *Glossanodon leioglossa*, Ⓐ 16 cm, with minute teeth only on front edge of tongue and maxillaries meeting in midline, from outer shelf and upper slope; and **Deepsea Smelt** *Bathylagus euryops* (**Bathylagidae**), Ⓑ 20 cm, with large eyes and minute fins, meso- and bathypelagic. Also **smoothheads** (**Alepocephalidae**), Ⓒ dark fishes, with large heads, and rear D and A, but no adipose fin: **Risso's Smoothhead** *Alepocephalus rostratus*, 47 cm, LL 50-55, may occur at edge of eastern Atlantic shelf.

Smelt

Capelin male

Capelin female

Argentine

Greater Argentine

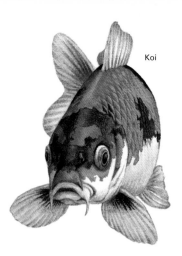

Koi

CARPS TO CATFISHES (SUPERORDER OSTARIOPHYSI)

The dominant group of freshwater teleosts, comprising, in the European fauna, **Carps and Loaches (Order Cypriniformes)**, and **Catfishes (Order Siluriformes)**. Their acuity of hearing is greatly enhanced by the anterior part of the swimbladder acting as a resonating chamber and transmitting vibrations to the inner ear via a chain of 3 small bones (Weberian ossicles).

CARPS (Cyprinidae)

Fusiform to more elongate fishes, typically midwater; 1 D more or less in middle of body, sometimes with a few simple spine-like rays; adipose fin absent; mouth protrusible, but lacking teeth on jaws, and instead, 1-3 rows of pharyngeal teeth on lower bones of gill arches, biting upwards onto horny pad. Often white nuptial tubercles on breeding males or both sexes. Spawning in schools, and hybridization is common. Generally, hybrids are intermediate in number of fin rays and lateral-line scales. Only common hybrids are noted. Many nominal species and subspecies in southern and eastern Europe need revision. North American Buffalo Suckers *Ictiobus* spp. (**Catostomidae**), may be established in eastern Europe. These are deep-bodied, with ventral mouth and numerous pharyngeal teeth (>100).

CARP *Cyprinus carpio*. Ponderous but cunning; farmed for food in many countries, but also as colourful ornamental varieties (Koi) originating from Japan. 4 barbels, 2 long and 2 short, on upper jaw, immediately distinguish Carp from Crucian Carp and Goldfish; LL 33-40; D with long base, a serrated anterior spine, III-V/17-22; A II-III/5; greenish-brown to brown, more yellow below. 103 cm; 42 yrs (reputedly to 100 yrs) (a: 34.35 kg). Slow or stagnant muddy, well-vegetated reaches of lakes and rivers, omnivorous. Breeds May-June or July, spawning over weed or grass in flooded shallows, one female with several males; fecundity to 2 million; eggs 1.0-1.8 mm, pale to yellowish, hatch at 4-6 mm in 5-8 days at 23-24°C. Sexually mature by 3-4 yrs (m), 4-5 yrs (f). Originally Black Sea rivers to Manchuria, but introduced into Europe and now worldwide. Cultivated varieties are Mirror Carp (with fewer, enlarged scales along midline and back) and Leather Carp (almost naked). Koi are now popular as pond fishes; the best examples are the most valuable individuals of any fish species. Hybridizes with Crucian Carp.

Carp

Carp, Mirror variety

Carp, Leather variety

CRUCIAN CARP *Carassius carassius*. Smaller carp, with brighter coloration and lacking barbels; LL 31-35; D with long base, slightly serrated anterior spine, III-IV/14-21; A II-III/6-8; gill rakers 22-33; olive or reddish-brown, paler below; P, V and A reddish; C base with dark spot. 50 cm (a: 2.01 kg). Stagnant and slow well-vegetated reaches of lakes and rivers; very resistant to deoxygenation; feeds on benthic and planktonic organisms. Breeds May-June (July); fecundity to 300,000; eggs golden or reddish, 1.4-1.7 mm, on vegetation. Sexually mature by 3 yrs (m), 4 yrs (f). Originally eastern Europe to Asia, now widely introduced in Europe. Farmed. Hybrids with Carp.

A ■
B ■

GOLDFISH *Carassius auratus*. Ⓐ Somewhat drab in nature, but transformed by man into the best-known pet fish. Similar but usually slimmer than Crucian Carp; LL 27-31; D with long base, serrated anterior spine, III-IV/15-19; A II-III/5 (5-6); more gill rakers (39-50); olive, golden to silvery below. 45 cm (a: 1.36 kg). Stagnant and slow waters of lakes and rivers. Breeds June-July, over weeds. Wild from eastern Europe (**Prussian Carp** or **Giebel** *C. a. gibelio* Ⓑ) to China (Asiatic Goldfish *C. a. auratus*), but feral throughout western Europe probably from imported Asiatic stock. Farmed as Prussian Carp, but chief value as ornamental fish, with domestic variants (originally Chinese and Japanese) in colour (golden, black, nacreous, etc.) and form (double and lengthened caudal fins, absent dorsal fin, protuberant and upturned eyes, bubble-eyed, skin excrescences, etc.). Prussian Carp are *gynogenetic*, males being rare and females spawning with males of other cyprinid species, whose sperm merely initiates development of eggs into female offspring without genetic fusion.

varieties of
Goldfish

TENCH *Tinca tinca*. Very rounded, sluggish 'doctor fish', covered with slime reputedly of medicinal value to other fishes and even mankind; mouth terminal, with 2 barbels; scales small, LL 95-120; D short-based, origin behind V origin, III/8; A III/6-8; V with second unbranched ray much thicker and longer in males; gill rakers long, 12-13 on first arch; dark green to almost black, eye reddish, golden-bronze tint to sides and below. 70 cm, 8 kg (a: 4.64 kg). Lakes and slow reaches of rivers, into slightly brackish water of eastern Baltic; nocturnal, bottom-feeding in a vertical posture, and may lie dormant in cold winters. Breeds May-July (August), in schools; highly fecund, to 900,000; small (1.0-1.4 mm) greenish eggs deposited on weed in shallows; hatch at 4-5 mm. Used in pond culture; Golden Tench is an ornamental variety. Hybrids with Crucian Carp.

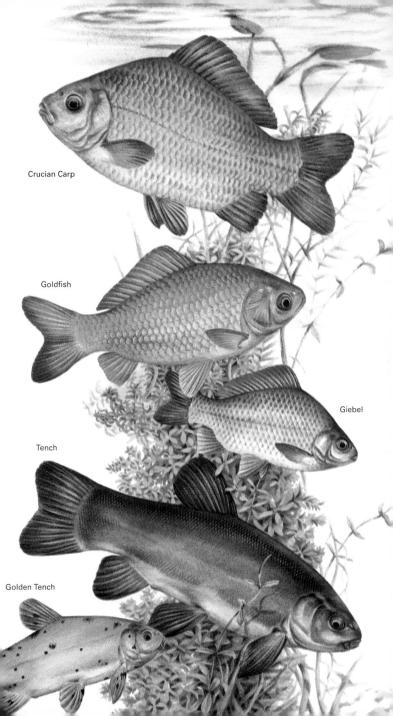

Crucian Carp

Goldfish

Giebel

Tench

Golden Tench

Barbel

A ■
B ▨
C ▧
D ■

BARBEL *Barbus barbus*. Ⓐ Moderately slender and fights vigorously when hooked; mouth inferior, 4 barbels, anterior near snout tip and not reaching to nostril when reflected; LL 55-65; D short-based, origin above V; D III/7-9, ray III thick, serrated; A III/5; gill rakers about 11; brownish to darker green, sides with slightly golden tint; fins green, origins reddish; young may have dark spots. 102 cm, 10 kg (a: 2.55 kg). Bottom-living in faster, clear reaches of rivers, feeding at night on benthic invertebrates, sometimes small fish and plant material. Breeds April-July after upstream migration; ovaries emetic to man; fecundity up to 30,000; yellow eggs (2.0-2.5 mm), deposited among stones of river bed; hatch at 7-8 mm. Sexually mature by 4-5 yrs. Originally in east coast rivers, today more widely distributed in Britain. **Dnieper Barbel** *B. b. borysthenicus*, has longer fins (D height one-fifth standard length) and is much more fecund. **Italian Barbel** *B. plebejus*, Ⓑ 60 cm, 4 kg, with numerous small dark spots, **Iberian Barbels** *B. comiza*, Ⓒ with 49-51 scales in lateral series, *B. bocagei*, *B. microcephalus*, *B. graellsii*, *B. scla-teri*, *B. guiraonis*, *B. haasi* and **Greek** *B. peloponnensius*, Ⓓ are nominal species needing further study.

SOUTHERN BARBEL *Barbus meridionalis*. Similar to Barbel, but barbels longer, anterior reaching to nostrils when turned back; LL 48-55; D ray III thin and smooth, and A longer, reaching lower C origin when depressed; coloration darker, including brown spots over body. 40 cm. Biology as Barbel, but tending to occur in higher reaches. Various subspecies: **Danubian Semling** *B. m. petenyi*; **Italian** *B. m. caninus*; and western Balkan *B. m. albanicus*. Hybrids with Barbel.

DALMATIAN BARBEL GUDGEON *Aulopyge hugeli*. Small cyprinid found only in western Balkans, and lacking scales. Body moderately elongated; snout long, mouth subterminal, jaw angle well before eye; 4 short barbels; D third spinous ray serrated; adult female deeper-bodied than male, with fleshy tubular process along front of anal fin, ending in anus and uro-genital opening; lateral line complete, somewhat wavy course; greenish back, silvery sides, with dark brown blotching. 13 cm. Bottom-living, in flowing water, including subterranean reaches of karst rivers; locally common, but overall classed as very endangered.

Southern
Barbel

Dalmatian
Barbel
Gudgeon

A
B
C
D

GUDGEON *Gobio gobio.* Ⓐ Similar to a miniature Barbel with somewhat elongated, cylindrical body; mouth subterminal, 2 barbels at jaw angle; LL 38-44; throat without scales; D origin somewhat before V origin, III/5-7, lacking conspicuous spine; A III/6-7; gill rakers short, widely spaced; brownish-green back becoming yellowish below, with several dark blotches along lateral midline, and median fins spotted. 20 cm, 220 g; 6 yrs. Bottom-living, in small schools, feeding chiefly on benthic insect stages, typically in fast-flowing rivers and also clear gravelly lake shallows. Breeds May-June (April-July), spawning by night, fecundity to 3,000 in several batches; eggs 1.3-2.0 mm, grey or bluish; hatch at 4-5 mm. Mature by 2-3 yrs. Various subspecies and related forms, from Danube and Russian rivers, such as: **White-finned Gudgeon** *G. albipinnatus,* Ⓑ with few D and C spots; **Kessler's Gudgeon** *G. kessleri,* Ⓒ 15 cm, with barbels reaching to vertical of rear margin of eye when reflected, D III/8 (8-9), and D and C with dark bands; and **Danubian Gudgeon** *G. uranoscopus,* Ⓓ as Kessler's Gudgeon, but even longer barbels, D III/7, throat scaled, less spotted but bluish lateral band more or less evident.

FALSE HARLEQUIN *Pseudorasbora parva.* Gudgeon-like but no barbels; mouth small, superior, transverse; LL 36-38; D III/7; A III/6; male with spiny tubercles under eye; greyish above, silvery sides and below, and dark lateral stripe from snout to C base; scales with thick dark edging. 11 cm. Originally Far Eastern species (Amur and Japan to China), accidentally introduced to Danube basin with Chinese carps in 1960, and now spreading in central and southern Europe. Another alien species with a dark stripe is **Fathead Minnow** *Promephales promelas,* 8 cm, from North America, also with incomplete lateral line, and males with spongy pad on back.

A
B
C

NASE *Chondrostoma nasus.* Ⓐ Slender-bodied, with prominent snout over mouth, with thick upper lip and horny lower jaw used for scraping food from stones; LL 53-66; D origin slightly before V origin, III/9-10 (8-10), no well-developed spine; A III/10-11 (9-12); gill rakers short, close-set; back grey to greenish, yellowish below, fins reddish. 50 cm, 10 yrs. Fast-flowing rivers, schools in deeper middle reaches, feeding chiefly on algae. Breeds February-May after upstream migration into shallower tributaries; fecundity to 100,000; eggs 1.5 mm. Sexually mature by 3-4 yrs. Relatives include **Italian Nase** *Ch. soetta,* Ⓑ 45 cm, deeper bodied, darker finned; and **Iberian Nase** *Ch. polylepis,* Ⓒ 25 cm, hybridizing with Pardilla.

Minnow Nase　　　　Soiffe　　　　　　Nase

A
B
C

SOIFFE *Chondrostoma toxostoma.* Ⓐ As Nase, but with more pointed snout, thin upper lip, strongly crescentic mouth, D origin directly above V origin, dark lateral band, and most fins yellowish. 20 cm. Streams and clear, well-oxygenated lake waters. Breeds late March-April, over upstream gravel beds. There are various subspecies, and the closely related **Italian Soiffe** *Ch. genei,* Ⓑ 25 cm; **Dalmatian Soiffe** *Ch. kneri,* Ⓒ 20 cm, LL 50-54, and other forms; and Iberian *Ch. t. miegii, turiensis* and *arrigonis.*

MINNOW NASE *Chondrostoma phoxinus.* Similar to Nase, but slimmer, minnow-like, and with many more scales (LL 88-110); dark back, silvery sides and below, yellowish fins and lateral band especially towards C. 15 cm. Fast streams of Dalmatia. Similar form, *Ch. lusitanicum,* in southern Portugal.

Gudgeon

False
Harlequin

Nase

Soiffe

Minnow Nase

ZIEGE *Pelecus cultratus.* Silvery cyprinid in midwater schools, with very compressed body and lower edge forming a sharp keel from throat to anus; mouth superior, jaws very oblique; LL 90-115; D well behind Vs origin, above A origin, III/7-8, much shorter than A, III/24-28; P long, pointed; lateral line complete but very curved near lower margin of body; gill rakers long, 18-23; olive, with silvery sides and below. 60 cm, 11 yrs. Midwater schools in brackish inshore waters, estuaries and into lower parts of rivers, feeding on small fish and crustaceans. Breeds May-July after springtime ascent into rivers; about 30,000 eggs, dispersed by current and may float in brackish water. Sexually mature by 3 yrs. Included in commercial fisheries in eastern Europe, but now rare in Baltic area.

ZÄHRTE *Vimba vimba.* Body moderately slender; snout projecting over inferior crescentic mouth; LL 53-61; D origin somewhat behind V origin, III/8 (8-9), without strong spine; A longer-based than D, III/19-21 (17-21); gill rakers short, well spaced; scaleless dorsal midline groove from head to D origin, and ridge between D and upper origin of C; back grey-blue, becoming yellowish towards underside; P, V and A yellowish; spawning male with black back and vivid orange to reddish underside. 51 cm (a: 1.14 kg). Lower reaches of rivers, feeding over muddy bottoms on invertebrates, and entering brackish water in Baltic, Black and Caspian seas. Breeds May-July after migration upstream or into river mouth, spawning over gravel in flowing water; fecundity to 200,000; eggs 1.4-2.0 mm, hatching at 6-8 mm; young initially in substrate. Several subspecies. Commercial fisheries in eastern areas. Hybrids with Silver Bream.

A ▓
B ▨

BREAM *Abramis brama.* Ⓐ An imposing fish with little fight; very deep but laterally flattened body, and small head; mouth inferior, thick-lipped; LL 49-60; D origin behind V origin, III/9 (8-10), without conspicuous spine; A long-based, with deeply concave edge, III/24-30 (22-32), origin under D base; scaleless keel behind V; above brownish or greyish, silvery sides and below, with somewhat bronze sheen in larger fish. 80 cm, 11.5 kg; 26 yrs (a: 6.01 kg). Slow lowland reaches of rivers, and also brackish water, but overwintering in deeper water in large numbers; bottom-feeding on invertebrates, such as midge larvae, sucked from mud with creation of a 'bream pit'. Breeds April-June, spawning in schools at night over weeds in shallows; fecundity to 340,000; eggs yellowish, 1.5-2.0 mm; hatch at 4.6-5.3 mm in 3-13 days. Mature at 22-24 cm (m), 18-24 cm (f), 4-6 yrs. Fisheries in eastern Europe. Danubian (*A. b. danubii*) and Caspian (*A. b. orientalis*) subspecies recognized. Hybrids with Roach, Rudd and Silver Bream. **Danubian Bream** *A. sapa,* Ⓑ as preceding, but LL 49-50 (48-53); A III/37-39 (35-42), and lower lobe of C noticeably longer than upper. 30 cm.

ZOPE *Abramis ballerus.* Similar to Bream, but body somewhat slimmer, mouth oblique and terminal, D narrow-based and higher (to three times base), A very long-based, III/35-44, LL 65-76; silvery, above bluish-green ('Blue Bream'); throat orange. 45 cm. Typically in slow reaches, feeding mostly on zooplankton.

SILVER BREAM *Blicca bjoerkna.* Also resembling Bream, but somewhat slimmer, eye larger (diameter equal to or longer than snout), and A origin below or behind end of D base; above greeny-brown or greyish, but sides silvery and white below; P and V bases orange to red. 35 cm. May feed in midwater as well as on bottom. Breeds June-July, spawning up to 110,000 yellowish eggs (1.5 mm) in batches over vegetation in stagnant shallows; young hatch at 5 mm and attach to weed. Mature by 2-4 yrs. Hybrids with Roach, Rudd, Zährte and Bream.

Ziege

Zährte male

Zährte female

Bream

Zope

Silver Bream

Roach

A ☐
B ☐
C ▦
D ▤
E ▥
F ▧

ROACH *Rutilus rutilus*. Ⓐ Among most frequently caught of coarse fishes; distinguished from Rudd by D origin above V base. Usually fairly deep bodied; mouth terminal; LL 42-45; D III/9-11, lacking conspicuous spine; A III/9-11; lateral line complete, curving to nearer ventral edge of body; gill rakers, about 10; rudimentary abdominal keel from V to A; rear part of swimbladder rounded; back dark bluish or green, sides brassy or golden, silvery-white underside, with V and A orange to red, and other fins darker; eye iris red; peritoneum pale. 50 cm, 2 kg; 12 yrs (a: 1.84 kg). Schooling, in lakes and slower parts of rivers, and may enter brackish water; bottom-feeder on invertebrates, especially molluscs, detritus and plant material. Breeds April-May (June) in fresh water, spawning 5,000-200,000 pale to greenish eggs (1.0-2.1 mm, with papillose sticky surface) over plants or sometimes gravel, usually in shallows; hatch at 4.5-6.5 mm. Mature at 2-3 yrs (m), 3-4 yrs (f). Hybrids with Rudd, Bleak, Chub, Bream and Silver Bream. Related species include **Rovella** *R. rubilio*, Ⓑ 30 cm, peritoneum usually dark, D 8, A 9, LL 39-40; and, all with pale peritoneum, **Danubian Roach** *R. pigus*, Ⓒ 50 cm, D 10, A 11, LL 47-49; **Triotto** *R. erythrophthalmus*, Ⓓ D 9, A 9, LL 38-39, dark lateral band; and **Basak** *R. basak*, Ⓔ D and A 9, LL 39-40, no obvious lateral band. Also small Iberian roaches, all with D III/9-10 and lateral dark band: **Berme Juela** *R. arcasii*, Ⓕ LL 42-46; **Pardilla** *R. lemmingii*, Ⓕ LL 59-63; and **Calandino** *Tropidophoxinellus alburnoides*, Ⓕ LL 38-44 (last species hybridizes with Iberian Chub). **Black Sea Roach** *R. frisii*, as Roach, but body more slender, cylindrical, LL 62-67, and rear end of swimbladder conical, pointed. 70 cm. Alpine subspecies *R. f. meidingeri*.

A ☐
B ☐

RUDD *Scardinius erythrophthalmus*. Ⓐ In contrast to Roach, D origin well behind V base; mouth upturned, without barbels; lateral scales 40-45; D III/8-9; A III/10-11; lateral line complete, regular; gill rakers, about 10; scaly keel from V to A; back and sides greeny-brown, yellowing to white underside, sometimes tinged gold; P, V and A red, bases greyish; eye iris gold, with upper red spot. 41 cm; 17 yrs (a: 1.58 kg). Lakes and slower reaches of rivers, and may enter brackish water; schooling in midwater, eating more surface insects and less plant material than Roach. Breeds April-June, often with other species, spawning 90,000-230,000 eggs, 1.4-1.8 mm, pale or yellowish, adhering to plants. Sexually mature by 2-3 yrs. A Romanian subspecies *S. e. racovitzai*, only 9.3 cm, is adapted to hot springs (28-34°C, algal diet); also **Greek Rudd** *S. e. graecus*, Ⓑ 40 cm. Hybridizes with Roach, Bream, Silver Bream, Bleak and Dace.

GRASS CARP *Ctenopharyngodon idella*. Asiatic carp with the ability to digest grass. Body slim, cylindrical, mouth subterminal; LL 43-45; D origin slightly in advance of V origin, III/7; A III/8; gill rakers, about 12; abdominal keel behind V; greenish-brown to brownish, sides paler, slightly golden, fins dark. 100 cm, 40 kg (a: 29.88 kg). Lowland rivers, feeding chiefly on faster-growing aquatic plants; breeds in summer, with planktonic eggs; hatch in 32-40 hours at 27-29°C. Originally from Far East, but widespread in pond culture, and also introduced to control water weeds. Other introduced Chinese carps are **Silver Carp** *Hypophthalmichthys molitrix*, 100 cm (a: 16 kg), with low-set eyes and LL 110-124, feeding on phytoplankton; and *H. nobilis*, with brown markings and more varied diet.

A ▪
B ▨
C ▤

CHUB *Leuciscus cephalus.* Ⓐ Moderately slender but robust, voracious but wary; mouth large, terminal; LL 43-46 (41-48); D origin behind V base, III/8 (7-9); A III/8-9, edge convex; gill rakers short, spaced, 8-11; back dark green or grey, silvery sides, yellowish below, with scales dark-edged, V and A reddish. 61 cm, 4 kg (a: 2.62 kg). Rivers, schooling or solitary near surface in clear, flowing reaches, sometimes in lakes or brackish water, taking invertebrates (including trout flies) and small fish. Breeds May-June, fecundity to 200,000; eggs 0.7-2.0 mm, pale yellowish-orange, on weed, stones or gravel. Subspecies from the Adriatic area and south-western Europe are *L. c. cabeda* and *L. c. albus*; other species include Iberian **Cacho** *L. pyrenaicus,* Ⓑ Tuscan *L. lucumonis* and Greek *L. beoticus.* Hybrids with Roach, Rudd, Bleak and Danubian Bleak. **Black Sea Chub** *L. borysthenicus,* Ⓒ 40 cm, with LL 36-40, has much lower fecundity (about 2,500 eggs). Related West Balkan species are *L. svallize,* D III/9 (8-10), A III/10 (9-10), LL 45-47 (44-49); and *L. illyricus,* D III/8, A III/9 (8-9), LL 47-51 (46-54).

A ▪
B ▪

SOUFIE *Leuciscus souffia.* Ⓐ Slender, minnow-like fish; mouth subterminal; LL 45-58; D origin slightly before V base; III/8-9; A III/8-9, edge slightly concave; back metallic-blue, sides with prominent dark band (lower edge iridescent in breeding male), silvery below. 12 cm. Schools in running water, and in some lakes, over gravel and stones, feeding mostly on benthic invertebrates. Breeds March-May, 6,000-8,000 eggs, on gravel. Subspecies *L. s. souffia, L. s. agassizi,* and *L. s. muticellus* around Alpine massif, in upper Danube basin, and in Italy; also related *L. pleurobipunctatus* Ⓑ from western Greece.

A ▪
B ▪

DACE *Leuciscus leuciscus.* Ⓐ Slender, darting, among the most lively of carps; mouth inferior; LL 48-51; D origin above V base, III/7; A edge concave, III/8; gill rakers 8 (6-9); back greenish-blue, sides silvery to yellowish below, fins grey (D, A, C) or yellowish (P, V). 30 cm. Schools near surface in fast-flowing, clear water, sometimes in lakes; feeds on plant material and invertebrates. Breeds February-May, in gravelly shallows; fecundity to 27,000; eggs yellow or greenish, 1.5-2.5 mm. Sexually mature by 2-3 yrs. Also Croatian *L. ukliva,* LL 62-64; *L. turskyi,* LL 70-72, broad, dark lateral band; and *L. microlepis,* LL 73-75, lateral band more or less developed. *L. danilewskii,* 22 cm, from the Don basin, has LL 43-46. **Bordallo** *L. carolitertii,* Ⓑ occurs in northern Iberia.

dorsal fin
of Dace

dorsal fin
of Chub

ORFE *Leuciscus idus.* More robust and larger than Dace but of similar habits; mouth terminal, oblique; LL 56-61 (55-63); D origin behind V origin, III/8; A III/9-10, longer-based than D and with more or less concave edge; gill rakers short, wide-spaced, 10-14; very slight keel between V and A; above dark, sides and below silvery, fins (except D) reddish, eye iris yellow. 102 cm, 8 kg (a: 2.52 kg). Slow rivers and lakes, entering brackish water, eating invertebrates. Breeds April-May, fecundity to 114,000; eggs 1.5-2.2 mm. Some local fisheries in Russia. Golden Orfe is a yellow ornamental variety, sometimes feral.

Chub

Soufie

Dace

Golden Orfe

Orfe

Minnow
female

Minnow male

MINNOW *Phoxinus phoxinus*. Small, slender schooling fishes, males with bright red bellies (not to be confused with the red-breasted male 'tiddler' – Three-Spined Stickleback); mouth sub-terminal; scales tiny, LL 85-100; D origin behind V origin, III/7; A III/6-7; lateral-line ends above A; gill rakers 8-11 (5-11); back brownish-olive, yellowing to belly, and sides with dark blotches often running into irregular band. 12 cm, 8 yrs. Clear, flowing waters of rivers, as well as lakes with coarse substrate; in winter solitary, beneath stones; feeds on invertebrates and plant material. Breeds April-August; eggs 200-1,000, 1.2-1.8 mm, grey-white to yellowish; mature at 1 yr, 3.5-4.0 cm.

SWAMP MINNOW *Phoxinus percnurus*. Deeper-bodied than Minnow, LL 68-80 (65-89), and coloration golden with numer-ous small dark spots but no larger lateral blotches; males lacking nuptial tubercles on head. 15 cm. Schools, especially in still, well-vegetated lakes and ponds. To eastern Siberia and Amur basin. Local variation has suggested a number of doubt-ful subspecies.

ALBANIAN MINNOW *Pachychilon pictum*. Body slender; mouth subterminal, lips thick, lower as continuous fold across apex of jaw; LL 43-44; III/11; A III/11-12; pale brown to white below, with numerous brown spots. 16 cm. Schooling, in rivers. Now introduced to Italy (River Serchio).

A ■
B ■

ADRIATIC MINNOW *Paraphoxinus alepidotus*. Ⓐ (Includes other Balkan minnows.) Body slender; jaws terminal; scales absent except for row along lateral line; lateral line variable in extent; back dark brown, steel-blue lateral band, and belly silvery. 10 cm. Related West Balkan species are **Croatian Minnow** *P. croaticus*, 10 cm, rudimentary scales, lacks dark spots; **Dalmatian Minnow** *P. ghetaldii*, 13 cm, cave waters, lacks scales on back and lower caudal peduncle; **South Dalmatian Minnow** *P. pstrossi*, 10 cm, dark spots chiefly above lateral midline; **Greek Minnow** *P. epiroticus*, 12 cm, deciduous scales; **Spotted Minnow** *P. adspersus*, 10 cm, spotted, many below lateral mid-line, Dalmatia; and *P. minutus*, 5.5 cm, fully scaled, Lake Ochrid. **Jarubago** *Anae-cypris hispanica*, Ⓑ from Iberian Guadiana and Guadalquivir, is a schooling, minnow-like fish with dark lateral band, LL 59-71, prominent scaleless keel from V to anus, and many gill rakers (to 120); is now facing extinction.

SUNBLEAK *Leucaspius delineatus*. Also termed Belica. Slen-der silvery fish, with large, easily-dislodged scales; mouth ter-minal, jaws very oblique; LL 40-46; III/8; A longer, III/10-13; V 10; lateral line short, along not more than first 10 scales; slight abdominal keel; back olive, sides with bluish longitudinal stripe, otherwise silvery. 12 cm, 5 yrs. Schools near surface in open reaches of slow, well-vegetated waters. Breeds April-May; eggs 1.0 mm, deposited by female via tubular genital fold, in spiral bands on aquatic plants, and guarded by male. Related are **Marida** *Pseudophoxinus stymphalicus*, 12 cm, from southern Greece and Pelopon-nese; and *Ladigesocypris ghigii*, 10 cm, from Rhodes. *Iberocypris palaciosi*, 17.5 cm, from southern Spain, has LL 45-53 and complete lateral line.

Swamp Minnow

Adriatic Minnow

Sunbleak

Bleak

BLEAK *Alburnus alburnus.* A 'Frolicsome' small fish, whose silver scales yield pearl essence, based on guanine crystals, once used to line artificial pearls (100 g from 4,000-5,000 fish). Slim; mouth terminal, jaws oblique; LL 48-55; D origin behind V origin, III/8-9; A long-based, III/16-20; gill rakers 17-22; sharp scaleless abdominal keel from V to A; greeny-blue, belly silvery, fins typically greyish but bases may be orange in breeding male. 20 cm, 40 g; 6 yrs. Schools near surface in clear, slow rivers and lakes, entering brackish water; feeds on surface insects and plankton. Breeds April-June, eggs about 5,000-6,000, 1.5 mm, yellow, with papillae on surface of capsule, in clumps on vegetation; hatch at only 3-4 mm. Sexually mature by 2-3 yrs. Eastern European fisheries for animal food and scales. Hybrids with Roach, Rudd, Chub and Dace. Related **Italian Bleak** *A. albidus,* B 14 cm, now endangered, has A III/13-18; and **Caucasian Bleak** *A. charusini,* C 12 cm, has deeper body and LL 41-47.

115

DANUBIAN BLEAK *Chalcalburnus chalcoides.* Very slender; mouth terminal; LL 61-68; D origin behind V origin, D II-III/8-9; A III/15-19; gill rakers long, close together, 22-23; short scale-less abdominal keel between V and anus; silvery, back dark green, below silvery-white. 35 cm. Slower rivers and lakes; also into brackish water. Breeds May-June in fresh water, fecundity to 40,000 eggs. Danube basin as *Ch. ch. mento;* typical subspecies, *Ch. ch. chalcoides,* 40 cm, D III/8 (7-9), A III/13-17, in Caspian Basin; other subspecies in Black and Aral basins. Hybrids with Chub.

 SCHNEIDER *Alburnoides bipunctatus.* Body deeper than Bleak; mouth terminal, subhorizontal; LL 44-51; D origin behind V base, III/7-8 (7-9); A III/12-17 (11-17); gill rakers short, well spaced; scaleless abdominal keel from V to anus; back dark, sides silvery, lateral line always dark; lateral dark band evident, especially in breeding season. 15 cm. Schools in clear, flowing water, over rocky beds, sometimes in lakes, feeding chiefly on benthic insect larvae and also surface drift organisms. Breeds May-June. Three Balkan subspecies recognized.

 ASP *Aspius aspius.* A hunting carp, with elongated, compressed body; mouth terminal, large, oblique, lower jaw with median knob fitting notch in upper jaw; LL 65-74 (64-76); D origin over V base, III/8; A III/13 (12-14); gill rakers short, about 10; scaled abdominal keel behind V; back dark green, otherwise silvery with reddish fins. 80 cm (even to 100 cm) (a: 5.66 kg). Middle reaches of rivers and also large lakes, entering brackish water; solitary predators chiefly on small fish. Breeds April-May.

 BITTERLING *Rhodeus sericeus.* Deep-bodied, small cyprinid which lays its eggs inside a mussel; mouth subterminal, small; LL 34-40; D origin slightly behind V origin, III/9-10; A III/8-9 (8-10); lateral line incomplete, on merely several scales; back greeny-grey, sides and belly silvery-white, with lateral bluish stripe especially nearer C, and fins tinged orange; breeding males with lateral iridescence and red D and A. 9.5 cm, 5 yrs. Lakes and slow-moving parts of rivers, feeding on benthic invertebrates and plant material. Breeds April-June, among marginal vegetation where eggs are laid in the gill chamber of a freshwater mussel, the female developing a long tubular ovipositor from the urogenital orifice immediately behind the anus, and the male fertilizing the eggs by ejaculating sperm into the inhalant current of the mussel; eggs pale yellow, oval, 3 × 2 mm; young remain within mussel until about 9-10 mm long, when the yolk sac is absorbed. Sexually mature by 2-3 yrs. Feral in England (spreading via canals from Lancashire and Cheshire) from imported ornamental fish. To the Far East.

Schneider

Asp

Bitterling male

Bitterling female

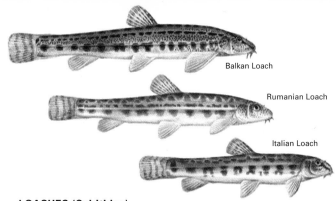

Balkan Loach

Rumanian Loach

Italian Loach

LOACHES (Cobitidae)

Long, slender, bottom-living fishes, feeding nocturnally on invertebrates; mouth inferior, with up to 10 barbels; 1 short dorsal fin. Some species may augment gill respiration by swallowing air at the surface and passing this through the intestine, parts of which are modified for gas exchange with the blood system.

A
B
C

SPINED LOACH *Cobitis taenia.* A Body compressed; mouth with 3 pairs of barbels; mobile, backwardly directed, bifid spine in skin fold below eye; D II-III/6-7; A II-III/5-6; C 14 branched rays; scales minute; brownish above, yellow below, with series of many dark brown spots along lateral midline. 14 cm. In sand or mud of slow streams or lakes, resting with just head exposed but sometimes coming to surface to swallow air. Breeds April-June, with yellowish eggs (0.8 mm) laid on stones and plants; breeding males have enlarged second P ray. At least 9 subspecies, and related species: **Lamprehuela** *C. calderoni* B and **Colmilleja** *C. maroccana* C in Spain; and **Balkan Loach** *C. elongata*, 16.5 cm, with thin dark line through lateral spots.

GOLDEN LOACH *Cobitis auratus.* As Spined Loach, but C 12 (12-13) branched rays, body with golden tint and lateral midline spots less distinct; mature males with wider body before D. 13.8 cm. In faster middle and upper parts of rivers. Breeds April-June. Other nominal species include **Rumanian Loach** *Sabanejewia romanica*, 12 cm, paler; and **Italian Loach** *S. larvata*, 10 cm, with Y-shaped mark on snout.

STONE LOACH *Barbatula barbatula.* Body more cylindrical; mouth with 3 pairs of barbels; cheek without spine; D III-IV/7; A III-IV/5; no scales; brownish-yellow with darker blotches, yellowish below. 12.5 cm. Usually under stones, in clear streams, and also lake shallows, as well as brackish water in Baltic (absence may denote pollution). Breeds April-August, spawning batches of small pale to greenish eggs (1.0-1.2 mm), reputedly under stones and guarded by female; ripe males have small papillae over P. To Far East.

WEATHER FISH *Misgurnus fossilis.* Reputedly a fish barometer, becoming active prior to thunderstorms; long cylindrical; mouth with 5 pairs of barbels; cheek without spine; D II-IV/5-7; A III-V/5 (5-6); scales minute, LL 135-175; brownish, with dark mottling and lateral banding, yellowish below. 35 cm. In muddy bottoms of lakes and stagnant water, often air-breathing; it may aestivate in mud if habitat dries out. Breeds April-June, spawning up to 150,000 reddish-brown eggs (1.5 mm) on aquatic plants; newly hatched larvae have external gill filaments.

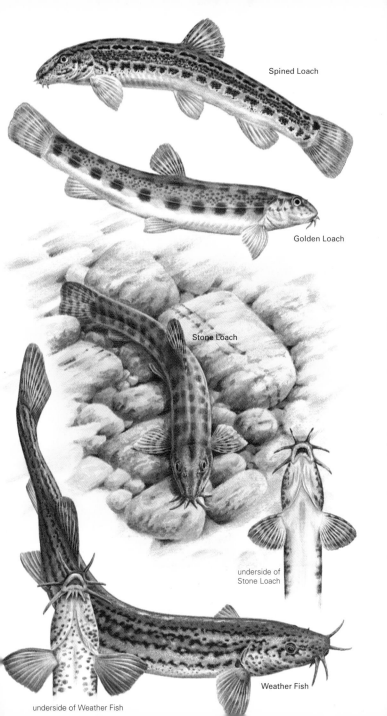

Spined Loach

Golden Loach

Stone Loach

underside of
Stone Loach

Weather Fish

underside of Weather Fish

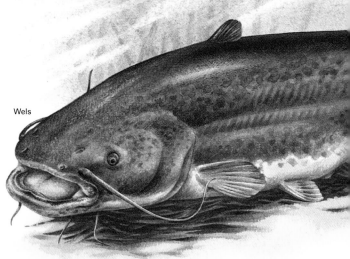

Wels

CATFISHES (ORDER SILURIFORMES)

Two of many catfish families; catfishes have jaw teeth and usually an adipose fin; barbels well developed; P typically with strong spine.

A ▪
B ▪

WELS *Silurus glanis* (**Siluridae**). Ⓐ Europe's largest freshwater teleost, reaching at least 500 cm, and, allegedly, big enough to eat swimming dogs and children. Body robust, with long compressed tail tapering to small C; D very small, 3-5; A 77-92; 1 pair of very long barbels on upper jaw, 2 pairs of short barbels on lower jaw; no scales or adipose fin; olive-green, back dark, sides mottled with whitish blotches, belly pale. Solitary, in holes or beneath sunken structures, in muddy, stagnant water bodies, feeding at night on fishes, and other small aquatic vertebrates. Breeds May-July in shallow areas, spawning numerous pale yellow-green eggs (3 mm) on nest of leaf litter in muddy depression among tree roots, excavated by male; both parents guard eggs and alevins (hatch at 7 mm). Sexually mature by 2-3 yrs (m), 3-4 yrs (f), at 50-80 cm. Established in some lakes in southern England, but could reduce native fish. Commercial fisheries and intensive angling in eastern Europe (a: 33 kg); eggs may be used as a caviare. **Aristotle's Catfish** *S. aristotelis*, Ⓑ with only 1 pair of small barbels on lower jaw, occurs in the Achelous area of western Greece.

BROWN BULLHEAD *Ameiurus nebulosus* (**Ictaluridae**). Representing a North American catfish family; 4 pairs of barbels, 1 pair (longest) on upper jaw, 1 pair behind nostrils, and 2 pairs on lower jaw; D moderate, with spine; adipose fin; C with only slightly concave rear edge; P spine serrated; grey or dark brown mottling to yellowish below; barbels brown or black. 40 cm (a: 2.59 kg). Slow or stagnant well-vegetated muddy water; an omnivorous nocturnal feeder; via the sharp chemical sense, this and related species are attracted by 'ripe' baits. Breeds May-June, spawning creamy-white eggs in a sheltered depression guarded by one or both parents; young remain near nest, often in dense schools. Originally from New England and Great Lakes to Mexico, but widespread in Europe after introductions since 1870s. The North American **Black Bullhead** *A. melas*, 50 cm (a: 3.62 kg), with dark or spotted chin barbels and smooth P spine, has been introduced to Italy and Spain; **Channel Catfish** *Ictalurus punctatus*, 90 cm (a: 26.3 kg), greyish, with scattered black spots and usually black barbels, and C deeply forked, is another alien. A marine mouth-brooding catfish, *Arius thalassinus* (**Ariidae**), with 3 pairs of barbels and deeply forked C, has entered Mediterranean via Suez Canal.

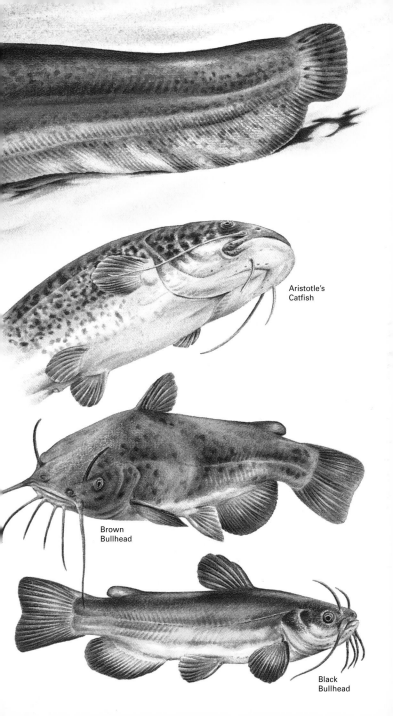

Aristotle's
Catfish

Brown
Bullhead

Black
Bullhead

STOMIIFORMS (SUPERORDER STENOPTERYGII)

Mostly dark, deep-sea species, mesopelagic in the ocean water column down to about 1,000 m. Characterized by small light organs, typically in 2 parallel rows along the lower edge of the body, probably serving to deceive predators from below by concealment against natural light from above. Mouth usually very large, with angle well behind eye, and teeth fang-like. Many approach the surface at night, migrating vertically for hundreds of metres each day, to feed on plankton, small crustaceans and fish. Very abundant in oceanic waters; examples of some species are occasionally taken nearer land or stranded. The following is a cross-section of several stomiiform families from temperate or warmer Atlantic waters off the continental shelf of Europe.

 BRAUER'S BRISTLEMOUTH *Cyclothone braueri* (**Gonostomatidae**). Mouth large, upper jaw curved but teeth relatively small; body elongated, D posterior, above longer-based A (18-20); P 9-10; whitish, with scattered areas of darker pigment. 2.6 cm (m), 3.8 cm (f). Adults 250-900 m, nearer surface in winter, and occasionally offshore shelf. Spawns April-October; up to 900 eggs, small, 0.5 mm. Worldwide. Also temperate eastern Atlantic, the mostly protandric hermaphroditic **Black Bristlemouth** *Gonostoma bathyphilum*, 15 cm (m), 20 cm (f), with adipose fin, A 22-26, P 11-14, and black coloration, has postlarvae near surface, although bathypelagic adults remain at 700-2000 m.

 BLACK SNAGGLETOOTH *Astronesthes niger* (**Astronesthidae**). A Large mouth with fang-like teeth; chin barbel; D well before A; dorsal and ventral adipose fins; mostly black. 16 cm. Usually deeper than 500 m by day. Warmer Atlantic. **Black Dragonfish** *Idiacanthus fasciola* (**Idiacanthidae**), B is eel-like, D and A long-based; mouth with fangs; P absent; chin-barbel in females; males also lack teeth and V; black. 7 cm (m), F larger. 500-2,000 m during day, females to 250 m or nearer surface at night; post-larvae with eyes on long stalks.

  SLOANE'S VIPERFISH *Chauliodus sloani* (**Chauliodontidae**). (lower-middle illustration) Body very elongated, with hexagonal patterning and gelatinous pellicle; head bulbous, with large jaws and prominent fangs, but barbel only in juvenile; D anterior, above P/V interspace, and first ray very long; silvery-blue. 30 cm. To 1,000 m by day. Worldwide in warmer seas.

 SCALY DRAGONFISH *Stomias boa* (**Stomiidae**). (lower illustration) Body as Sloane's Viperfish, but head smaller, D very posterior, over A, no adipose fins, and short chin barbel, with a few filaments on terminal bulb; iridescent silvery. 30 cm. To 1,000 m by day. West Africa into western Mediterranean (*S. b. boa*, A with 83-86 (82-88) ventral IC photophores) and north to Iceland and British Isles (*S. b. ferox*, B with 87-89 (85-91) IC photophores).

 LONG-BARBELLED DRAGONFISH *Grammatostomias flagellibarba* (**Melanostomiidae**). A Body moderately long, tapering to D and A before small C; eyes small; jaws long, with fangs; chin barbel fragile, reported several times body length; black, with pale loop of luminous tissue on body behind opercle. 20 cm. Over 500 m by day. **Black Loosejaw** *Malacosteus niger* (**Malacosteidae**), B has body as preceding; head prominent, with eyes at tip and very long jaws; lower jaw with fangs, and lacking membranous floor and barbel; large light organ below eye, and smaller one behind; black. 24 cm. Mesopelagic by day.

HATCHET FISH *Argyropelecus hemigymnus* (**Sternoptychidae**). (upper illustration) Small, very compressed silvery fishes, with dorsal bony blade of several spines before D, abdominal keel with rear spines; eyes somewhat tubular, upwardly directed; mouth small, vertical; dark above, sides silvery, with prominent photophores in paired abdominal rows between V and A, and above A base. 2.8 cm (m), 3.9 cm (f). 50-800 m by day. Breed in summer (North Atlantic), all year (Mediterranean), 50-500 eggs. Worldwide.

PEARLSIDES *Maurolicus muelleri* (**Sternoptychidae**). (upper-middle illustration) Photophores as Hatchet Fish but body more normally fish-like, not greatly compressed and without dorsal blade and ventral keel; eyes lateral; dark above, sides silvery. 6.5 cm. 10-400 m by day. Spawns as Hatchet Fish, 200-500 eggs, 1.3-2.0 mm, near surface. Eastern Atlantic.

LIZARDFISHES AND LANTERNFISHES
(SUPERORDER SCOPELOMORPHA)

Mostly oceanic fishes with large heads, jaws, and prominent eyes; 1 rayed D and an adipose fin. Perhaps lizardfishes are best known in the form of 'Bombay duck', a dried Indian Ocean species, but lanternfishes are of great importance in oceanic food webs because of their abundance and diversity.

A ▪
B ▨

ATLANTIC LIZARDFISH *Synodus saurus* (**Synodontidae**). Ⓐ Elongated, cylindrical body, with long head and jaws, their angle well behind eye; D small, behind P, over large V, 8; no photophores; back with several dark bars, becoming indistinct at larger size. 43 cm. Bottom-living, shelf, from inshore, especially around islands, rarely upper slope; moves over substrate on pelvic fins, but typically a 'sit-and-wait' predator for fish and shrimps. Indo-Pacific **Brush-toothed Lizardfish** *Saurida undosquamis*, Ⓑ 50 cm, V 9, 8-10 well-defined dark spots along lateral line, is a Suez Canal colonist of the Levant Sea.

LANTERN FISH *Myctophum punctatum* (**Myctophidae**). Small fishes with very large eyes, set forward with very short snout and long jaws, angle well behind eye; D (13-14) and A (20-22) large; photophores on head and body below lateral line; 107 mm. Oceanic, mesopelagic (mostly 700-800 m), rising to epipelagic (45 m-surface) at night, feeding on small crustaceans and larval fish. Breeds late winter-spring (Atlantic) into summer (Mediterranean). The family is extremely rich in genera and species, requiring specialist identification by photophore pattern. Occasionally stranded on shore.

FLAGFIN *Aulopus filamentosus* (**Aulopidae**). Large eyes, lower edge meeting upper jaw, and prominent D, 16, origin above P; enlarged horizontal scales on C wrist; no photophores; browny-green. 44 cm. Bottom-living, shelf and upper slope, to 1,000 m.

BARRACUDINA *Paralepis coregonoides* (**Paralepidae**). Somewhat like a Barracuda, in being elongated with large jaws, whose angle is below eye; V small; no photophores; silvery. 40 cm. Oceanic, to mesopelagic, but straying to shelf and even included within British angling records. Similar *P. rissoi kroyeri*, 30 cm, has A 31-34, P 11-15.

A ▪
B ▨
C ▩

LANCETFISH *Alepisaurus ferox* (**Alepisauridae**). Ⓐ 200 cm, D 39-42 and sail-like, jaws with large fangs; and *Anotopterus pharao* (**Anotopteridae**), Ⓑ 50 cm, head and jaws long, fins tiny. Other unusual oceanic fishes include the **Pearleye** *Scopelarchus analis* (**Scopelarchidae**), Ⓒ 127 mm, eye upturned with lateral lens pad.

Lancetfish

Atlantic
Lizardfish

Lantern Fish

Flagfin

Barracudina

SUPERORDER PARACANTHOPTERYGII, COD-LIKE FISHES (ORDER GADIFORMES)

The Cod and its relatives are very familiar species, but unusual among teleosts in that they have 3 dorsal and 2 anal fins, as well as a caudal fin that has a tapering base. Other forms within this group have 1-2 dorsal fins and 1 anal fin. Spinous fin rays are absent, and V are below or in advance of P origin. Typically marine fishes of the continental shelf and upper slope, they include many species of considerable economic importance.

CODS (Gadidae)

C separate from D and A; V origin before P; barbels often present; eggs typically planktonic.

Cods with 3Ds and 2As:

COD *Gadus morhua*. For centuries a prime component of demersal fisheries throughout the cold North Atlantic, with the traditional salt cod an important item of trade, but now greatly diminished. Chin barbel present, equal to eye diameter; upper jaw projecting beyond lower jaw, angle of jaws below eye; lateral line continuous to below D3; A1 base less than distance from snout to anus, A1 origin below D2; A2 17-19; greenish-brown, back and sides with dense darker mottling, lateral line white, white below. 190 cm, 20 yrs (a: 44.79 kg). Demersal, shelf, usually 150-200 m, to upper slope, in schools; feeds on fish (often smaller cod) and invertebrates. Migrates to spawning grounds, such as central North Sea, in February-April; spawns February-April, then moves to feeding areas associated with herring abundance; pre-spawning courtship behaviour involves fin display and grunting by males, then movement towards surface where spawning occurs as pair swims in circles with male inverted below female; fecundity to 9 million; eggs planktonic, 1.16-1.89 mm, with thick yellow unsegmented yolk but no oil globule, and embryo with only black pigment; hatch at 4.0 mm in 8.5-23 days at 3-14°C; larvae drift to nursery areas (as in southern North Sea or east coast of Scotland), becoming demersal at 20 mm after 2-2.5 months; as codling, on rough ground for 1.5-2 yrs, then mature at 68-78 cm, 4-5 yrs (North Sea). Nominal subspecies in Baltic Sea (*G. m. callarias*); other subspecies in western Atlantic. Two Polar inshore relatives are **Navaga** *Eleginus navaga*, 42 cm, with less conspicuous lateral line, continuous only to D2, A2 19-26; and **Arctic Cod** *Boreogadus saida*, 32 cm, lower jaw protruding, tiny barbel, and very wavy, dark lateral line.

HADDOCK *Melanogrammus aeglefinus*. Another important economic species, distinguished from Cod by tiny chin barbel, much less than eye diameter, dark lateral line, and dark blotch on LL above P; upper jaw projecting beyond lower jaw, angle of jaws before eye; lateral line continuous to C; A1 base less than distance from snout to anus, A1 origin below D2; A2 22-23; dark greenish-brown, sides paler, white below. 112 cm, 14.5 kg; 22 yrs (a: 5.3 kg). Benthic, offshore usually 80-200 m (10-450 m), in schools; feeds mostly on bottom-living invertebrates such as worms, shellfish and echinoderms. Spawns March-May (North Sea), May-June (Iceland); fecundity to over 1.8 million; eggs 1.2-1.7 mm, otherwise as Cod; hatch at 3.5-4.0 mm in 10-20 days at 4-10°C; after metamorphosis, juveniles have longer pelagic life than Cod, at first living beneath large jellyfish; demersal at about 5 cm, but do not migrate inshore; mature at 23-29 cm, 3-5 yrs.

Cod

Navaga

Arctic Cod

Haddock

BIB *Trisopterus luscus*. Also called Pouting; common inshore, but more important in sea angling than in fisheries. Deep-bodied; chin barbel present, almost equal to eye diameter; upper jaw projecting beyond lower jaw, angle of jaws below eye; body depth greater than head length; lateral line continuous to C; A1 30-34, base long, more than distance from snout to anus, A1 origin below or behind D1 origin; coppery, with 4-5 dark bars often evident, lateral line dark. 45 cm, 4 yrs. Demersal, adults offshore shelf, 30-100 m; feeds chiefly on crustaceans. Spawns March-April, requiring temperatures of at least 8-9°C; eggs 0.9-1.23 mm; hatch at about 3.0 mm in 10-12 days; mature at 21-25 cm, 1 yr.

POOR COD *Trisopterus minutus*. As Bib, but body depth less than head length; A1 25-29, its base somewhat shorter than distance from snout to anus, A1 origin below middle of D1; brownish-yellow above, sides coppery, silvery below. 40 cm. Offshore shelf and uppermost slope, 30-300 m, young more inshore; feeds chiefly on shrimp-like crustaceans and small fish. Spawns March-April (February-June); eggs 0.95-1.03 mm, as Cod but embryo with both black and yellow pigment; hatch at 2.3-2.4 mm; mature at 11-12.5 cm, 2 yrs. Two subspecies are *T. m. minutus* (Gibraltar to Norway), and *T. m. capelanus* (Morocco and western Mediterranean).

NORWAY POUT *Trisopterus esmarki*. Less likely inshore than Bib and Poor Cod; otherwise similar, but chin barbel much shorter than eye diameter; latter at least equal to snout length; lower jaw projecting beyond upper jaw; brownish-grey above, sides silvery, paler below. 26 cm, 5 yrs. Offshore shelf, on muddy grounds in 100-200 m (50-300 m), schooling; feeds chiefly on planktonic crustaceans. Spawns March-May (January-July); fecundity to 384,000; eggs 1.0-1.19 mm; hatch at only 3.2 mm. Sexually mature at 2 (1-2) yrs, 11-15 cm.

POLLACK *Pollachius pollachius*. Common near the shore, and frequently caught by sea-anglers; chin barbel absent; lower jaw projecting beyond upper jaw; gill rakers 25-28; lateral line curved over P, continuous to C; A1 27-30, base more than half distance from snout to anus; A1 origin below D1; above brown to olive, sides and below paler. 130 cm (a: 12.41 kg). Inshore, demersal and midwater, over coarser ground, schooling in breeding season; feeds on small fish; breeds March (January-May); fecundity to 2.5 million; eggs 1.1-1.22 mm.

SAITHE *Pollachius virens*. Also termed Coalfish, more northerly in abundance than Pollack, and fished commercially. As Pollack, but minute barbel and smaller eye; lateral line straight; gill-rakers 35-40; brownish-green to olive, paler sides, including lateral line, and below. 130 cm, 25 yrs (a: 21.14 kg). Shelf, schooling. Breeds January-May; fecundity to 4 million; eggs 1.03-1.22 mm, with black pigment on yolk but no oil globule; hatch at 3.4-3.8 mm in 6-9 days at 6-9°C. Also Greenland and western Atlantic.

WHITING *Merlangius merlangus*. Common in coastal fisheries. Chin barbel minute or absent (present in young at 2.5 cm); eye less than snout length; upper jaw slightly before lower jaw; lateral line continuous to rear D3; A1 origin below D1; browny-yellow to blue above, sides yellowish, silvery or white below; P base with dark spot. 70 cm, 10 yrs (a: 2.33 kg). Usually inshore, midwater to surface, feeding on fish, especially sandeels. Breeds January-July; fecundity to 285,000; eggs 0.97-1.32 mm, without oil globule but yolk vacuolated and capsule appears rough; hatch at 3.2-3.5 mm; pelagic young from 20-50 mm occur under or near large jellyfish. Subspecies *M. m. euxinus*, with chin barbel and longer P, in Mediterranean and Black Sea.

Bib

Poor Cod

Pollack

Saithe

Whiting

A ▪
B ▨

BLUE WHITING *Micromesistius poutassou*. Ⓐ A small oceanic species, whose vast abundance deserves harvesting. Chin barbel absent; lower jaw projecting slightly beyond upper; latter under eye; lateral line continuous to C; A1 33-39, its base longer than distance from snout to anus; A1 origin before or below D1 origin; Ds well spaced, D2/3 interspace longer than D1 base; above blue-grey, sides silvery, white below. 50 cm; 20 yrs. Offshore, pelagic at 300-400 m (150 to >1,000 m), schooling, young sometimes inshore; feeds mostly on crustaceans. Breeds February-May at shelf edge or beyond; eggs 1.04-1.28 mm; hatch at 2.0-2.2 mm; sexually mature at 20 cm, 2-4 yrs. Also western Atlantic. Another offshore pelagic codlet is **Silvery Pout** *Gadiculus argenteus*, Ⓑ 15 cm, eye large (longer than snout), no barbel, Ds close together, and A1 11-16, base short; *G. a. thori* is the Mediterranean subspecies.

Cods with 1-2 Ds, 1 A:

TORSK *Brosme brosme*. Long-line fisheries in colder areas. Chin barbel present, equal to eye diameter; snout barbels absent; 1 D; D and A connected to C; brownish-grey, D and A with dark band near edge. 110 cm, 20 yrs (a: 15.15 kg). Bottom-living, offshore shelf and upper slope, usually 150-450 m (20-1,000 m), on coarse ground. Breeds April-July (north-western Scotland); fecundity to 2.25 million; eggs 1.29-1.51 mm, with brownish to pink oil globule and fine pitting of surface; hatch at 4.0 mm, post-larva with 3 long V rays. Also western Atlantic.

LING *Molva molva*. Large elongated gadoids, taken by angling in deeper coastal waters, as well as by commercial fisheries, and renowned for their fecundity (perhaps to 60 million eggs in one female); chin barbel present, longer than eye diameter; latter not more than about one-fifth of head length; snout barbels absent; upper jaw projecting before lower jaw; 2 Ds; V 6, short; greeny-bronze above, marbled, paler below, Ds and A with dark mark at rear corner, pale-edged. 220 cm, 10-14 yrs (a: 37.2 kg). Offshore shelf and upper slope, 100-400 m (15-600 m), but young more inshore, on rocky ground; feeds mostly on fish. Breeds March-August; eggs 0.97-1.13 mm, with one colourless or pale green oil globule carrying black pigment; hatch at 3.2 mm; postlarvae have very elongated V; demersal from 8 cm; mature at 80 cm (m), 90-100 cm, 6-8 yrs (f). Also western Atlantic.

BLUE LING *Molva dypterygia*. As preceding, but lower jaw projecting beyond upper, eye larger, more than one-fifth head length; uniform coppery. 155 cm, 20 yrs (a: 16.05 kg). Offshore, shelf edge and upper slope, 350-500 m (150-1,000 m). Breeds May-June. Two subspecies: **Spanish Ling** *M. d. macrophthalma*, V tip behind vertical of P tip (Morocco and western Mediterranean to Ireland); and *M. d. dipterygia*, V tip below P (Ireland to Barents Sea, Iceland and Spitzbergen); also western Atlantic.

BURBOT *Lota lota*. Virtually a fresh-water Ling, but much smaller and relative-ly less fecund (to a mere 3 million eggs); chin barbel present, at least equal to eye diameter; snout barbels absent, other than short processes from anterior nostrils; 2 Ds; brown, yellowish-olive to greenish, mottled, especially in smaller fish, sides paler, white below. 120 cm, 32 kg, 15 yrs (a: 8.27 kg). Bottom-living in lakes and rivers, nocturnal; feeds on invertebrates, fish when larger. Breeds November-March, in shallows over gravel; eggs 1.0-1.8 mm, with oil globule, just demersal and easily drifted. Sexually mature by 3-4 yrs. Also Siberia and North America; once abundant in eastern England but now presumed extinct.

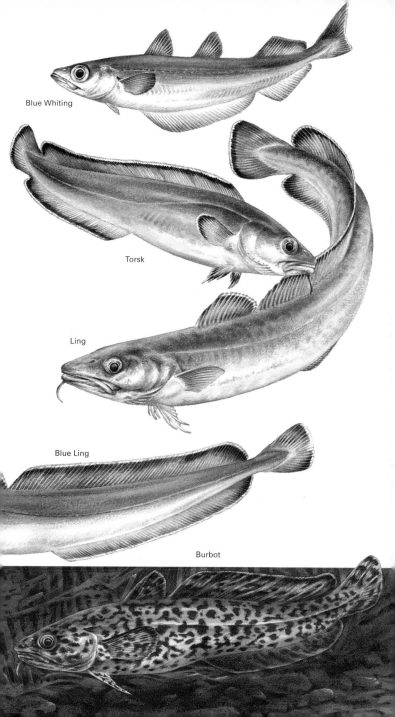

Blue Whiting

Torsk

Ling

Blue Ling

Burbot

SHORE ROCKLING *Gaidropsarus mediterraneus.* Reddish shore fishes with 2 Ds, D2 long but D1 with prominent first ray, followed by short rays set in a groove and forming a vibratile membrane believed to waft water over sensory organs on the rays; chin barbel present, longer than eye-diameter; snout with 2 barbels, one on each anterior nostril; D2 long; P 15-18; reddish to dark brown, paler below. 50 cm. Intertidal under stones and in pools, to 60 m; feeds on invertebrates and small fish. Breeds July-August (British Isles), winter to early spring (Mediterranean); eggs similar to those of Five-Bearded Rockling, but surface smoother; silvery juveniles (mackerel midges) once thought to be a distinct genus, in midwater of pools.

THREE-BEARDED ROCKLING *Gaidropsarus vulgaris.* A As Shore Rockling but P 22-23, above and sides with brown blotches or bars, background and below pink to whitish. 60 cm. Inshore, to 120 m, and intertidal, usually below LWN, under stones. Breeds spring-summer. Other three-bearded forms are: **Grant's Rockling** *G. granti*, 36 cm, with pale wavy band below D2 base, and *G. guttatus*, 26 cm, with numerous pale spots; offshore **Big-Eyed Rockling** *G. macrophthalmus*, B with large canine teeth in front of upper jaw, 10 cm, D2 53-59, A 45-50, and *G. biscayensis*, C 40 cm, D2 49-54, A 41-46; and **Silvery Rockling** *Onogadus argentatus*, D 30 cm, D1 first ray at least twice as long as eye diameter, in cold offshore waters.

FOUR-BEARDED ROCKLING *Enchelyopus cimbrius.* Chin barbel present; 3 snout barbels, one on each anterior nostril and a median barbel on upper lip; Ds as preceding rocklings; reddish-brown to sandy above, paler below, D2 and A with dark blotch on rear tip. 41 cm. Shelf and upper slope, to 550 m, on soft deposits. Breeds May-August (January-October); eggs 0.66-0.98 mm, with greenish or yellowish oil-globule.

FIVE-BEARDED ROCKLING *Ciliata mustela.* A Commonest shore rockling. Chin barbel present; 4 snout barbels, 1 on each anterior nostril and 2 above upper lip; Ds as preceding; reddish to dark brown, paler below. 25 cm. Intertidal, under stones, and sublittoral. Breeds offshore, January-August (western Channel); fecundity 84,000 at 25 cm; eggs 0.66-0.98 mm, with one pale green or yellow oil-globule and somewhat corrugated surface. Very similar **Northern Rockling** *C. septentrionalis*, B with row of additional small barbels along upper jaw, occurs inshore as well as to shelf edge.

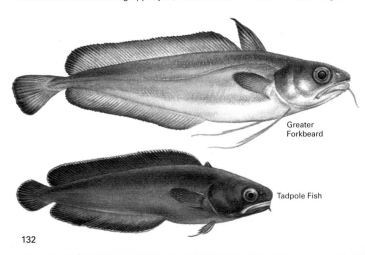

Greater Forkbeard

Tadpole Fish

Shore Rockling

Three-bearded Rockling

Four-bearded Rockling

Five-bearded Rockling

A
B

GREATER FORKBEARD *Phycis blennoides.* A Representing off-shore hake-like fishes, but may be caught in coastal waters. Chin barbel present; snout barbels absent; 2 Ds, 1 A; V 3, with one ray very long, reaching beyond origin of A; LL about 100, 5-6 scales between lateral line and D1 base; brownish to grey, with D2, A and C dark-edged. 110 cm. Offshore shelf, on softer deposits, 150-300 m, sometimes in shallower water (to 10 m). Breeds spring-early summer. More southerly *P. phycis,* B 60 cm, with LL 120-140 and 11-12 scales between lateral line and D1 base, occurs on rocky ground in 100-200 m. **Squirrel Hakes** *Urophycis chuss* and *U. tenuis,* 100-130 cm, are western Atlantic species, recorded off western Ireland and Iceland respectively.

TADPOLE FISH *Raniceps raninus.* So called because of large head and tapering tail, a resemblance especially striking in small fish. Chin barbel present, shorter than eye; snout barbels absent; 2 Ds, 1 A; D1 3, minute; V 6, short; dark brown. 30 cm. Bottom-living, solitary, inshore shelf, to 20 m, rarely deeper; young sometimes intertidal. Breeds July-September; eggs 0.75-0.91 mm, yolk unsegmented and one oil globule, embryo and globule yellow; hatch at 2.16-2.9 mm.

HAKES AND HAKELINGS

A
B

HAKE *Merluccius merluccius* (**Merlucciidae**). Ⓐ Important commercial fisheries from Scotland southwards. Slender predator, with large, black-lined mouth and prominent, hinged teeth; barbels absent; 1 A; D2 and A with concave outline; back greyish, paling to white below. 140 cm, 15 kg. Offshore shelf and upper slope, 70-400 m (30-1,000 m), bottom-living by day, feeding in midwater at night on fish, and moving into shallower water in summer. Breeds all year, chiefly winter and spring (Mediterranean) to May-September (western Scotland); fecundity to 2 million, with batches spawned at about monthly intervals; eggs 0.93-1.03 mm, yolk unsegmented with large oil globule; hatch at 3.0 mm; mature at 28.5 cm, 3-4 yrs (m), 70-78 cm, 8-10 yrs (f). Southern **Black Hake** *M. senegalensis*, Ⓑ 87 cm, has black back and more gill rakers (12-19).

HAKELING *Mora mora* (**Moridae**). Representing a deep-water family, with unusual swimbladder projections to skull; chin barbel, minute; snout barbels absent; 2 Ds, 2 As. 60 cm. Benthic, upper slope, locally common. Also *Lepidion eques*, 44 cm, 1 A and elongate D1, on   edge of shelf and slope.

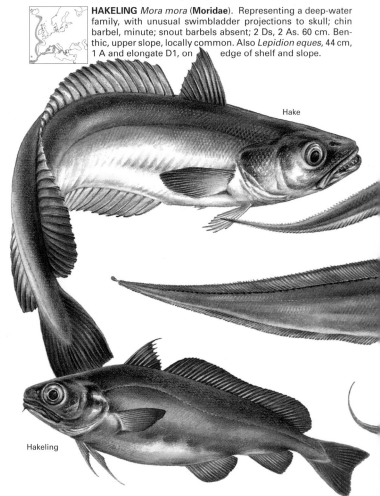

Hake

Hakeling

GRENADIERS (Macruroidei)

Related to the cods, the grenadiers (**Macrouridae**), also termed rat-tails, comprise many deep-sea species on the European continental slope, some appearing in commercial catches. Head prominent, with more or less conical snout, but body compressed and tapering into attenuated tail, much the greater part of overall length; D1 short-based, D2 and A long.

Include: **Rough-Headed Grenadier** *Macrourus berglax*, 100 cm, dark grey, with D1 anterior edge serrated, D2 rays much shorter than A rays; **Long-Snouted Grenadier** *Trachyrhynchus trachyrhynchus*, 50 cm, greyish brown, with snout very long and pointed, D2 rays as long as those of A; and **Black-Spotted Grenadier** *Coelorhynchus coelorhynchus*, 38 cm, mouth and belly black.

Rough-headed Grenadier

Long-snouted Grenadier

Black-spotted Grenadier

CUSKEELS, PEARLFISHES AND EELPOUTS (ORDER OPHIDIIFORMES)

Long tapering body, with single long-based D and A merging with C at tip of tail; V when present always before vertical of P base ('jugular'); systematic position uncertain, eelpouts often being placed with blennies.

CUSK EEL *Ophidion barbatum* (**Ophidiidae**). V very far forward, under lower jaw, and of only single bifid ray; 5-6 gill rakers; reddish above, silvery or paler below; D and A edged black. 25 cm. Bottom-living, shelf, to 150 m. Breeds July-October (Mediterranean), with planktonic eggs held together by transparent mucus. Other Mediterranean cuskeels include the very similar *O. rochei*, 30 cm, 4 gill rakers; *Parophidion vassali*, 25 cm, red fins; and *Benthocometes robustus*, 14 cm, deeper-bodied, with V just before P base and opercle with two small spines.

A
B

PEARLFISH *Echiodon drummondi* (**Carapidae**). Ⓐ At least some species of pearlfish take refuge inside the body of seacucumbers, entering via the anus, sometimes feeding on the reproductive organs, and liable to sudden ejection if the seacucumber decides to turn out its guts! No V; anus below P fin; reddish, silvery below. 30 cm. Offshore shelf. Breeds spring and summer; eggs planktonic, elliptical, 1.25-1.32 × 1.08-1.1 mm, in slimy masses; hatch at 4.5-4.7 mm. Mediterranean pearlfishes are: *E. dentatus*, Ⓑ 17 cm, as *E. drummondi* but without lateral-line pores; and *Carapus acus*, 20 cm, anus below or before vertical from P base. Pearlfish have a distinctive vexillifer planktonic larval stage, with a long tentacle behind head.

VIVIPAROUS BLENNY *Zoarces viviparus* (**Zoarcidae**). Common between tidemarks on Scottish and North Sea shores, especially near freshwater drainage, but not warmer coasts. Elongated, with large mouth; D outline with distinct depression (short spinous rays) near tip of tail; yellowish to greenish-brown above, yellower below, with dark blotches along lateral midline and D base; breeding males with reddish jaws and edges of P and D. 52 cm. Bottom-living, intertidal, under stones, and sublittoral to 40 m, and in estuaries. Viviparous, mating in August-September; embryos (10-400) develop in ovarian cavity, nourished by secretion from ovary lining; born December-February at 3.5-4.5 cm.

A
B

VAHL'S EELPOUT *Lycodes vahli*. Ⓐ Most eelpouts inhabit colder and deeper water, and are characteristic benthic fishes of Arctic seas, often like large-headed plump eels. D with uniform outline; lateral-line canal pores around mouth minute; chin with crests; body depth at A origin 8-10 per cent total length; young banded, adults brownish with black spots on anterior part of D. 52 cm. Bottom-living, offshore shelf and upper slope. Breeds July (Iceland); oviparous; eggs large (4.5 mm), and only 27-93. Also western Atlantic, to Nova Scotia. **Sars' Eelpout** *Lycenchelys sarsi*, Ⓑ 19 cm, with large pores along upper and lower jaws, no chin crests, and more elongated (body depth at A origin 5-6 per cent total length), occurs in similar habitat.

TOADFISHES (ORDER BATRACHOIDIFORMES)

TOADFISH *Halobatrachus didactylus* (**Batrachoididae**). Bottom-living, sedentary, robust 'sit-and-wait' predator, with flattened head, large mouth and frilly lower jaw; eyes dorsolateral; anterior nostril with short processes; D1 very small, III; V before vertical of P base; mottled brownish above, with vertical dark bands; paler below. Inshore to about 50 m, concealed in sand, mud or among rocks. Warm temperate distribution but once from Kattegat.

Cusk Eel

Pearlfish
emerging from
sea-cucumber

Pearlfish

Viviparous
Blenny

Vahl's Eelpout

Toadfish

ANGLERFISHES (ORDER LOPHIIFORMES)

Appropriately, all the anglers have a 'fishing rod' *(illicium)*, which is the first ray of D1, shifted anteriorly onto head; the 'bait' *(esca)* is a fleshy flap, sometimes much elaborated.

ANGLER *Lophius piscatorius* (**Lophiidae**). Large well-concealed predator, waiting on sea-bed for fish and bigger invertebrates; touching of the esca causes a snapping reflex, which has sometimes provided angler fish with larger prey like seabirds, but also with more indigestible items such as a brass tea-tray! With head removed, angler tails are a valuable fish product (termed Monk). Head broad and flattened; mouth very wide, semicircular; head and body outline edged with small skin processes; D1 rays free from membrane, first 2 rays on snout; P lobes arm-like, usually downturned; D2 11-12; A 9-10; P 24-26; brown to greenish-brown above, mottled darker, white below; V dark-edged or dusky above; peritoneum pale. 200 cm. Bottom-living, from inshore shelf to upper slope in about 500 m. Breeds March-June (February-August) on slope; eggs 2.3-3.1 mm, with 1-9 oil globules, in long gelatinous ribbon, to 11 m long by 60-90 cm wide; hatch at about 4.5 mm, postlarval D and V rays very elongated.

BLACK-BELLIED ANGLER *Lophius budegassa.* More southerly species, often confused with Angler, but D2 8-9, A 8-9, P 22-24; peritoneum dark, and V white. 100 cm.

FROGFISH *Histrio histrio* (**Antennariidae**). Typically on floating sargassum weed, closely matched in coloration. Body short, compressed, skin with numerous flaps or filaments; mouth very oblique; D1 rays stout, with filaments; P lobe prehensile; mottled brown and yellow with small spots and white lines. 14.1 cm. Tropical Atlantic, but carried northwards, once even to Vardo, Norway. Other Frogfish (*Antennarius* species), with spiny skin and no filaments, bottom-living, rarely from Madeira and the Azores, and young of **Big-Eyed Frogfish** *A. radiosus*, 18 cm, with large dark 'eye-spot' near D2 base, have been found off western Ireland.

DEEPSEA ANGLERFISHES
(ORDER LOPHIIFORMES: CERATIOIDEI)

Mesopelagic or bathypelagic midwater anglers, deep-bodied, lacking V fins and with typically dark coloration. At least 10 families in north-eastern Atlantic but absent from Mediterranean. Some families have parasitic males, permanently attached to larger female with fusion of tissues and blood systems.

Species include **Atlantic Football Fish** *Himantolophus groenlandicus* (**Himantolophidae**), 40 cm (f), 3.5 cm (m), female with scattered bony plates, stout illicium, esca with bunch of filaments, male with fine spinelets on skin; **Deepsea Angler** *Ceratias holboeli* (**Ceratiidae**), 70 cm (f), 12 cm (m), females with 2 club-shaped processes on back, long illicium with simple esca, male parasitic; and **Lucifer Angler**, *Linophryne lucifer* (**Linophrynidae**), 23 cm (f), 2.9 cm (m), female with long chin barbel with double leaf-like appendages, male parasitic.

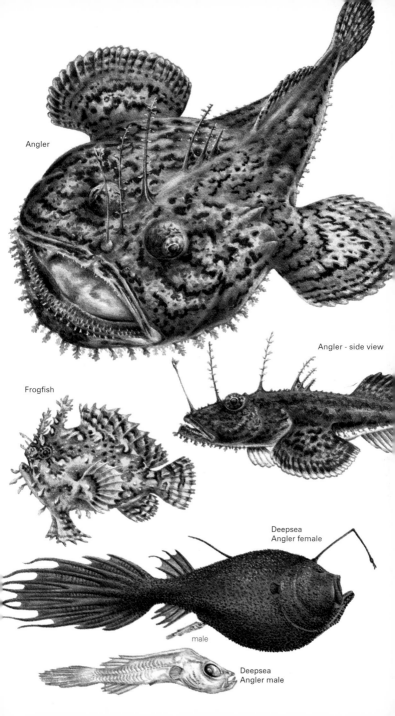

Angler

Angler - side view

Frogfish

Deepsea
Angler female

male

Deepsea
Angler male

ORDER BELONIFORMES
Surface fishes with a propensity for taking to the air.

FLYING FISHES (Exocoetidae)
Characteristic of tropical and subtropical oceans, with 1 rear-sited D and A, and deeply forked C. Often in schools, flying fishes leap from the water and glide, spreading enlarged Ps and sometimes Vs as rigid aerofoil surfaces; by repeating this with tail beats on descent, helped by longer lower C lobe, several hundred metres may be covered and predators escaped. Breed all year in tropics; eggs planktonic, often with filaments which attach to floating objects; young usually with long chin barbels.

FLYING FISH *Exocoetus volitans.* 'Two-winged' with V short, not to A, and origin nearer to P origin than to that of A; upper jaw not protrusible; P reaching behind A base; gill rakers 29-37; typically 6 scale rows between D origin and LL; metallic to iridescent-blue above, silvery below. 18 cm. Eggs without filaments; juveniles without barbels. Cosmopolitan in warm seas. **Blunt-Nosed Flying Fish** *E. obtusirostris*, 20 cm, with gill rakers 24-29 and 7 scale rows between D origin and LL, also strays to Portugal and into Mediterranean. Records of unspecified *Exocoetus* also northwards to western Channel.

A
B
C

ATLANTIC FLYING FISH *Cheilopogon heterurus.* Ⓐ As Flying Fish, but 'four-winged' with V long, to behind A origin, and origin nearer A than to P origin; A origin below third or subsequent D ray; D with 3-5 more rays than A; PD scales 32-36 (30-38); blue-grey above, silvery below; P with pale transverse band. 34 cm. Epipelagic, but usually within 65 km of land. Breeds mid-May-July (Naples), eggs with filaments; young to about 4 cm with barbels. Tropical Atlantic. Also ranging northwards are *C. pinnatibarbatus*, Ⓑ 38 cm, PD 42-44 (39-47), D with 0-4 rays more than A; young with single, fringed barbel; and perhaps *C. exsiliens*, Ⓒ 22 cm, PD 21-30, D with 3-6 more rays than A, C upper lobe paler.

A
B

SWALLOW FISH *Hirundichthys rondeletii.* Ⓐ Also 'four-winged', but origin of A before or below first three rays of D; D rays never exceeding 1 more than A; P purpley-brown with narrow pale edge. 25 cm. Oceanic. Breeds in summer (Mediterranean); eggs with 1, and group of filaments respectively at opposite poles; young lack barbels. Tropical Atlantic and other oceans. *H. speculiger*, Ⓑ 25 cm, P with broad pale edge and pale triangular transverse marking, is recorded once from the southern North Sea. Red Sea and Indo-Pacific *Parexocoetus mento*, 10 cm, immigrant via Suez Canal; has protrusible upper jaw and P not reaching rear A base.

Flying Fish

Atlantic Flying Fish

Swallow Fish

Enlarged pectoral fins and an asymmetrical tail allow flying fish to glide away from predators

HALFBEAKS (Hemiramphidae)

Long, silvery, surface fishes, with lower jaw usually extending far in advance of upper jaw; P and V short, latter abdominal; D and A set far back. Often leaping. Eggs have adhesive filaments.

PICART'S HALFBEAK *Hyporhamphus picarti.* Ⓐ Ridge before eye; scales on snout; A 13-17; C moderately forked; young without vertical bars. 14 cm. Inshore shelf and estuaries. Tropical eastern Atlantic. Indo-Pacific **Spotted Halfbeak** *Hemiramphus far,* Ⓑ 33 cm, with a A 9-12, several dark bars on body, and no scales or ridge on snout, is established in Mediterranean; *Hyporhamphus dussumieri* is another immigrant.

NEEDLEFISHES (Belonidae)

Long, cylindrical fishes, upper and lower jaws forming thin beak, with sharp teeth; D and A placed far back; P and V small, latter abdominal; bones green. Eggs with adhesive filaments, young with lower jaw longer like that of halfbeaks. Surface dwellers, frequently leaping, in warmer seas; at night, needlefish leap towards lights, and their sharp beaks may cause injury on collision with fishermen.

GARFISH *Belone belone.* Ⓐ Common garfish of temperate seas, bright green to dark blue above, sides silvery, yellowish below; gill rakers 27-40; 94 cm, 11 yrs. Shelf and more oceanic, inshore in warmer months and entering estuaries, feeding on fish. Breeds May-June (North Sea); eggs to 11,000, 3.0-3.5 mm; hatch at 9-13 mm, larva heavily pigmented black and yellow. Subspecies: *B. b. belone*, Celtic Sea northwards; *B. b. gracilis*, Ⓑ Biscay southwards and Mediterranean; and *B. b. euxini*, Ⓒ Black Sea basin. **Short-Beaked Garfish** *B. svetovidovi*, 57 cm, has gill rakers 38-52, and smaller and closer, 13-21 along one eye-diameter length in middle of upper jaw.

AGUJON NEEDLEFISH *Tylosurus acus.* Similar to Garfish, but D longer (20-27), and no gill rakers; caudal peduncle with thin black lateral keel; young with high rear lobe of D dark. 95 cm (a: 3.71 kg). More offshore than Garfish. Tropical Atlantic. Red Sea *T. choram*, 70 cm, with longer head, is a Suez immigrant.

SAURIES (Scomberesocidae)

SKIPPER *Scomberesox saurus.* Similar to needlefishes, but with small finlets behind D and A fins. Typically oceanic, epipelagic in schools, but over shelf in warmer months and sometimes stranded on shore by autumn cooling; bright silver band above lateral midline, above olive-green to blue, otherwise golden or silvery to belly; P 13-14 (12-15); 46 cm. Breeds October-December (Naples); eggs planktonic, filaments non-adhesive. Cosmopolitan in warm seas. The tropical offshore *Nanichthys simulans*, 12.5 cm, has lower jaw much longer than upper jaw, P 10-11, and gill rakers 19-26.

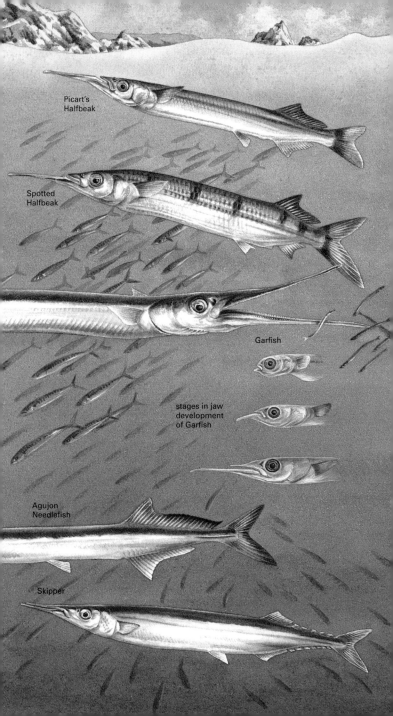

Picart's
Halfbeak

Spotted
Halfbeak

Garfish

stages in jaw
development
of Garfish

Agujon
Needlefish

Skipper

TOOTHCARPS (ORDER CYPRINODONTIFORMES)

Better known to many as tropical aquarium Killifishes. European native species are less colourful, small euryhaline fishes, head more or less flattened, with mouth upwardly directed for surface-feeding; 1 D and 1 A, former somewhat posterior; V abdominal; body lateral-line absent. Eggs demersal. Hybridization a frequent occurrence.

SPANISH TOOTHCARP *Aphanius iberus* (**Cyprinodontidae**). D 9-10 (9-11); A 9-10; olive to bluish-green above, paler below; male with 10-15 vertical dark bands, separated by silvery lines; C of male with 2-5 dark bands. 5 cm (f), 2 yrs. Brackish lagoons, pools, etc.; breeds April-August. Also Algeria. Endangered by habitat destruction and introduction of Mosquitofish.

A ■
B ■

SOUTH-EASTERN TOOTHCARP *Aphanius fasciatus*. Ⓐ Similar to Spanish Toothcarp, but D 10-12 (8-13), A 9-12 (9-13); male with only 1 C dark band. 7 cm. Brackish, hypersaline and in-shore marine. Breeds March-June (Sardinia). Hybridizes with Spanish Toothcarp in Algeria, and *A. dispar*, Ⓑ 6 cm (m), 8 cm (f), D 9-10, male C with 2-3 bands, a larger Red Sea species reported from the eastern Mediterranean.

A ■
B ■
C ■

VALENCIAN TOOTHCARP *Valencia hispanica* (**Valenciidae**). Ⓐ Similar to preceding, but body more compressed, and A 14 (12-14); dark spot above P base; D, A and C dark-edged, last with 4-7 dark bars. 8 cm. Typically freshwater. Also regarded as endangered. Western Greek *V. letourneuxi*, Ⓑ 7 cm, in slow well-vegetated fresh waters, A 12 (11-13); C 2-4 bars. **Mummichog** *Fundulus heteroclitus*, Ⓒ 15 cm, a brackish-water North American species (Gulf of Mexico to St Lawrence), is now established in Iberian peninsula; differs from native killifish in D 12 (11-12), A 10 (10-11), and males with dark and silvery bars.

LIVEBEARERS (Poeciliidae)

MOSQUITOFISH *Gambusia affinis*. A 'livebearer' related to those of tropical aquaria; similar to egg-laying toothcarps in general appearance, but viviparous; male with rod-like *gonopodium*, modified anterior rays of A fin; LL 30-32. 3.5 cm (m), 6 cm (f). Freshwater, in pools and ditches; mostly surface feeding, especially on insect larvae. Breeds in summer, producing several broods of up to over 200 young, 8-9 mm at birth, and mature at 6 weeks. Originally Mexico and southern United States, but introduced worldwide for mosquito control; now established in Mediterranean region and south-western France. **Guppy** *Poecilia reticulata*, 3 cm (m), 6 cm (f), also reported as feral, with LL 26-28, males with dark spot on side, but many cultivated variants in coloration; females similar to Mosquitofish, but without dark spots on C.

Sandsmelt

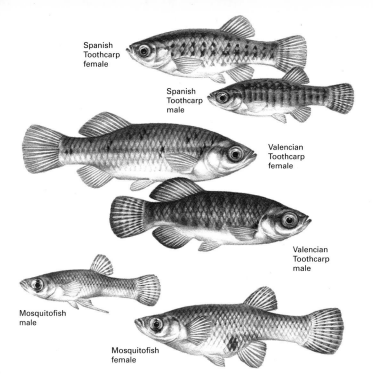

Spanish Toothcarp female

Spanish Toothcarp male

Valencian Toothcarp female

Valencian Toothcarp male

Mosquitofish male

Mosquitofish female

ORDER ATHERINIFORMES

SILVERSIDES (Atherinidae)

Small slender fishes, schooling inshore, sometimes barely moving; body somewhat translucent, olive above, with broad silvery lateral stripe, more or less dark-edged. 2 short-based, well-separated Ds, as in Grey Mullet, but differ from latter in having oblique jaws. Plankton-feeding. Eggs demersal, with filaments; young with very long caudal region of body, found in small dense schools.

SANDSMELT *Atherina presbyter*. D1 7-9; preopercle with regular edge; lower jaw expanded upwards into mouth; LL 52-57; vertebrae 46-52. 20 cm. Coastal, sometimes into brackish water. Breeds June-July (western Channel); eggs 1.85-1.95 mm, hatch at 7 mm.

BIG-SCALED SANDSMELT *Atherina boyeri*. As Sandsmelt but LL 44-48 (39-49), vertebrae 40-47. 13 cm. Intertidal, lagoons, and some freshwater populations. *A. hepsetus*, 20 cm, LL 59-65, vertebrae 53-57, has similar distribution and also occurs in Caspian Sea.

A ▮
B ▮

NOTCHED SANDSMELT *Atherinomorus lacunosus*. Ⓐ D1 shorter, 4-7; preopercle notched; LL about 40. 14 cm. Inshore shallows. Red Sea and Indian Ocean, now established in eastern Mediterranean via Suez Canal. The plankton-eating South American *Odonthestes bonariensis*, Ⓑ 70 cm, LL 49-59, has been successfully introduced into Lake Nemi, near Rome, to replace whitefishes.

OPAHS TO OARFISH (ORDER LAMPRIFORMES)

Mostly oceanic fishes, of great diversity and in bizarre shapes, but all with 1 D lacking spines; V usually thoracic; mouth protrusible.

OPAH *Lampris guttatus* (**Lamprididae**). Colourful, very deep oval body; mouth small, toothless; 1 D, long-based, with anterior rays drawn out into sickle-shaped lobe; P base horizontal, fin upturned; V long, also sickle-shaped; dark blue above, sides greenish, golden or lilac, pink below, many white spots, fins red. 180 cm, 70 kg (a: 55.33 kg). Oceanic, epipelagic, down to 400 m, feeding mostly on squid, but sometimes more inshore and stranded. All tropical and temperate seas.

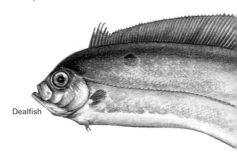

Dealfish

DEALFISH *Trachypterus arcticus* (**Trachipteridae**). Ⓐ Long, plank-like body; head small; D long-based, anterior rays elongated in young; A absent; P and V tiny; C fan-like, probably upturned; silvery, with 1-5 dark spots along upper flank, fins red. 300 cm. Oceanic, epipelagic and mesopelagic, to 900 m, but nearer surface at night; sometimes stranded or found moribund at surface. Mediterranean **Ribbonfish** *T. trachypterus*, Ⓑ 150 cm, is similar, but with greatest body depth immediately behind head, and axis of tail region curved upwards in adults. **Scalloped Ribbonfish** *Zu cristatus*, 100 cm, has irregular belly profile, much-narrowed tail region, and more symmetrical C. **Crested Oarfish** *Lophotus cepedianus*, 180 cm, has prominent triangular nape crest, tiny A near tiny C, and emits black ink from urogenital opening.

OARFISH *Regalecus glesne* (**Regalecidae**). Similar body form to Dealfish but fragile despite large size; its great length (700 cm) and undulating mode of swimming may suggest a 'sea-serpent'. Crest of first 10-15 D rays, elongated, mostly free from membrane and tips lobed; P and C tiny; V of one very long ray in adult, also lobed at tip; skin with bands of small tubercles, especially ventrally; silvery, with oblique dark striae, fins red. Oceanic, mesopelagic to 1,000 m, occasionally found floating or stranded. Breeds July-December (Mediterranean), with planktonic eggs.

Oarfish

Opah

Ribbonfish

Oarfish

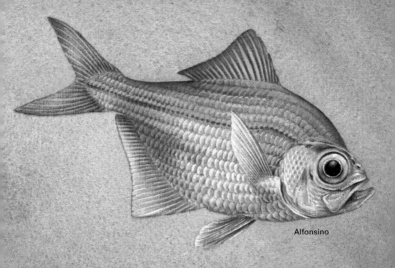

Alfonsino

ORDER BERYCIFORMES

Marine fishes of typically more conventional oval, compressed body shape; anterior D and A rays spiny; V thoracic, with a spinous ray and usually more than 5 soft rays.

ALFONSINO *Beryx decadactylus* (**Berycidae**). A Uniform red or orange, with large eyes; 1 D, IV/16-20, A III-IV/24-31, base ending well behind A origin, V I/6; barbel absent; scales ctenoid. 61 cm. Offshore shelf and upper slope (120-600 m), demersal. More southerly *B. splendens*, B 40 cm, is slimmer (body depth less than two-thirds standard length), with D base ending above A origin, and, internally, only 23-30 pyloric caeca.

ROUGHFISH *Hoplostethus mediterraneus* (**Trachichthyidae**). Unprepossessing fish, but highly edible and with body oil so similar to that of sperm whales as to spare the latter from exploitation. Head large, rough, with prominent spine at angle of preopercle; lateral line spiny; abdomen with median keel; scales ctenoid; D VI/12-14; A II/12-14 V I/6-7; silvery, head ridges and fins pink. 29 cm. Edge of shelf and upper slope, 200-600 m. **Orange Roughie** *H. atlanticus*, 60 cm, D soft rays 15-18, A 11, is cosmopolitan, in 900-1,700 m over seamounts, with potential Atlantic fishery like that off New Zealand.

RED SOLDIERFISH *Sargocentron hastatus* (**Holocentridae**). A Eye large and lower rear angle of preopercle with long spine; 2 shorter spines at upper corner of opercle; D XI/15 (14-15), outline deeply notched between spinous and soft sections; A IV/10, third spine greatly enlarged; LL 48-51; red, with dark longitudinal lines. 25 cm. Inshore, bottom-living, nocturnal, in 50-100 m. To West Africa. *S. ruber*, B 22 cm, LL 34-39, is an Indo-Pacific species now present in the eastern Mediterranean.

BEARDFISH *Polymixia nobilis* (**Polymixiidae**). Body oval; pair of long barbels under lower jaw; 1 D, IV-VI/30-38; grey or greenish, median fins edged dark. 35 cm. Offshore shelf and upper slope. Tropical Atlantic.

Roughfish

Red Soldierfish

Beardfish

John Dory

DORIES AND BOARFISHES (ORDER ZEIFORMES)

A
B

JOHN DORY *Zeus faber* (**Zeidae**). A Very deep body, with large head and highly protrusible jaws, but so laterally compressed as to be inconspicuous when viewed head on: an effective means of approaching prey. D IX-XI/21-25; A IV(III-V), strong, separate from 20-24 branched rays; D and A bases flanked by small spiny plates; V long; yellowish-brown to grey, paler below with large black spot, yellow-edged, on each side near P. 66 cm. Usually inshore, to 100 m; slow-swimming, stalking fish which are sucked in by sudden protrusion of mouth. Breeds June-August, eggs planktonic, 1.96-2.0 mm, with pale greenish-yellow oil globules; hatch at 4.3 mm. Also southern and tropical Africa. West African **Sail-finned Dory** *Zenopsis conchifer*, B 75 cm, has concave head profile and large bony shields along D and A bases; bottom-living and midwater on offshore shelf.

A
B

BOARFISH *Capros aper* (**Caproidae**). A Reddish rhomboidal body, with large eyes and small but highly protrusible mouth; small, ctenoid scales; D IX-X/23-25; A III, short/23- 25; typically yellowish-red, to brick-red from deeper water. 18 cm. Offshore shelf and slope canyons, probably bottom-living over yellow or pink coral-encrusted rocks, and sometimes brought inshore by upwelling events. Breeds June-August; eggs planktonic, 0.9-1.01 mm, with yellow oil globule. Also to Senegal. Tropical Atlantic **Deep-bodied Boarfish** *Antigonia capros*, B 30 cm, has D VII-VIII/32-26, A III/31-34.

PIPEFISHES AND RELATIVES (ORDER SYNGNATHIFORMES)

Pipefishes, seahorses and the related snipefishes all have a small mouth at the tip of a long tubular snout.

SNIPEFISH *Macrorhamphosus scolopax* (**Macrorhamphosidae**). Oval compressed body, with large eye; 2 D, short-based, posteriorly sited, D1 typically with very long, serrated second spine (but shorter and smooth in *gracilis* variety); reddish or bluish-grey, young silvery. 20 cm. Adults bottom-living to midwater, especially at night, in schools on offshore shelf to upper slope. Worldwide in warm seas.

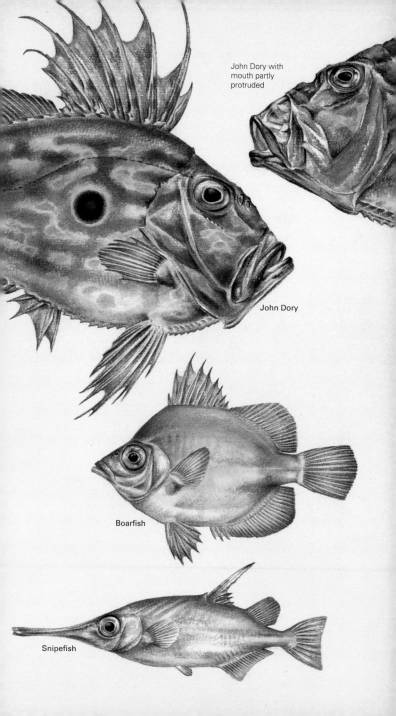

John Dory with
mouth partly
protruded

John Dory

Boarfish

Snipefish

PIPEFISHES AND SEAHORSES (Syngnathidae)

Long, thin, hard but flexible bodies, completely encased in seg-mental bony rings; V always absent; 1 D. Males carry developing eggs in pouch or on surface of abdomen.

LONG-SNOUTED SEAHORSE *Hippocampus ramulosus*. One of the best known of bizarre-shaped fishes, seahorses are more precisely distinguished from Pipefishes by having the head bent downwards from the upright body, and a prehensile tail, lacking C. This species has snout at least one-third head length, D 19 (18-21); P 16-17 (15-18); brown or darker, reddish or yel-low, usually with many bluish-white spots. 16 cm. Inshore shal-lows, among algae. Breeds April-October, eggs about 2 mm, incubated for 3-5 weeks; young hatch at 15-16 mm.

SHORT-SNOUTED SEAHORSE *Hippocampus hippocampus*. As Long-snouted Seahorse but snout less than one-third head length, D 17-18 (16-19), P 14 (13-15); brown to black, some-times with pale blotches; D with dark band near edge. 15 cm. Also West Africa.

DEEP-SNOUTED PIPEFISH *Syngnathus typhle*. P, A and C pre-sent; snout deep, profile straight, its depth similar to that of head at eyes; trunk rings (P base to anus) 16-20, tail rings (behind anus) 31-39; pale to greenish-brown, head with small brown dots. 35 cm. Inshore and estuaries, among sea-grass, often with body aligned with blades, and in brown algae on rocks. Breeds June-August, developing eggs carried by male in pouch along underside of tail behind anus.

Greater
Pipefish

A
B
C

GREATER PIPEFISH *Syngnathus acus*. Ⓐ As Deep-snouted Pipefish but snout profile concave, depth less than that of head at eyes; snout length less than half head length; head with medi-an ridge; rings 17-21 and 38-43; brownish, with green to dark vertical bars. 46 cm. Inshore shelf, on coarse to muddy grounds, or among weed and sea-grass. Breeds May-August, with up to more than 400 incubating eggs, 1.6-2.5 mm, hatching after 5 weeks, young leaving pouch at 25-35 mm. Three Mediterranean shorter-snout-ed pipefishes, lacking head ridge, are: *S. taenionotus*, 19 cm, rings 16-18 and 33-39, with dark band along lateral body ridge, only from Italian Adriatic; *S. tenuirostris*, 39 cm, rings 17-19 and 41-44, from Adriatic and Black seas, per-haps western Mediterranean; and the small *Minyichthys sentus*, Ⓑ 6 cm, very blunt-snouted, rings 20-21 and 41-42, Algeria to Canaries. **Variegated Pipefish** *S. variegatus*, Ⓒ 30 cm, brown with pale banding, has slight head ridge, rings 19-21 and 38-41, and is restricted to Black Sea and Sea of Azov.

Short-snouted
Seahorse

Long-snouted
Seahorse

Deep-snouted
Seahorse

LESSER PIPEFISH *Syngnathus rostellatus.* Often caught in shrimping nets at the edge of the sea; similar to Greater Pipefish, but rings 13-17 and 37-42; D base above 9-12 rings. 18 cm. Inshore and estuarine, on sandy shores and among weed. Breeds June-August; eggs pinkish-white, 1.5 mm, about 100 in pouch of male 12.7 cm; hatch after 3 weeks at 13-14 mm, and young pelagic for a time.

 SHORE PIPEFISH *Syngnathus abaster.* Similar to preceding, but D short, above only 6-11 rings; brownish-green, with thin pale or dark markings, often pale striations every 3-5 rings; D base usually with dark band. 15 cm (21 cm in Black Sea). Inshore, estuarine, and may even enter fresh water, on soft grounds and vegetation. Breeds mid-May-November (Gulf of Naples); incubating eggs 1.6-2.0 mm, hatching at about 23 mm.

 SPINY PIPEFISH *Syngnathus phlegon.* Bony rings with somewhat spiny rear edges; rings 17-19 and 47-50, D base over 12-14; bluish, each ring usually with dark blotch, silver below. 20 cm. Offshore, pelagic. Breeds usually April-October; 300-400 eggs, 1.3-1.4 mm, hatching at 18 mm.

A ■
B ■

 WORM PIPEFISH *Nerophis lumbriciformis.* Ⓐ Thin wiry body, lacking P, A and C; rings 17-19 and 46-54, D base mostly over tail rings; dark, olive-green to black, mottled white below. 17 cm. Inshore and intertidal, under stones on weed-covered rocky shores and among sublittoral weed holdfasts. Breeds May-September, males with up to 150 yellowish eggs, 1.0-1.2 mm, attached to undersurface of abdomen; hatch at 10 mm. Mediterranean **Spotted Worm-pipefish** *N. maculatus,* Ⓑ 30 cm, has 20-23 and 65-74 rings, males with pale tail bars, females with red markings on belly.

Straight-nosed
Pipefish

 STRAIGHT-NOSED PIPEFISH *Nerophis ophidion.* As preceding, but rings 28-33 and 68-82; greenish-brown above, sides pale green; adult female, blue lines along belly. 25 cm (m), 30.5 cm (f). Inshore among weeds, especially sea-grass and *Chorda filum,* entering brackish and fresh water. Breeds May-August, 120-150 yellowish eggs, 1.0-1.4 mm; young hatch at 9 mm, planktonic for 3-4 months, and embryonic P fins lost at about 12 mm.

Snake Pipefish

 SNAKE PIPEFISH *Entelurus aequoreus.* Similar to Worm pipefishes, but minute C usually present; rings 28-31 and 60-69, D base mostly over trunk rings; brown or yellowish, with bright blue to white vertical lines across each ring and ring junction. 40 cm (m), 60 cm (f). Shelf, among weed or in midwater, to 165 m and also pelagic. Breeds June-July, eggs 1.2 mm, on belly of male, hatching at 11-12 mm, with embryonic P.

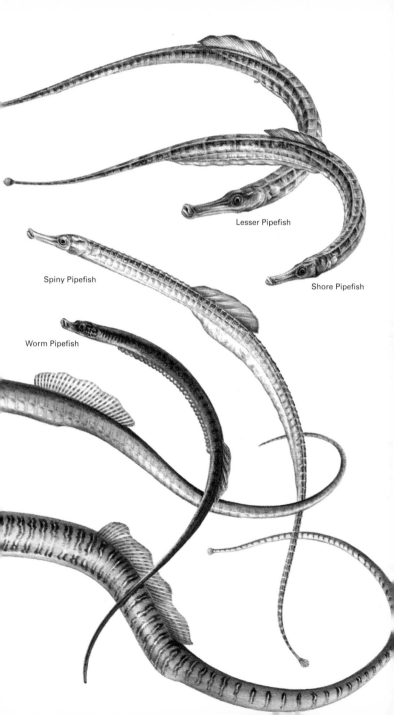

Lesser Pipefish

Spiny Pipefish

Shore Pipefish

Worm Pipefish

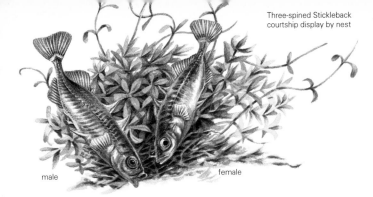

Three-spined Stickleback
courtship display by nest

male   female

STICKLEBACKS (ORDER GASTEROSTEIFORMES)

Temperate and low Arctic small fishes, sticklebacks (**Gasterosteidae**) have 3-16 dorsal spines before a single soft D and narrow tail; normally with bony plates along lateral midline. Frequently used in behavioural and variation studies on fish.

THREE-SPINED STICKLEBACK *Gasterosteus aculeatus*. One the commonest small freshwater fishes, traditionally caught on bent pin and worm, and even studied by Mr Pickwick. 3 (2-4) spines before D, third usually much smaller; V with long erectile spine and 1 ray, but V sometimes absent; silvery bluish-green to dark above, white below; breeding males with bright red belly and underside of head. 11.5 cm. Three main forms of the species distinguished by extent of lateral bony plates: complete series ('*trachurus*'), from P origin to base of C, forming lateral keel along sides of tail wrist; partial ('*semiarmatus*'), with plates in short series along sides of abdomen and on tail wrist; and low, with plates only on sides of abdomen ('*leiurus*') or completely absent ('*gymnurus*'). *Trachurus* inshore marine and estuarine, including saltmarsh and high-shore pools, in cooler areas; other varieties mostly freshwater. Breeds in fresh water (*trachurus* anadromous), March-July; 50-100 (450) eggs, demersal, 1.5-1.9 mm, initially with about a dozen oil globules; nest of weed fragments bound together by kidney secretion, constructed on bottom and guarded by male; eggs hatch at 2.0-4.5 mm. Temperate to low-Arctic marine and fresh waters of Eurasia and North America.

A
B

NINE-SPINED STICKLEBACK *Pungitius pungitius*. Ⓐ 9 (9-10) spines before D, directed alternately left or right from dorsal midline; median bony plate between Vs; bony plates along lateral midline, and bony keel along tail wrist; olive-green to dark above, sides sometimes barred, silvery below; breeding male black, with white V membrane. 10.0 cm. Fresh and brackish waters, inshore marine in arctic areas. Breeds April-July in fresh water; nest in weed above bottom, built and guarded by male; eggs 1.0-1.2 mm, with oil globules. Eurasia and North America. **Ukrainian Nine-spined Stickleback** *P. platygaster*, Ⓑ 7 cm, has serrated V spine but no tail keel.

FIFTEEN-SPINED STICKLEBACK *Spinachia spinachia*. Larger, entirely marine stickleback. Elongated body, tapering to long and slender tail, encased in complete series of lateral plates, with keel on tail wrist, as well as upper and lower rows; 15 (14-17) small spines before D; V spine short; brownish-olive, sides barred, greenish-white below; breeding male bluish. 19 cm; most adults die after first breeding season, usually at 1 yr. Marine, inshore and intertidal pools, and lower estuaries, especially juveniles, among seaweed and sea-grass. Breeds April-July; nest of plant fragments above bottom, often in brown weed *Halidrys*, in shore pools or sublittoral; eggs 2.0 mm, amber, hatch at 4.5-6.0 mm.

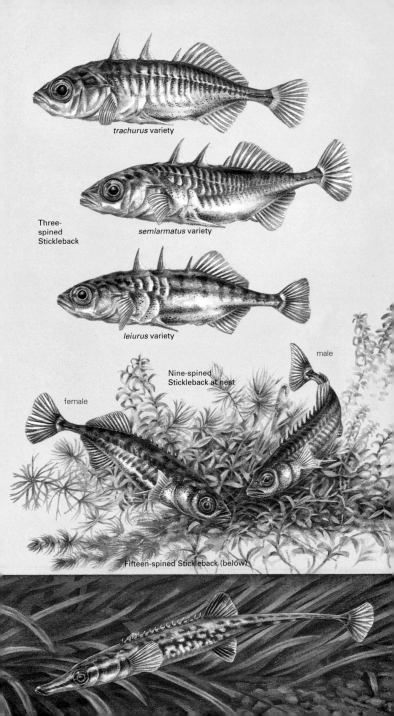

trachurus variety

Three-
spined
Stickleback

semiarmatus variety

leiurus variety

male

Nine-spined
Stickleback at nest

female

Fifteen-spined Stickleback (below)

MAILCHEEKS (ORDER SCORPAENIFORMES)

Typically, spiny rayed fishes with large heads that carry an array of spines; P usually large; V thoracic. Regardless of outer form, one of the bones below the eye projects back to meet the preopercular bone forming the rear edge of the cheek on all mailcheeks; this feature is also found in sticklebacks.

SCORPIONFISHES (Scorpaenidae)

Marine mailcheeks of some commercial importance; head typically with 3-5 cheek spines, 2 diverging spines on upper opercle, as well as other spines and fleshy processes; 1 D; most have internal egg fertilization and some are livebearing.

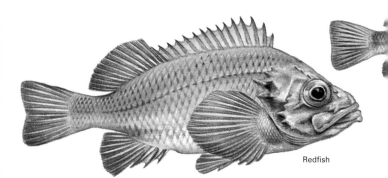

Redfish

REDFISH *Sebastes marinus.* With other Redfish species, the Norway Haddock or Ocean Perch of fisheries in colder waters; deep-bodied, large-eyed, with spiny cheek edge but relatively smooth, steep nape; head and body without fleshy processes; D XV (XIV-XVI)/14-15 (13-16); A III/7-10; P 19 (18-21), middle rays longest; lateral line with tubular scales; infraorbital ridge without spine; 2 upper preopercle spines of similar size directed backwards, lower 3 downwards; breast scaled; LL 34 (31-39); orange or yellowish-red with dark patch on opercle. 100 cm (a: 4.69 kg). Schooling, pelagic, over offshore shelf and slope, 100-1,000 m, but young more inshore. Ovoviviparous; mates October-January (Iceland and Greenland), but eggs not fertilized by stored sperm until February-May; young born April-August, as postlarvae at 5-7 mm; fecundity 40,000-360,000. Also Western Atlantic. Very similar **Deepwater Redfish** *S. mentella,* 55 cm, brighter red, with preopercular spines more prominent and lowest often obliquely forwards.

LESSER REDFISH *Sebastes viviparus.* A smaller, more coastal Redfish, with D XIV-XVI/13-14 (12-15); A III/6-8; and preopercular spines directed backwards, lowest also more or less downwards; breast scaled; LL 32 (30-33); bright red with several dark bands or blotches persisting after death. 35 cm. Bottom-living on shelf (10-200 m). Ovoviviparous; young born May-August, at 4-5 mm; fecundity 11,800-29,300 at 19-30 cm.

SPINY SCORPIONFISH *Trachyscorpia cristulata.* Large spiny head, with spiny cheek ridge but few fleshy processes; P 20-23, with upper rays longer; D XII/9 (8-9); dark, rear spinous D with dark blotch. 50 cm. Bottom-living on muddy grounds, edge of shelf to 2,500 m.

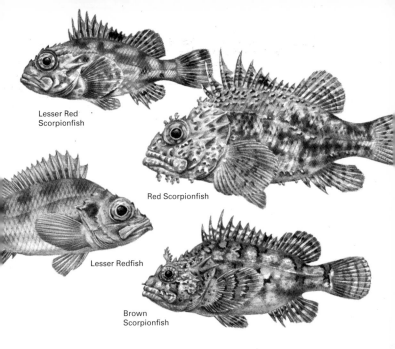

Lesser Red Scorpionfish

Red Scorpionfish

Lesser Redfish

Brown Scorpionfish

RED SCORPIONFISH *Scorpaena scrofa.* Sedentary, well-concealed 'sit-and-wait' predators. Small flap above eye; larger flap before eye and 2 flaps on lower edge of cheek; lower jaw fringed by smaller tentacles; 2 pores at apex of median space between lower jaws; occipital pit present; spiny cheek ridge; D XII/9; P 19 (18-20), uppermost rays not longest; LL about 45, scales ctenoid, tubular along lateral line; mottled, pale pink to bright red, rear spinous D with dark band. 50 cm. Bottom-living on coarser grounds of shelf, juveniles in seagrass; feeding particularly on fish. Breeds May-September (Algeria).

LESSER RED SCORPIONFISH *Scorpaena notata.* As preceding, but with additional cheek and snout skin flaps but none along edge of lower jaw; P 18 (17-19); reddish-brown with prominent black spot on rear part of spinous D. 20 cm. Inshore rocky ground and sea-grass, to 150 m, sometimes deeper; feeds mostly on shrimps and prawns. Breeds July-September (Algeria).

BROWN SCORPIONFISH *Scorpaena porcus.* Tentacle above eye about equal to eye diameter; spiny cheek ridge; edge of lower jaw lacking flaps; P 16-17 (16-18); scales small, LL 65-70; brownish, rear spinous D with patch area. 25 cm. Shelf and upper slope, on rocky ground and among seaweed and sea-grass; feeds particularly on crabs. Breeds July-September (Algeria). Also to Senegal. Other southerly scorpionfishes include: *S. loppei*, 10 cm, upper jaw with crest, LL 35-40; *S. elongata*, 50 cm, with large snout and rear cheek flaps, and LL 45-50, also with skin flaps; and *S. laevis*, 35 cm, fringed tentacle over eye, and lower jaw with row of skin flaps; P with large brown spots on inner face. *Scorpaenoides arenai*, 11 cm, with D XIII/9-10, is known only from the Straits of Messina; *Sebastapistes nuchalis*, 10 cm, similar to *Scorpaena* but with scaled breast, is a Suez Canal immigrant.

BLUEMOUTH *Helicolenus dactylopterus.* Head spines less prominent, but cheek ridge spiny and second preopercular spine longest; no skin flaps or nape pit; D XII (XI-XIII)/11-12 (10-14); LL 55-80; P 19 (16-21), upper rays longest, lowest rays partly free from membrane; red to rose-pink below, often with 3-5 dark bands or blotches; mouth and throat leaden-blue. 45 cm, 25 yrs. Edge of shelf and upper slope on rocky ground, 200-1,000 m, shallower in cooler areas. Oviparous, chiefly November-December. To southern Africa and also western Atlantic, from Venezuela to Nova Scotia; increasing fisheries.

KUHL'S SCORPIONFISH *Pontinus kuhlii.* Spiny head, lacking flaps and upper preopercular spine longest; D XII/9, spinous rays II and III elongated in adult; LL 60-65; reddish and yellow, with dark blotches; yellow areas on head especially below cheek ridge; mouth white with red patch near upper gullet. 23 cm. Bottom-living on coarse offshore grounds of shelf and upper slope, 100-450 m. To southern Africa.

GURNARDS (Triglidae)

Large, hard head with steep snout, all encased in bone; body tapers to slender tail; 2 D, spiny D1 much shorter-based; P large, with lowest 3 rays thickened and separate, used for walking on substrate and for detection of invertebrate prey. Grunt or growl by use of swimbladder. Eggs planktonic. Some commercial value.

GREY GURNARD *Eutrigla gurnardus.* Head with shallow transverse groove behind eyes, smooth; scales small; LL scales somewhat enlarged, with spiny keel, 72-77; body lacking transverse skin ridges; D1 II not elongated; P to origin of A; spine above P to anterior quarter of P; slate-grey to brownish-grey, above and sides more or less reddish, usually with many small white or cream spots (rosy variety off Sicily); D1 with large black blotch. 50 cm. Inshore, typically on sand, to 140 m, but may approach surface at night; enters estuaries in summer. Breeds January-August (Channel); eggs (200,000-300,000) 1.27-1.55 mm, with reddish or yellowish oil globule and dark pigment on unsegmented yolk; hatch at 3.0-4.0 mm; postlarvae have enlarged Ps.

RED GURNARD *Aspitrigla cuculus.* As preceding but LL scales (70-73) expanded vertically into long plates, lacking spines; D1 II slightly elongated; deep red, paler below; V rosy, A with white edge; D and P sometimes yellowish. 50 cm. Shelf, sandy to rocky grounds, 20-250 m. Breeds April-August (Channel), eggs 1.42-1.61 mm, with coppery oil globule.

LONG-FINNED GURNARD *Aspitrigla obscura.* Differs from preceding in LL scales plate-like but not expanded vertically, and elongated D1 II; above red, below pinky-white, with LL pearly-pink; P dark blue, other fins reddish. 40 cm. Shelf, on soft deposits and about rocks.

A
B

LARGE-SCALED GURNARD *Lepidotrigla cavillone.* Ⓐ Head with deep, spiny, transverse groove behind eyes; bilobed snout with larger outer spines; 2 spines before eyes; P to origin of A, but longest free ray short of anus; spine above P about one-third P length; scales large, firmly attached; pinkish, P dark blue. 20 cm. Shelf and uppermost slope, on finer deposits. Breeds May-July (Mediterranean). **Spiny Gurnard** *L. dieuzeidei,* Ⓑ 15 cm, has smooth groove behind eyes, no spines before eyes; shorter spine above P and looser scales; P dark towards tip.

Bluemouth

Grey Gurnard

Red Gurnard

Long-finned Gurnard

Large-scaled Gurnard

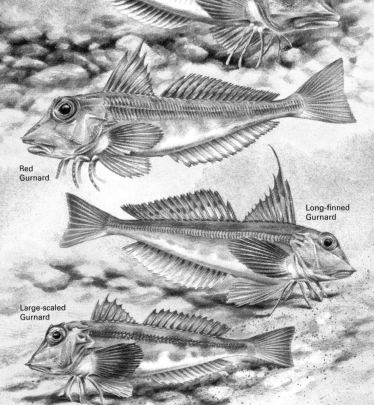

Tub Gurnard

TUB GURNARD *Trigla lucerna*. Head lacks deep transverse groove; scales small, LL scales little enlarged, tubular; body lacks transverse skin ridges; D1 II not elongated; P long, to above A 2-4; spine above P short, above anterior quarter of P; dull reddish, below white or golden; P reddish outer face, inner side bright blue with dark mark. 75 cm. Shelf, chiefly 50-150 m (to 300 m), on gravel to mud. Breeds May-July (Channel). **Piper** *T. lyra*, as preceding but spine above P very long, to above middle of P; bright red above, sides rosy, silvery below; D and P dark. 60 cm. Offshore, to 700 m.

STREAKED GURNARD *Trigloporus lastoviza*. Head strongly spinous and ridged but no deep transverse groove behind eyes; body with close-set transverse skin ridges; LL scales (62-67) enlarged, with small spines; P to well behind origin of A; spine above P short, over merely origin of P; dull red, with dark blotches on head and body; P greyish-violet, with rows of blue spots along fin membranes, especially on inner face. 40 cm. Typically inshore, on rocky ground or adjacent sand, 30-150 m. Breeds June-August.

ARMED GURNARD *Peristedion cataphractum*. Body encased in spiny plates, 17-21 along lateral midline; snout with paired long bony projections; lower jaw with barbels, 2 long and fringed; P free rays 2; pink or reddish, paler below. 40 cm. Bottom-living on coarse to muddy grounds, 30-500 m. Also West Africa.

FLYING GURNARDS (Dactylopteridae)

Gurnard-like with bony head and steep snout, but strictly classified in a separate order (**Dactylopteriformes**).

FLYING GURNARD *Dactylopterus volitans*. Lower corner of preopercle with very long spine; P very long, to near C; D1 VI, I and II free; D2 I/8; scales scute-like, LL 60-62; above brown to greenish-olive, sides paler with reddish or salmon-yellow blotches; P with bright blue streaks and blue spots and bars, may be flashed to deter predators. 50 cm (a: 1.81 kg). Bottom-living, inshore to 80 m, on finer grounds, walking on Vs; may leap and glide above surface. Tropical Atlantic.

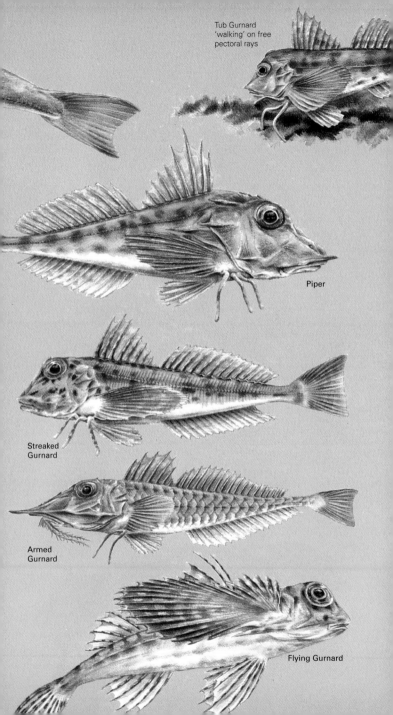

Tub Gurnard 'walking' on free pectoral rays

Piper

Streaked Gurnard

Armed Gurnard

Flying Gurnard

BULLHEADS (Cottidae)

Bottom-living fishes, with large heads, more or less spiny, and body often lacking scales, although never encased in bony plates; Ps large, lowest rays not free. 2 Ds. Somewhat sedentary but voracious feeders on crustaceans and small fish. Eggs demersal.

SHORT-SPINED SEASCORPION *Myoxocephalus scorpius.* Gill membranes joined by fold across isthmus; upper preopercular spine straight, directed obliquely upwards, larger than second spine; 1 spine in middle of opercular edge; body with small prickly bony plates, but not along LL; LL pores in 3 rows; no gap between D1 and D2; A 9-15; V I/3; vertebrae 34-36; dark green to brownish, variously blotched and barred; yellowish below, but males with reddish, white-spotted belly. 60 cm. Inshore to 50 m and intertidal on cooler shores, such as northern and eastern British Isles. Breeds December-March (North Sea); eggs (to 2,700) demersal, 1.8-2.5 mm, yolk bright yellow to red, fertilized within female and fist-sized clumps guarded by male after deposition; hatch at 7.4-8.6 mm. *M. s. groenlandicus*, vertebrae 37-39, and skin spicules with 8 rear spines, occurs in western Atlantic.

LONG-SPINED SEASCORPION *Taurulus bubalis.* Gill membranes joined to isthmus but lacking transverse skin fold; nape with prominent ridges and paired spines; upper preopercular spine long, straight, directed obliquely upwards, to beyond opercle flap; opercular edge with 2 spines; fleshy flap over eye; small tentacle on rear end of upper jaw; skin lacking folds, bony plates or spicules; LL more or less spiny; V I/3; P 14-16; brownish to red, with dark blotches; below blue-green; axilla of male with large spots and V marked black and white. 17.5 cm. Inshore to 30 m; intertidal rock pools on sheltered weedy shores; young in estuaries. Breeds February-April, eggs 1.5-1.8 mm, greenish to yellowish with oil globule and pimpled capsule, in walnut-sized clumps guarded by male until hatching at 5.5-5.8 mm in 6-7 weeks.

NORWAY BULLHEAD *Microenophrys lilljeborgi.* Similar to preceding, but smaller; V I/2 and row of bony spinules above lateral-line spines; reddish-olive with dark crossbands; males with red markings on head and sides. 7.4 cm. Sublittoral to 90 m, on coarse grounds. Breeds March-May.

BULLHEAD *Cottus gobio.* The 'Miller's Thumb', its flattened shape said to resemble the thumb of a miller splayed from testing flour. Gill membranes joined to isthmus but lacking transverse fold; relatively smooth, broad head, but upwardly directed preopercular spine; body naked; LL pores uniserial, about 30-35, to C base; no gap between D1 and D2; V I/4 (3-4), inner and outer rays of similar length; above brownish, mottled or barred; V pale. 15 cm. Freshwater, in clear streams and lake edges, under stones and vegetation, and also in brackish water of Baltic, feeding chiefly on invertebrates but not averse to small fish. Spawns March-May, eggs 2.0-2.5 mm, yellowy-red, in clump beneath stone and guarded by male; hatch at 6-7 mm.

ALPINE BULLHEAD *Cottus poecilopus.* Similar to preceding but with LL ending below D2 (20-25 pores), and V with dark transverse banding; inner V ray much shorter than outer ray. 15 cm. Streams (above reach occupied by Bullhead) and lakes, to brackish water. Breeds May-June.

Short-spined
Seascorpion

Long-spined
Seascorpion

Norway
Bullhead

Bullhead

Alpine
Bullhead

FOUR-HORNED SCULPIN *Triglopsis quadricornis.* Nape with 2 pairs of bony knobs, sometimes enlarged; gill membranes joined to isthmus with distinct fold; 4 preopercular spines, uppermost directed obliquely upwards; body above LL with bony plates, male with spinules on D2 and P; D1 and D2 separated by small gap; brownish to greenish above, bony knobs on nape yellowish; pale below. 36.5 cm. Bottom-living (to 20 m) on soft deposits in sea, estuarine and fresh waters. Breeds November-February, eggs dark green, hatching after >3 months. Arctic basin but relict lake populations around Baltic.

A ■
B ▥
C ▨
D ▧

ATLANTIC HOOK-EARED SCULPIN *Artediellus atlanticus.* Ⓐ Preopercle with uppermost spine hook-like, curving upwards; nape relatively smooth; gill membranes joined with transverse fold; body lacking plates; LL pores uniserial, 17-24; greenish-brown with oblique dark bands across body, narrower on fins. 13.5 cm. Shelf and slope on softer grounds, 35-875 m. Breeds August-September (Barents Sea); eggs large (4 mm), only 50-150. Other Arctic basin sculpins are: **Arctic Staghorn Sculpin** *Gymnacanthus tricuspis*, 30 cm, with nape covering of bony plates and straight preopercular spine; **Two-horned Sculpin** *Icelus bicornis*, Ⓑ 15.7 cm, with numerous plates on upper body and serrated LL; and **Moustache Sculpin** *Triglops murrayi*, Ⓒ 19.2 cm, slender, with oblique, finely serrated skin folds below LL. Offshore and slope: **tadpole sculpins** (**Psychrolutidae**), with low fleshy D1 continuous with D2; **Polar Sculpin** *Cottunculus microps*, Ⓓ 20 cm, dark-banded, with rough spiny skin and nape knobs; and **Pallid Sculpin** *C. thompsoni*, 35 cm, uniform grey. Related to sculpins, but with first D1 spine very short, 3 Red Sea **flatheads** (**Platycephalidae**) have entered eastern Mediterranean: *Platycephalus indicus* (LL pores >65, a: 2.15 kg); *Sorsogona prionata*; and *Papilloculiceps longiceps*.

POACHERS (Agonidae)

A ■
B ▨

POGGE *Agonus cataphractus.* Ⓐ Hard, elongated body and thin tapering tail encased in rows of more or less spiny bony plates; snout with paired curved prongs; underside of head and branchiostegal membrane with numerous short unbranched barbels; D1 and D2 short, contiguous; dorsal plates 31-34; dark brown above, banded; underside white. 21 cm. Inshore, but to edge of shelf in winter in colder areas or entering shallower waters further south. Breeds January-April (North Sea); eggs 1.75-2.23 mm, yellowish-orange, with oil globule, in small bean-sized clumps often among oarweed holdfasts; hatch at 6.3-8.0 mm, but only after very long developmental time of 10-12 months. Arctic basin **Atlantic Poacher** *Leptagonus decagonus*, Ⓑ 21 cm, has branching barbels on underside of head but none on branchiostegal membrane, and 41-45 plates in dorsal row.

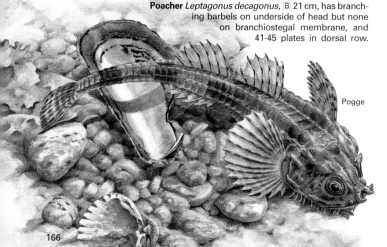

Pogge

Four-horned
Sculpin

Atlantic Hook-
eared Sculpin

Two-horned
Sculpin

Polar Sculpin

LUMPFISH and SNAILFISHES (Cyclopteridae)

A
B

LUMPSUCKER *Cyclopterus lumpus*. Ⓐ Deep-bodied, flabby fishes with rounded pelvic sucker derived from Vs; body with 3 rows of larger bony tubercles and scattered smaller platelets (tubercles and lumps less prominent in Baltic fish); D1 as 6-8 spines concealed in high fleshy ridge followed by notch and paired tubercles before D2; green to greenish-yellow, becoming dark above, sides slate-blue, often spotted; breeding males very dark above, sides and below pink or brick-red to orange. 51 cm (m), 61 cm (f); 14 yrs. Inshore to uppermost slope (400 m), typically epipelagic in top 50-60 m, under floating seaweed, feeding on comb jellyfish, worms, crustaceans, fish eggs and young. Breeds January-May, moving inshore to spawn, usually among kelp, sometimes at low water of spring tides, where males establish territories; eggs (100,000-400,000) 2.2-2.6 mm, bluish-red to yellowish, laid in 2-4 batches, forming thick, usually ovoid masses (20-30 cm) attached to rocks between LW and midtide, guarded and ventilated by male even at low water; hatch at 5.5-7.4 mm after 6-10 weeks, and young may be abundant in shore pools; mature at 5 or more yrs. Eggs, cured in brine and usually dyed black, are marketed as a form of caviare. Also Greenland to Maryland. Arctic **Spiny Lumpsucker** *Eumicrotremus spinosus*, Ⓑ 13 cm, also from Greenland to Massachusetts, has distinct D1, and body with often close-set tubercles.

COMMON SEASNAIL *Liparis liparis*. Smaller fishes also with pelvic sucker; large head and tapering tail, with loose skin; single D and A long, attached to at least basal quarter of C; A 26-29; sandy to brownish, often with longitudinal dark stripes. 18 cm. Bottom-living, inshore to 300 m, and estuarine in winter. Breeds November-February (North Sea); eggs 1.35-1.67 mm, in walnut-sized, colourless to pale yellow clumps, usually on hydroids; hatch at 5.5 mm.

MONTAGU'S SEASNAIL *Liparis montagui*. Differs from common seasnails in D and A to only base of C; A 22-25. 6 cm. Intertidal to 30 m, under stones or among weed. Breeds January-April (North Sea); eggs 1.03-1.2 mm, yellow to rose, in clumps usually attached to red algae; hatch at 3.3-3.8 mm, after about 6 weeks.

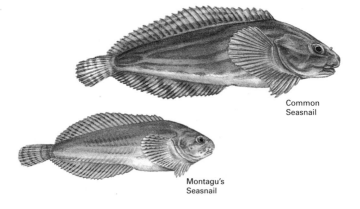

Common Seasnail

Montagu's Seasnail

Lumpsucker
female

Lumpsucker
juvenile

Lumpsucker
male

Bass

PERCH-LIKE FISHES (ORDER PERCIFORMES)
Series Percomorpha

These, and other groups derived from them, are the 'higher' teleosts with typically a full suite of advanced features such as spinous rays in D, A and V, ctenoid scales, V at least thoracic and I/5; P lateral, with vertical base; mouth protrusible, the upper jaw edge formed only by premaxilla; and swimbladder physoclistous. The perciforms comprise at least 150 families, with near 8,000 species; in this book, they are presented in groups of families or distinct suborders.

BASSES (Moronidae)

BASS *Dicentrarchus labrax*. Active sportfishes, sought especially in estuaries, and also important commercially, trawled at sea and today much more valuable than salmon. Ds contiguous, D1 VIII-IX (VIII-X), D2 I/12-13; A III/10-12; LL modally 70 (52-74); vomerine teeth in transverse crescent; rear angle of cheek with fine serration; silvery, above grey to blue, below white to yellowish; juveniles (to about 10 cm) often with dark spots. 100 cm, 30 yrs (a: 9.4 kg). Shelf, in schools, entering estuaries from spring to autumn; feeds on fish, crustaceans and squid. Mature at 32-36 cm (m), >42 cm (f). Spawns offshore February-June (south-western Ireland); fecundity to over 2 million; eggs planktonic, 1.2-1.5 mm (British Isles), 0.9-1.2 mm (Mediterranean), with unsegmented yolk and 2-3 oil globules that coalesce; hatch at 3.61-4.05 mm; young in estuaries. To Senegal.

SPOTTED BASS *Dicentrarchus punctatus*. As Bass, but adults with many small black spots over body; LL modally 60 (57-65); vomerine teeth patch with median rearward extension. 70 cm.

Spotted Bass

Comber

GROUPERS and SEAPERCHES (Serranidae)

Deeper-bodied perch-like fishes with Ds continuous; many species are hermaphrodite.

COMBER *Serranus cabrilla.* Head lacking bony ridges; C moderately concave; soft D and A mostly without scales; V base lacking upper scaly flap; maxilla lacking scales and supramaxilla; interorbit naked; LL 72-78; D X/13-15; A III/7-8; yellowish-grey to reddish, 7-9 dark bars on upper body; head with a few yellow to orange lines across cheek and opercle. 40 cm. Shelf and upper slope, to 400 m, on coarse grounds, solitary but inquisitive. Breeds July-August (Channel), April-July (Mediterranean); eggs planktonic, 0.9-0.97 mm, with oil globule; hatch at about 2.0 mm. To southern Africa.

Brown Comber

BROWN COMBER *Serranus hepatus*. Interorbit scaly; LL 44-50; D X/11-13; A III/6-7; brownish, with 2-5 dark bars, that under soft D divided at top; D with dark blotch in middle; V black, white-edged; head with 3 yellow lines. 15 cm. Inshore shelf, in sea-grass beds and on finer deposits. Breeds March-August (Mediterranean), eggs planktonic. To Senegal.

A
B

BLACK-TAILED COMBER *Serranus atricauda*. Ⓐ Similar to Comber, but large dark blotches along sides; LL 80-90; D X/15-16; A III/8. 35 cm. Inshore, to 90 m, on rocky and coralline ground. **Painted Comber** *S. scriba*, Ⓑ as preceding, but 5-7 dark bars and head with many blue wavy lines and red spots; LL 65-75; D X/14-16; A III/7-8. 36 cm. Inshore, among algae-covered rocks, solitary. Breeds April-August (Mediterranean).

DUSKY PERCH *Epinephelus guaza*. A large grouper, often spear-fished. Head lacking bony ridges; teeth depressible; C rounded; soft D and A mostly covered with small scales; P base with upper scaly flap; LL 120-130; D XI/13-16; A III/8-9; P not reaching to above anus; chocolate-brown, with light blotches above; yellow-ish below. 150 cm (a: 5.3 kg). Shelf, among rocks, usually solitary and territorial; feeds chiefly on cephalopods, as well as fish and crustaceans. To southern Africa; also western tropical Atlantic. Somewhat similar in form, but with numerous small dark spots over vertical bars, Indo-Pacific **Malabar Grouper** *E. malabaricus*, 88.5 cm (a: 10 kg), LL 102-115, is a Suez Canal immigrant into Levant Sea.

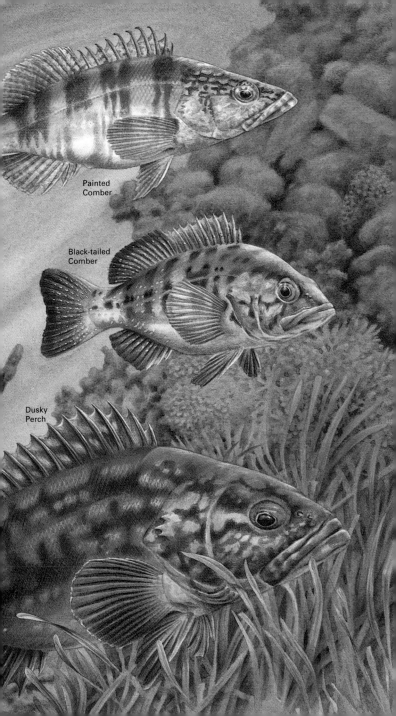

Painted Comber

Black-tailed Comber

Dusky Perch

WHITE GROUPER *Epinephelus aeneus.* More slender than Dusky Perch, greenish-grey, with somewhat indistinct lateral dark bars but a few conspicuous pale lines across cheek and opercle; D X-XI/14-16; LL 90. 115 cm (a: 6.85 kg). Shelf, on sand and mud. Also tropical eastern Atlantic.

A
B

GOLDEN GROUPER *Epinephelus alexandrinus.* Ⓐ As White Grouper, but C truncated to concave; LL 90; D XI/16-18; juveniles reddish-brown with dark lines along body and 2 oblique lines across cheek and opercle; adults more uniform greyish-brown, with lateral gold blotch in life. 140 cm. Rocks and softer deposits, to 300 m; young may form school. To Gulf of Guinea. Of similar distribution, and also with slightly concave C, **Dog-toothed Grouper** *E. caninus*, 150 cm, greyish-purple, has 2-3 dark streaks across cheek and opercle in smaller fish, D XI/13-14. **Ben-Tuvia's Grouper** *E. haifensis,* Ⓑ has large head, and small, rounded C; P reach to above anus; D XI/14-15; A III/9; brown, with dark fins. 40 cm. Offshore shelf.

COMB GROUPER *Mycteroperca rubra.* Similar to other groupers; C truncated; preopercle with small notch near lower corner; D XI/15-17; A III/11-12; reddish-brown with irregular dark mottling and pale blotches, especially in juveniles, which also have dark saddle on tail. 80 cm. Shelf, in rock crevices; mostly fish-eating. Tropical Atlantic.

STONE BASS *Polyprion americanum.* Very large and robust, grouper-like but closer to Bass; head with rough bony ridges; C rounded; LL 90-114 strongly ctenoid scales; D XI/11-12; A III/8-10; soft D and A with swollen fleshy base; brown to greyish, yellowish below; juveniles marbled. 200 cm (a: 48.5 kg). Bottom-living, shelf and over slope, perhaps to 1,000 m; smaller individuals epipelagic, often under floating objects (wreckage, driftwood, weed). To southern Africa; also western Atlantic.

SWALLOW-TAILED SEAPERCH *Anthias anthias.* Deep compressed body; 2 flat spines on upper opercle; C deeply forked; scales large, LL 36-39; D X/15, III elongated; A III/7; V longer than P; reddish-pink, oblique yellow lines on cheek and opercle. 27 cm. Offshore shelf and upper slope (150-300 m), on rocky areas and in caves; feeds on small fish and invertebrates. Females become males; breeds spring-summer (Mediterranean). To West Africa.

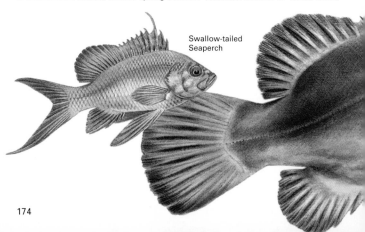

Swallow-tailed
Seaperch

White Grouper

Golden Grouper

Comb Grouper

Stone Bass

Pollack (food of
Stone Bass)

Parrot Seaperch (below)
Cardinalfish (below left)

Grunt

PARROT SEAPERCH *Callanthias ruber.* More slender than Swallow-tailed Seaperch, and C lobes elongated into filaments, but lateral-line shorter, ending on tail; LL 24-26; D X/10-11, rear part much higher; A III/9-10; V and P of similar length; reddish above, sides and below rose with pearly highlights; fins yellow. 20 cm. Shelf and upper slope, on rocks and mud, and in caves. Breeds December-January (Mediterranean).

A ⬛
B ▨

CARDINALFISH *Apogon imberbis* (**Apogonidae**). Ⓐ Small, compressed body; eyes large, diameter longer than snout; 2 Ds, D1 VI, D2 I/9-10; A II/8-9; LL scales large, 22-30; reddish, darker above; base of C with 2-3 dark spots. 15 cm. Marine, shelf rocky ground. Breeds June-September (Mediterranean); eggs fertilized internally and mouth-brooded by male. To West Africa. *A. taeniatus*, 13 cm, D1 VII, brown, is a Suez Canal immigrant.

Bullseye *Epigonus telescopus,* Ⓑ 60 cm, from deeper shelf and upper slope, dark brown to black, has scales behind eyes and on bases of Ds, A and C; *Microichthys coccoi* and *M. sanzoi* are rare pelagic species from the Straits of Messina, with a dark herring-bone pattern on sides, P 16 and 20 respectively.

GRUNTS (Haemulidae) and perch-like families

A ⬛
B ▨
C ▧

GRUNT *Pomadasys incisus.* Ⓐ Oval, somewhat compressed body; chin with 2 pores and median groove or depression; 1 D, XII/16, spinous part higher; A short, III/11-13, base more or less raised; LL 47-53; dark above, silvery below; opercle rear corner dark. 35 cm. Inshore, to 50 m. To West Africa. Related *P. stridens*, 15 cm, 3 longitudinal brown stripes, A II/8-10, LL 54-61, is a Red Sea immigrant into the Mediterranean. West African grunts ranging northwards are: **Striped Grunt** *Parapristipoma octolineatum,* Ⓑ 50 cm, brownish with 4 bluish longitudinal stripes, 6 chin pores, LL 53-58, A III/7; **Guinean Grunt** *P. humile,* Ⓒ 36 cm, uniform brown above, D XIII/15; **Big-eyed Grunt** *Brachydeuteras auritus,* Ⓒ 25 cm, D XII (X-XIII)/11-13 and deeply notched fin outline, A III/9-10, 3 chin pores but no groove; and **Rubber-lipped Grunt** *Plectorhinchus mediterraneus,* Ⓑ 80 cm, D XI-XII/17-19, A III/8-9, LL 54-57. Grunts do grunt, by rubbing their pharyngeal teeth and amplifying sound by resonation of the swimbladder.

Tripletail (top)
Bluefish (above)

 TRIPLETAIL *Lobotes surinamensis* (**Lobotidae**). Grouper-like in finnage but nape steep and body deeper, compressed; cheek and opercle lacking spines but cheek rear edge serrated; D XI-XII/14-16; A III/11; soft D and A bases scaled; LL 37-45; above dark grey, sides and below silvery. 100 cm (a: 19.2 kg). Inshore, sometimes swimming head down or on one side. Warm seas.

 BLUEFISH *Pomatomus saltator* (**Pomatomidae**). Very voracious and active predator; long compressed body; small eyes; jaws large with single series of strong teeth; D1 low, VII-VIII, contiguous with D2, I/23-28; A II/23-27; LL scales small, 95-106; dark green above, sides and below silvery; dark blotch on P base. 110 cm (a: 14.40 kg). Neritic over shelf, in schools, especially when small. Breeds July-September (Mediterranean), eggs planktonic. Worldwide in warm seas.

 COBIA *Rachycentron canadum* (**Rachycentridae**). Long cylindrical body with flattened head and lunate C; D with VII-VIII (VII-IX) separate short spines, then 30-31 branched rays; A III/20-23; above dark brown, sides with longitudinal brown band, edged white. 200 cm (a: 61.5 kg). Shelf and pelagic, usually solitary, and often near fixed or floating structures. Worldwide in warm seas (? Suez Canal immigrant to Levant Sea).

 ATLANTIC BIGEYE *Priacanthus arenatus* (**Priacanthidae**). Similar to Cardinalfish but bright red; 1 D, X/13-14; A III; V large, jugular, joined to body by membrane; P dark, with black spot near base. 40 cm (a: 1.13 kg). Inshore rocky and coral grounds, nocturnal; young pelagic. Tropical Atlantic. **Glass-eye** *P. cruentatus*, 30 cm, has dark dots on D, A and C, and noticeable cheek spine to edge of opercle flap; *P. hamrur* is another Suez immigrant, as are the **Terapons (Teraponidae)** *Pelates quadrilineatus*, 15 cm, and *Terapon puta*, 15 cm, with 1 D, spines higher than soft rays and body with longitudinal dark stripes, 4 and 5-6 respectively.

177

Zander

PERCHES (Percidae)

Freshwater species, with usually 2 Ds, contiguous at least; A I or II; include both active predators and bottom-living species. Eggs demersal. Larger, more vigorous species are important sportfish.

PERCH *Perca fluviatilis*. Head lateral-line canals around eye and along rear cheek not expanded into cavities; upper jaw rear corner not covered by bony plate before eye; D1 and D2 only slightly separated; D1 XII-XVII; D2 I-III/12-16; A II/7-10; Vs close together; LL 58-67; dark green above, sides with several dark vertical bars, single or split, paler below; D1 with dark blotch at rear end. 51 cm, 4.75 kg, 10 yrs. Lakes and slower rivers, usually near sheltering structures such as roots or vegetation, entering brackish water in Baltic Sea; larger adults solitary; feeds on fish, including perch, and invertebrates. Breeds late April-May; females accompanied by several males spawn over weed and other ramified objects, usually in 0.5-3 m; fecundity to 210,000; eggs 1.5-2.5 mm, pale or yellowish, with oil globule, bound by mucus into long white strands; hatch at 4.8-6.4 mm; sexually mature by 3-4 yrs. Commercial and sport fisheries. Hybridizes with Ruffe.

A
B
C

ZANDER *Stizostedion lucioperca*. A More slender ('Pikeperch') shape, mouth large, angle to below rear edge of eye, and teeth include fangs; D1 XIII-XV, D2 I-II/19-23; A II/11-13; Vs well spaced; LL 80-95; dark green above, below white or silvery; sides with several broad, more or less irregular dark bars; Ds with rows of dark dots. 130 cm, 18 kg; 19 yrs (a: 11.42 kg). Lakes and larger rivers, in more open water, schooling when young, but solitary predators when larger; also in brackish water of Baltic; from about 5-10 cm, feed on fish, usually pursued rather than ambushed. Breeds April-May (late February-July), typically on sandy or stony shallows, where a flat nest depression is made; fecundity to over 500,000; eggs 1.0-1.5 mm, guarded by both parents, hatch at about 6.0mm in 3-11 days at 10-15°C. Sexually mature by 3-5 yrs, at 35-45 cm. Important sportfish. Recently established in eastern England. **Sea Zander** *S. marina*, B 62 cm, is variety from brackish water of Black Sea and Caspian estuaries and adjoining sea, with more heavily scaled head; commercial fisheries. **Volga Zander** *S. volgensis*, C 45 cm, 1.4 kg, is similar but has D1 X-XIV, higher than D2; LL 70-83, no canine teeth in adults. North American **Walleye** *S. vitreum*, similar to Zander, has been introduced to European waters.

Minnow (typical food of Perch)

Perch

A
B

RUFFE *Gymnocephalus cernuus.* Ⓐ Head lateral-line canals expanded into cavities around eye and along rear cheek; Ds continuous, XII-XVI/11-15; A II/5-6; LL 35-40; above and sides dark green, with many dark spots; yellowish below; D and C with dark dots. 15 cm, 6 yrs. Lakes and slow rivers, near bottom, in small schools; feeds on invertebrates, small fish and fish eggs, notably on those of Powan after introduction of Ruffe to Loch Lomond. Breeds March-June; eggs yellowish, 0.5-1.0 mm, to 200,000 per female, in strands on stones and vegetation; hatch at 3-4 mm; sexually mature by 2 yrs. To Far East. Hybrids with Perch. Similar Danubian **Balon's Ruffe** *G. baloni,* Ⓑ has 2 small spines along edge of opercle, and 4-6 dark bars.

A
B
C

SCHRAETZER *Gymnocephalus schraetzer.* Ⓐ Similar to Ruffe, but D XVII-XIX/12-14, A II/6-7; LL 55-62; yellowish, with 3-4 longitudinal narrow dark stripes. 24 cm. Danube basin. **Don Ruffe** *G. acerina,* Ⓑ 21 cm, has same D spinous ray count, A II/5-6, LL 50-55; scattered small dark spots but no stripes, and occurs in rivers of northern Black Sea. **Percarina** *Percarina demidoffi,* Ⓒ 7 cm (m), 10 cm (f), from the northern Black Sea and Sea of Azov, has expanded head canals but Ds contiguous, D1 IX-XI, D2 II-III/10-13; A II/8-11, LL 33-37; yellowish with dark spots along back. Fished commercially.

ZINGEL *Aspro zingel.* Slender, cylindrical body tapering to tail; head lateral-line canals not expanded; mouth inferior, upper jaw upper rear corner covered by bony plate before eye; Ds well separated, D1 XIII-XV; D2 I/18-20; A I-II/11-13; D2 base longer than caudal peduncle; mottled dark on yellow-brown, with somewhat irregular dark oblique bands. 48 cm. Shallow fast streams, bottom-living among stones; feeds nocturnally on invertebrates and fish spawn. Breeds March-April.

Streber

A
B

STREBER *Aspro streber.* Ⓐ As Zingel, but more slender, D1 only VIII-IX, D2 I/12-13; A I/10-12; D2 base equal to or shorter than caudal peduncle; 4-5 distinct oblique dark bands across sides. 22 cm. Habitat as Zingel, but in higher, faster reaches. Also Greek *A. s. balcanicus* and Rumanian *A. s. nerensis.* **Rhône Streber** *A. asper,* Ⓑ 22 cm, is very similar, but D2 base is longer than caudal peduncle.

RUMANIAN BULLHEAD-PERCH *Romanichthys valsanicola.* Discovered in 1950s, now endangered with restricted distribution in upper River Arges of Rumania, and now further reduced. Zingel-like, but eyes dorsally sited on flattened head; Ds adjoining; D1 IX, D2 I/15-16; A I/7; LL 58-67; grey-brown with darker mottling. Under stones in fast streams, often with bullheads (*Cottus*); feeds chiefly on stonefly larvae.

180

Ruffe

Schraetzer

Zingel

Rhône
Streber

Rumanian
Bullhead-perch

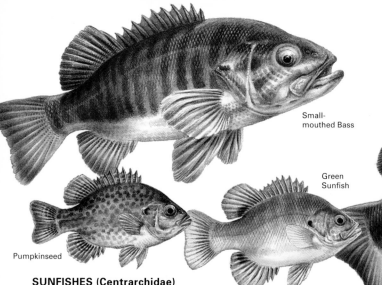

Small-mouthed Bass

Green Sunfish

Pumpkinseed

SUNFISHES (Centrarchidae)

Freshwater perches of eastern North
America; somewhat deep-bodied; single D; A usually with 3 spines.
Several species introduced to temperate waters worldwide as sportfish, so that wider European distributions indicated are very approximate. For spawning in late spring or early summer, the male digs a
round shallow nest-pit in a sheltered position. Eggs from usually a
number of females are guarded by the male until hatching, and his care
of the young in the nest may continue for some days afterwards until
their yolk sacs are absorbed and the young become free-swimming.

 SMALL-MOUTHED BASS *Micropterus dolomieu*. Also important for sportfishing in North America. As Large-mouthed Bass,
but mouth smaller, jaw angle to below pupil; D outline with deep
notch but spinous and soft parts obviously connected; A III; LL 68-
78; scales on bases of D and A; brownish, with irregular dark bars
and vertical markings. 58 cm (a: 5.41 kg). Clear, cooler reaches of
rivers and lakes. Breeds late April-early June. Originally Lake
Ontario and Ohio system; established in France, Denmark and Finland.

 PUMPKINSEED *Lepomis gibbosus*. Easily caught but fights,
hence the starting fish for many anglers. Deep-bodied, with
small mouth, jaw angle before front edge of eye; A III; LL 40-
47; olive with dark mottling; head with blue-green lines radiating from snout; opercular spot with red tip. 22 cm, 9 yrs (a:
0.63 kg). Shallows, feeding on small fish and invertebrates.
Breeds May-October, with nests in groups. Eastern Canada and
Dakotas to Georgia and Tennessee; widely established in western Europe and
Danube basin, including southern England.

 GREEN SUNFISH *Lepomis cyanellus*. Stouter sunfish, with
larger mouth, jaw angle below eye; above and sides olive-
green with brass tints; opercular spot with pale edging. 30 cm
(a: 0.96 kg). Lakes and rivers to artificial ponds, adaptable to
adverse conditions. Breeds May-August (North America).
Established in Germany (Frankfurt-am-Main).

Large-mouthed Bass

Rock Bass

 RED-BREASTED SUNFISH *Lepomis auritus*. As Pumpkinseed, but sides yellowish, red below, and opercular spot may be elongated, without coloured edging. 24 cm (a: 0.79 kg). Especially common in rivers. New Brunswick to Florida; established in Italy.

 LARGE-MOUTHED BASS *Micropterus salmoides*. Important gamefish in North America. Moderately elongated, substantial body; large mouth, jaw angle to rear of eye; dorsal fin with spinous and soft parts merely contiguous at base; LL 59-68; bases of D and A without scales; greenish to bronzy-green, with dark lateral blotches. 83 cm (a: 10.09 kg). Quiet, shallow, well-weeded lakes or backwaters, feeding on fish, frogs and larger invertebrates. Breeds March-July, with solitary nests up to 90 cm in diameter; fecundity to over 30,000. Established in many parts of Europe, from Spain to USSR, and England (Surrey and Dorset).

 ROCK BASS *Ambloplites rupestris*. Robust body; jaw angle below pupil; A VI; LL 39-40; dark olive above, sides blotched brown and metallic; several lines of dark dots below lateral line; opercular dark spot edged gold or white. 34 cm (a: 1.36 kg). Around rocks in lakes and deeper streams, feeding on invertebrates and small fish. Breeds May-July. Vermont and Manitoba to Gulf states; established for a time in at least England (Oxfordshire).

CICHLIDS (Cichlidae). Tropical aquarium species reported as feral are: **Oscar** *Astronotus ocellatus*, **Chanchito** *Cichlasoma facetum*, and **Tilapia** *Tilapia zillii*, 30 cm. Cichlids resemble sunfishes, but have only 1 nostril on each side of snout and interrupted lateral line

183

SHARKSUCKERS (Echeneidae)

Elongated fishes that attach themselves to sharks by the oval head sucker (derived from D1 rays of typical perch-like fishes). Traditionally regarded as feeding merely on scraps from the host's diet, sharksuckers may in fact cause skin injury to the host.

 SHARKSUCKER *Echeneis naucrates*. Head sucker with 21-28 transverse laminae; D2 and A long-based; brown, with lateral stripe; D2, A and C dark. 100 cm (a: 2.3 kg). Inshore in tropical seas.

 COMMON REMORA *Remora remora*. Similar to Sharksucker, but shorter-bodied, with sucker length at least equal to distance from its rear edge to D2 origin; 16-20 laminae; bluish-brown. 62 cm. Offshore, recorded from at least 12 shark species; feeds largely on parasitic copepods. Worldwide in tropics. There are several other Mediterranean or more southerly *Remora* species.

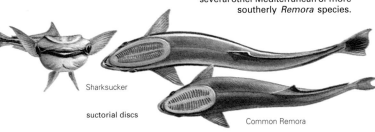

Sharksucker

suctorial discs

Common Remora

JACKS (Carangidae)

Of very varied body form, and many species important in commercial and sport fishing. C always deeply forked; 2 Ds; first few A spines separated from rest of fin. Usually schooling, midwater to pelagic, with planktonic eggs.

A ▨
B ▨
C ▨
D ▨

ATLANTIC HORSE-MACKEREL *Trachurus trachurus*. Ⓐ 'Scad' are fished commercially, especially by trawling for industrial use. Body moderately slender; all LL scales expanded, 66-75, forming lateral keel; accessory dorsal lateral line back to rear part of D2; P at least as long as head; D1 VIII, as high as D2; D2 I/29-33; A II, I/24-29; grey-blue to greenish, sides silvery, white below. 60 cm. Shelf, midwater schools, deeper in winter, migrating northwards in summer; feeds on invertebrates and small fish. Breeds June-August (Celtic Sea), November-May (Adriatic); eggs tiny, 0.81-1.04 mm, with reddish oil globule and segmented yolk; hatch at 2.5 mm, with yolk sac projecting in advance of head; young fish (10-70 mm) beneath large pelagic jellyfish; mature at 3-4 yrs. To West Africa and southern Africa (as *T. t. capensis*). Very similar **Mediterranean Horse-mackerel** *T. mediterraneus*, Ⓑ 50 cm, more coastal, has accessory lateral line to opposite anterior part of D2, LL 75-89; **Blue Jack-mackerel** *T. picturatus*, Ⓒ 60 cm, as preceding but LL 93-100; and West African **Cunene Horse-mackerel** *T. trecae*, Ⓓ 35 cm, accessory lateral line only to opposite D1, LL 71-78.

A ▨
B ▨

MACKEREL SCAD *Decapterus macarellus*. Ⓐ Elongate, with all lateral-line scales enlarged but relatively small, 77-84; D2 and A followed by separate finlet; D2 I/33-37; A II, I/28-32; rear edge of opercular opening with 2 short fleshy flaps; above dark blue, sides and below silvery; white spot inside middle of upper jaw; 35 cm. Schools offshore. Worldwide in tropics. **Ox-eyed Scad** *Selar boops*, Ⓑ 25 cm, also with opercular flaps, has rear lateral-line scales markedly enlarged, LL 58-72, but no D2 and A finlets, and gold lateral stripe; recorded from Sezimbra Bay, Portugal, but otherwise Indo-Pacific.

Sharksucker

Common Remora

Common Remora on Blue Shark

Atlantic Horse-mackerel

BLUE RUNNER *Caranx crysos*. Oval body outline, compressed; only rear lateral-line scales expanded, 46-56; accessory dorsal lateral-line not back to D1; P sickle-shaped, longer than head; D1 lower than D2, latter A with long front rays; D1 VIII; D2 I/22-25; A II, I/19-21; rear edge of opercular opening lacking fleshy flaps; upper jaw with outer row of canines and inner small teeth; olive to bluish-green above, silvery to golden below; black spot on rear corner of opercle. 55 cm (a: 3.83 kg). Inshore schools, feeding on fish. Tropical and warm-temperate Atlantic.

A
B
C
D

CREVALLE JACK *Caranx hippos*. Ⓐ As Blue Runner, but lateral-line expanded scales 23-37 and P with dark blotch; D2 I/19-22; A II, I/16-18. 101 cm (a: 26 kg). Also worldwide **Black Jack** *C. lugubris*, Ⓑ 89 cm (a: 17 94 kg), greyish-brown or darker, front rays of D2 elongated, also with low scute count (26-32); **False Scad** *C. rhonchus*, Ⓒ 60 cm, D1 similar in height to D2, dark blotch in upper front corner of D2, and almost separate D2 and A rear finlets; and **Shrimp Scad** *Alepes djedaba*, Ⓓ 30 cm, rear lateral bony plates 41-48, opercular dark blotch surmounted by white spot, and jaw teeth comblike, in single row, an Indo-Pacific immigrant into the Levant Sea.

GUELLY JACK *Pseudocaranx dentex*. Similar to *Caranx* species but single row of blunt teeth in jaws (adult) and D1 VIII, as high as D2, I/24-26; A II, I/22-23; above greenish, sides silvery with yellow lateral stripe, and opercular dark spot. 80 cm (a: 11.53 kg). Schools inshore, feeding on benthic invertebrates. Worldwide in warm seas, to Azores and Portugal, and to Mediterranean.

PILOT FISH *Naucrates ductor*. Long known as a follower of large moving objects. Oval body; mouth small, jaws with bands of tiny teeth; D1 IV-V, a series of low spines; D2 I/25-29, longer than A, II, I/15-17, with A spines indistinct; no enlarged LL scales; tail wrist with transverse groove on upper and lower surface, and keel along lateral midline; bluish, with 5-7 broad dark bands. 63 cm. Epipelagic, associated with sharks, rays, turtles, sailing vessels and driftwood, probably feeding on food debris, small fish and invertebrates; young under jellyfish. Warm seas.

Pilot Fish swimming with Hawksbill Turtle

Blue Runner

Crevalle Jack

False Scad

Guelly Jack

Pilot Fish

GREATER AMBERJACK *Seriola dumerili*. More elongate, mouth larger, but teeth minute; gill rakers 11-19; D1 small, VII; D2 I/29-35, longer than A, II, I/18-21, spines indistinct; no enlarged LL scales; transverse grooves on tail wrist but no keel; above bluish or green, sides silvery and reddish below, smaller fish (less than 17 cm) with several vertical bars, dividing ventrally. 188 cm; 80.6 kg (a: 70.59 kg). Schooling, over continental shelf, feeding on fish. Warm seas. Other species are: **Guinean Amberjack** *S. carpenteri*, B over 48 cm, gill rakers 19-23; **Lesser Amberjack** *S. fasciata*, C 67.5 cm, 4.6 kg, gill rakers 23-26, also western Atlantic; and **Almaco Jack** *S. rivoliana*, D 97 cm (a: 35.38 kg), similar but rear of upper jaw very deep, tropical seas.

VADIGO *Campogramma glaycos*. Jaws large, with single row of canine teeth; D1 VI-VII low spines; D2 I/26-28, little longer than A, II, I/23-25; no enlarged LL scales; transverse grooves on tail wrist not obvious, and no keel; above greenish-grey, forming digitate edge along lateral midline, silvery below. 60 cm. Inshore shelf. To Senegal.

DERBIO *Trachinotus ovatus*. Similar to Vadigo but mouth small with band of small teeth; D1 VI, low separate spines; D2 I/23-27; A II, I/22-25; above dark green, sides silvery with row of several small dark markings on LL; C tips and anterior tips of D2 and A black. 70 cm. Schooling inshore over sand, feeding on invertebrates and small fish. To West Africa.

LEERFISH *Lichia amia*. Similar to preceding, but body outline rhomboidal, with large mouth; teeth small but pointed, in bands; D1 VII separate spines; D2 I/19-21; A I/17-21; lateral line wavy, then straight along midline below rear D2; brownish above, sides silvery, and D2, A and C tips black. 180 cm (a: 23.79 kg). Inshore and into estuaries. Also Indian Ocean and West Africa.

POMPANO *Alectis alexandrinus*. Very deep, compressed body; D1 VII, but absent in fish above 15 cm fork length; D2 I/20-22; A II (lost), I/18-20; anterior tips of D2 and A elongated, rays filamentous in small fish; rear LL scales only slightly enlarged, 4-20; bluish-silvery, vertical bars in small fish. Over 70 cm (a: 2.7 kg). Inshore, young pelagic; feeds on squid and fish. To West Africa. Tropical Atlantic **Lookdown Scad** *Selene dorsalis*, B 32.5 cm, also deep-bodied, D2 and A never elongate, D1 VIII low spines, D2 I/23-24, scales not evident.

188

Greater Amberjack

Vadigo

Derbio

Leerfish

Pompano

POMFRETS to BUTTERFISHES (Pelagic Families)

RAY'S BREAM *Brama brama* (**Bramidae**). Ⓐ Deep, oval, compressed body; high, rounded head profile; 1 long-based D, 35-38, arising above P base; A 29-32, spines not prominent; D and A with high anterior tip, scales on fin; C deeply forked, no keel on tail root; LL 80-95; body uniform silvery-black. 70 cm. Pelagic, in small schools, feeding on small fish and squid. Breeds August-September (Mediterranean). Warm seas, seasonally northwards.

Offshore Atlantic relatives are: **Long-finned Bream** *Taractichthys longipinnis*, Ⓑ LL 39-45, pale-edged D, A and C; **Rough Pomfret** *Taractes asper*, Ⓒ 50 cm, LL scales spiny, 43-46, tail wrist with keel; and **Silver Pomfret** *Pterycombus brama*, Ⓓ 40 cm, sail-like D, 48-53, and A, 40-43, D origin on head, rear of D and A pale.

COMMON DOLPHIN (FISH) *Coryphaena hippurus* (**Coryphaenidae**). Ⓐ Not to be confused with small whales; elongated, with high, rounded head profile, becoming steep with bony crest in males; 1 long-based D, 58-66, arising on head; A with concave outline; C forked; LL 200; rich blue, sides green to yellowish, sometimes barred; in death, deep blue to purplish and greenish-yellow; white to golden below. 200 cm (a: 39.46 kg). Pelagic, often in pairs or small groups, inquisitive, around floating objects, including ships, and capable of bursts of speed to near 50 knots. Breeds all year in tropics, especially spring. Worldwide in warm seas. Also more southern **Pompano Dolphin** *C. equiselis*, Ⓑ 75 cm, D 52-59, A convex outline, LL.

Rough Pomfret

Ray's Bream

Silver Pomfret

Common
Dolphin

Long-finned
Bream

Blackfish

BLACKFISH *Centrolophus niger* (**Centrolophidae**). Sizeable, deep-bodied, oceanic and offshore, with 1 long-based D, and small P and V; C forked. D spinous rays weak and merging into soft rays or rear part; D origin usually behind base of P; scales tiny, LL 160-230; brownish to bluish, young with bars. 150 cm. Epipelagic and mesopelagic, sometimes over shelf; feeds on fish and pelagic invertebrates. Smaller individuals often below large jellyfish or floating objects.

A
B

CORNISH BARREL-FISH *Schedophilus medusophagus*. Ⓐ D spinous rays soft, total rays 44-50; body soft and flabby; D origin before vertical of P base; brown, young mottled, deeper-bodied. 50 cm. Epipelagic and mesopelagic, young feeding mostly on jellyfish tentacles and gonads. **Imperial Blackfish** *S. ovalis*, Ⓑ 80 cm, has stronger spinous rays, and D VI-VIII/31-32.

A
B

BARREL-FISH *Hyperoglyphe perciformis*. Ⓐ D spinous rays much lower than soft rays, VII-VIII/19-21; dark green to black. 80 cm. Slope, in canyons, but young near surface and over shelf, around floating structures but not jellyfish. Probably dispersed from western Atlantic. **Cigar-fish** *Cubiceps gracilis* (**Nomeidae**), Ⓑ 80 cm, often but not invariably with jellyfish, has 2 Ds, contiguous, D1 IX-XI, D2 22-24, and C deeply forked; brown or black; epipelagic and mesopelagic.

A
B

ATLANTIC SQUARETAIL *Tetragonurus atlanticus* (**Tetragonuridae**). Ⓐ Long-bodied, prominent head, 2 small Ds, in middle of body; lower jaw closes to within upper jaw; C rear edge with central notch; LL 73-95, scales with prominent ridges, forming paired keels on tail wrist; brown to black. 50 cm. Epipelagic and mesopelagic, young nearer surface and often living inside pelagic sea-squirts; feeds on jellyfish and salps (pelagic sea-squirts). Worldwide; eastern Atlantic to south-western British Isles. **Cuvier's Squaretail** *T. cuvieri*, Ⓑ 70 cm, has snout about twice eye length, D1 origin not before P tip, and LL 97-114.

BUTTERFISH *Stromateus fiatola* (**Stromateidae**). Deep, compressed body, head and mouth small; 1 D, long-based, total rays 42-50; C long, deeply forked; scales small; above bluish, spotted; below silvery-white; young with bars. 50 cm. Shelf, young with jellyfish. Also southern and West Africa.

Cornish Barrel-fish

Barrel-fish

Atlantic
Squaretail

Butterfish

SEABREAMS (Sparidae)

There are commercial fisheries for many seabream species, which are entirely unrelated to freshwater breams. Typically deep-bodied, compressed; 1 D; A with III spines; C forked; mouth small but jaw teeth may be differentiated variously into flat incisors and conical canines in front, or rounded molars along the side, depending on species. Many seabreams are hermaphroditic.

ANNULAR GILTHEAD *Diplodus annularis*. A Body oval, compressed; mouth small, each jaw with 8 front incisors and laterally 2-4 rows of molars; D XI/11-13; LL 48-56; silvery-grey or yellow, with dark band around tail root behind D and A; young also with 5 narrow vertical dark bars on body. 24 cm. Inshore, usually on sand or sea-grass beds, young into brackish water. Most individuals either male or female, few changing from male to female; breeds April-June (Atlantic and western Mediterranean). Also **Senegal Seabream** *D. bellottii*, B 30 cm, similar coloration, but dark spot at start of LL, longitudinal dark stripe below LL, and only 1 row of molars.

WHITE SEABREAM *Diplodus sargus*. Like Annular Gilthead, but body with 9 bars, alternately dark and paler, and tail wrist with dark saddle; LL 58-67. 45 cm. Inshore, over or near rocks; young in brackish water and sea grass beds. Some males change to females; breeds March-June (western Mediterranean). Two subspecies: *D. s. cadenati*, Cape Verdes to Biscay, and *D. s. sargus*, Mediterranean and Black Sea, losing black bars when over 25 cm.

COMMON TWO-BANDED SEABREAM *Diplodus vulgaris*. As preceding, but D XI-XII/13-16; LL 51-61; greyish to green or brown, with dark nape before D, and tail wrist including rear bases of D and A (less extensive in young). 45 cm. Inshore, to 90 m; young in brackish water and sea grass beds. Hermaphroditic; breeds October-November (western Mediterranean). To West Africa.

ZEBRA SEABREAM *Diplodus cervinus*. As preceding, but incisors 10-12 (upper jaw), 8 (lower jaw), both with gap before start of molars; D XI-XII/11-14; silvery to golden, with 3 broad dark bars and double bar across tail wrist and ends of D and A; dark transverse mark across eyes from cheek to cheek. 55 cm. Inshore, over rocks, or deeper, on mud to 300 m in Mediterranean; feeds on algae and invertebrates. Breeds January-April. To Cape Verdes.

SHARP-SNOUTED SEABREAM *Diplodus puntazzo*. As preceding, but snout noticeably pointed; molars few and small; D XI/12-15; LL 53-64; silvery, with about a dozen bars, alternating dark and paler, and including band on tail wrist. 60 cm. Inshore, over rocky ground; feeds on algae and invertebrates. To Cape Verdes.

COUCH'S SEABREAM *Pagrus pagrus*. A Body oval, compressed; head profile with slight convexity; jaws with front canines, 6 (lower) and 4 (upper), rear lateral teeth molar-like; D XI-XIII/9-10; LL 50-56; pinkish-silvery, C dark with pale tips. 75 cm (a: 2.29 kg). Shelf, usually inshore, sometimes in lagoons, feeding on invertebrates and fish. Breeds April-June, most individuals being female. Also West African **Red-banded Seabream** *P. auriga*, B 80 cm (a: 3 kg), D rays from III onwards filamentous, but I and II very short, D XI/10-12, pink with 4-5 reddish bars successively broad and narrow, and red V, especially in juveniles; and **Blue-spotted Seabream** *P. coeruleostictus*, C 90 cm (a: 9.17 kg), as Red-banded Seabream, but numerous blue spots over head and body and no bars; V greyish.

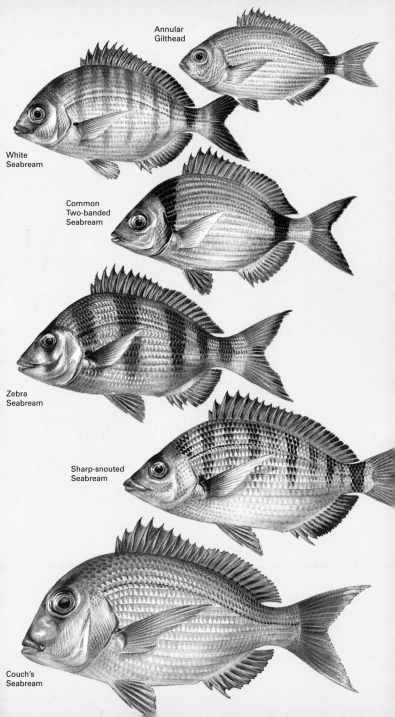

Annular
Gilthead

White
Seabream

Common
Two-banded
Seabream

Zebra
Seabream

Sharp-snouted
Seabream

Couch's
Seabream

COMMON DENTEX *Dentex dentex*. Body oval, compressed; jaws with rows of canine teeth; D XI/11-12, III and IV much longer than I and II; LL 62-68; greyish or pinkish, with many small black spots more or less evident. 100 cm (a: 9.85 kg). Shelf, usually inshore over rocky ground, feeding on fish and molluscs. Sexes mostly fixed, some hermaphroditic; breeds May (Mediterranean). To Senegal.

A ▨
B ▨
C ▨

PINK DENTEX *Dentex gibbosus*. Ⓐ Similar to Common Dentex, but D III and IV filamentous in juveniles, small black spot immediately after D base, and LL 56-62. 100 cm (a: 6.55 kg). Hermaphroditic, males changing to females. Also to West Africa: **Morocco Dentex** *D. maroccanus*, Ⓑ 41 cm, D XII and LL 46-51; and **Large-eyed Dentex** *D. macrophthalmus*, Ⓒ 65 cm, also D XII, but eye longer than snout.

GILTHEAD *Sparus auratus*. Deep oval body; jaws with 4-6 prominent front canines, and rows of large molars; D XI/13-14; LL 73-85; greyish-silvery, with golden band between eyes; large dark blotch over rear corner of opercle. 70 cm, 5 kg. Inshore, over sand and sea-grass, and into brackish water; feeds on fish, invertebrates and vegetable matter. Males change to females; breeds October-December. To Cape Verdes.

STRIPED SEABREAM *Lithognathus mormyrus*. Oval compressed body; jaws with outer row of small canines and inner lower teeth, becoming molar-like to rear of jaw; rear nostril slit-like; D XI-XII/11-12; LL 59-65; silvery, with about 15 thin, dark bars down flanks. 55 cm. Inshore on sandy ground and sea-grass meadows, feeding on invertebrates. Males change to females; breeds in spring and summer.

RED SEABREAM *Pagellus bogaraveo*. Similar teeth to Striped Seabream, but body slimmer, rear nostril porelike, and never striped; D XII-XIII/ 11-13; A III/11-12; LL 68-74; reddish, with large dark blotch above root of P; mouth reddish-orange. 70 cm. Shelf and upper slope, to 700 m; feeds on invertebrates and fish. Males usually change to females; breeds August-October (British Isles), January-May (Mediterranean).

SPANISH SEABREAM *Pagellus acarne*. Similar to Red Seabream but eye shorter than snout, and A III/9-10; pink, with dark mark on and above upper origin of P. 36 cm. Shelf, to 500 m. Breeds March-April and November (Atlantic). To Senegal.

Spanish Seabream

196

Common
Dentex

Gilthead

Striped Seabream

Red Seabream

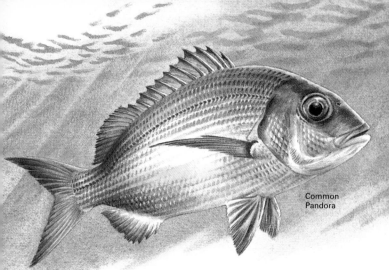

Common
Pandora

COMMON PANDORA *Pagellus erythrinus.* A Similar to preceding seabreams, but mouth pale or grey, A III/8-9, and LL 55-65; pink with tiny blue dots; P base and opercle edge reddish. 60 cm (a: 1.56 kg). Shelf, usually inshore. Breeds spring-autumn (Mediterranean). To Cape Verdes. West African **Red Pandora** *P. bellottii,* B 42 cm, has pale mouth, body silvery-red with longitudinal rows of blue dots, and reddish edge to opercle and start of LL.

BLACK SEABREAM *Spondyliosoma cantharus.* Oval, compressed body; jaws with 4-6 rows of slender canines, larger in front; D XI/11-13; LL 66-75; silvery, tinged bluish to pink, with broken longitudinal golden lines. 60 cm. Inshore shelf, often in schools, feeding on seaweed and invertebrates. Females change to males; breeds February-May; eggs demersal on sand. To Cape Verdes.

SADDLED SEABREAM *Oblada melanura.* Body more elongated, compressed, with shorter snout; jaws with outer row of 8-10 incisors and smaller lateral teeth, and inner belt of low blunt teeth; D XI/13-14; LL 64-67; dark silvery, with thin, dark striae along scale rows towards C; tail wrist with prominent dark bar, edged white. 30 cm. Inshore, over rocks and sea-grass, eating small invertebrates. Sexes mostly fixed, but few females change to male; breeds April-June (Mediterranean). To West Africa.

SALEMA *Sarpa salpa.* Similar in form to Saddled Seabream; jaws with single row of incisors, upper notched, lower pointed, and roots exposed inside mouth; D XI-XII/14-17, LL 70-80; bluish-grey, with gold striae along scales to C but no dark bar across wrist. 46 cm. Over algae and sea-grass inshore, herbivorous and may be ciguatoxic. Protandrous hermaphrodites; breeds in spring and autumn. To southern Africa. Suez immigrant **Karanteen Seabream** *Crenidens crenidens* is similar but has 2-3 rows of incisors.

BOGUE *Boops boops.* An elongated seabream; eye prominent; jaws with single row of small incisors, edges with 4-5 serrations; D XIII-XV/12-16; LL 69-80; above green or blue, sides silvery with thin longitudinal gold lines; upper edge of P base with small dark blotch. 36 cm. Shelf, usually inshore, midwater, at night towards surface. Females usually become male; breeds March-May (Atlantic), April-May (western Mediterranean).

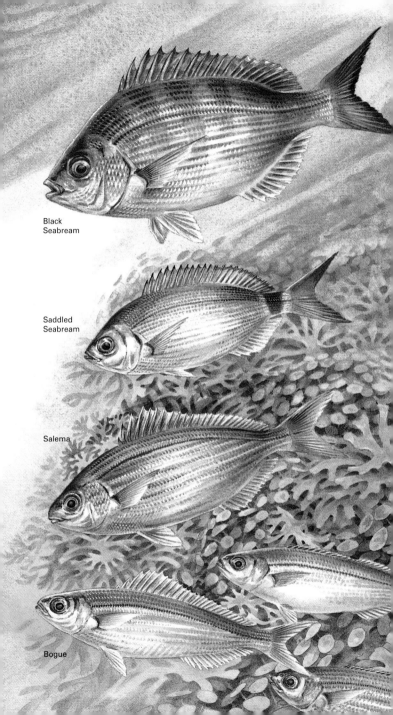

Black
Seabream

Saddled
Seabream

Salema

Bogue

MENOLAS (Centracanthidae) and Related Families

Menolas resemble seabreams but they are more elongate and are plankton-feeding; single D; mouth very protrusible, with small teeth in bands; C forked.

IMPERIAL JERRET *Centracanthus cirrus*. Body elongate, snout pointed and eyes large; D XIII/9-10, upper outline of fin deeply concave in middle; A III/9-10; LL 86-90; reddish above, pale below. 20 cm. Shelf, over coarser ground, in schools. Breeds in summer, eggs planktonic. To West Africa.

ZERRO *Spicara smaris*. Moderately elongate; D XI-XII/10-12, upper outline of fin not deeply concave; A III/8-10; LL 75-81; above brownish, with bluish makings and dark blotch above tip of P; silvery below. 20 cm (m), 15 cm (f). Inshore, over sea-grass beds and muddy deposits. Breeds February-May.

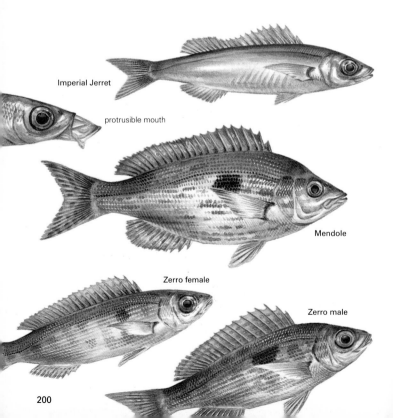

Imperial Jerret

protrusible mouth

Mendole

Zerro female

Zerro male

200

MENDOLE *Spicara maena*. As Zerro, but deeper-bodied and nape convex in larger individuals; LL 68-70; D XI/12; A III/9-10; greyish-blue above, silvery sides with small dark spots as well as lateral blotch. 25 cm (m), 21 cm (f). Sea-grass meadows, rocky and muddy ground, to 100 m, feeding on benthic as well as planktonic organisms. Breeds August-October, spawning among sea-grass in nest site cleared by male. **Garizzo** *S. flexuosa*. As Mendole, but head shorter than body depth, D XI/10-12; yellowish to darker brown, front of D black. 21 cm (m), 18 cm (f). Inshore to 130 m, over finer deposits; food mostly plankton. Breeds March-May, eggs demersal.

SILVERY SILLAGO *Sillago sihama* (**Sillaginidae**). Also elongate, with 2 D and forked C, but small mouth and flattened opercular spine; D1 XI, D2 I/20-23; dark above, sides and below silvery. 25 cm. Inshore sandy ground, eating worms and other invertebrates. Indo-Pacific Suez Canal immigrant into Levant Sea.

Bermuda Sea Chub

BERMUDA SEA CHUB *Kyphosus sectatrix* (**Kyphosidae**). Ⓐ Oval body; mouth small, with long curved incisors; cheek rear edge serrated; D single, XI/11-13; LL 51-58; C forked; grey-brown with numerous yellow longitudinal lines. 75 cm (a: 5.64 kg). Inshore, and may be associated with floating objects; feeds on seaweed and small invertebrates. Also tropical Atlantic. Similarly sporadic **Yellow Sea Chub** *K. incisor*, Ⓑ 90 cm, has D XI/13-15.

Garizzo

201

DRUMS (Sciaenidae)

Drums are somewhat slender sea-perches, whose swimbladder usually has numerous side branches; associated drumming muscles produce sound ('croaks') by resonation. Lateral-line canals of head conspicuous. C never forked; spinous and soft D contiguous at base; A base very short.

MEAGRE *Argyrosomus regius.* Elongate, mouth large but no chin barbel; teeth in bands; C truncate or slightly convex; D1 IX-X; D2 I/26-29; A II/7-8; silvery-bronze, mouth yellowish-orange. 140 cm (a: 48 kg). Shelf, into lagoons; feeds on fish and nektonic crustaceans. Breeds April-July (Mediterranean). To West Africa; also penetrating Suez Canal to Gulf of Suez.

BROWN MEAGRE *Sciaena umbra.* Deep-bodied, with steeply ascending predorsal profile; mouth smaller than Meagre; D1 high, X-XI, D2 I/23-26; swimbladder simple; dark grey or brown; V, A, D2 rim and lower edge of C black. 50 cm. Shelf, mostly inshore. Breeds March-August (Mediterranean). To Senegal.

CORB *Umbrina cirrosa.* Similar in form to preceding, but mouth definitely below snout, and chin with small stiff barbel; D1 IX-X; D2 I/23-25; greyish to brownish-silvery, with dark lines along upper body; opercle edged black; fins dark. 70 cm. Inshore, young into estuaries, feeding on benthic invertebrates. Through Suez Canal to Gulf of Suez.

CANARY DRUM *Umbrina canariensis.* Similar to preceding but D2 I/27-31; also with thin dark lines along upper body, but rim of opercle dark brown, and V, A, D2 and C edged black. 63 cm. Shelf and slope edge, over sand and softer deposits, feeding on invertebrates. **Fusca Drum** *U. ronchus*, 77 cm, has pale opercle edge and D2 I/25-27.

BUTTERFLYFISHES (Chaetodontidae) and DAMSELFISHES (Pomacentridae)

HOEFLER'S BUTTERFLYFISH *Chaetodon hoefleri.* This and the following species belong to families normally associated with coral reefs. Very deep, compressed body with tiny mouth; D XI/21-24; A III/16-18; LL 39-45; vivid coloration of yellow with 4 vertical dark bars. 15 cm. Inshore, feeding on invertebrates. To West Africa.

A ▣
B ▨

DEMOISELLE *Chromis chromis.* Ⓐ Deep, compressed body, with small mouth; teeth small, conical, in band; D XIII-XIV/10-11; A II/10-12; LL 24-30; brown with pale spot on each scale; young bluish. 15 cm. Small groups over inshore rocks and seagrass. Eggs demersal, attached by filaments and guarded by male. **Cape Verdean** *Abudefduf luridus*, Ⓑ 15 cm, is uniform darker brown with bluish markings, and has incisor-like teeth in single row, and D XIII/15-16.

Two other coral fish families are represented by recent Suez Canal immigrants: **River Snapper** *Lutjanus argentimaculatus* (**Lutjanidae**), 80 cm, seabream-like but preopercle notched, bronze to silvery-red; and **Vanikoro Sweeper** *Pempheris vanikolensis* (**Pempheridae**), 18 cm, very deep coppery body and large eye, A III/39-43 but D only VI/9, a nocturnal forager now established in Levant Sea.

Meagre

Brown Meagre

Corb

Hoefler's
Butterflyfish

Demoiselle

BARRACUDAS (Sphyraenidae)

Elongate, torpedo-like predators, with large jaws and fangs; may attack humans, usually aiming at male genitals. Traditionally linked with grey mullets, but may be more closely related to tunas.

GREAT BARRACUDA *Sphyraena sphyraena*. Ⓐ Preopercle scaled; widely separated short Ds; V below D1 origin, behind vertical off P tip; C forked; LL 125-145; dark above, silvery below, with yellow band along side. 160 cm (a: 38.55 kg). Inshore, midwater, in groups, inquisitive, feeding usually on fish, as well as squid and crustaceans. Tropical Atlantic. Some fisheries. **Yellowmouth Barracuda** *S. viridensis*, Ⓑ 65 cm (a: 8.2 kg), has naked rear edge of preopercle and dark bars on sides above LL; Indo-Pacific **Obtuse Barracuda** *S. chrysotaenia*, Ⓒ 32 cm, V below middle of P, is now established in Levant Sea.

RED MULLETS (Mullidae) and BANDFISH (Cepolidae)

STRIPED RED MULLET *Mullus surmuletus*. Ⓐ Moderately elongate body, with steep snout and 2 long, highly mobile barbels on chin; upper jaw lacking teeth; 2 Ds, well spaced, D1 VII-VIII, D2 I/7-8; LL 33-37; reddish to pink, with 3 yellow stripes along sides; D1 with dark markings. 40 cm. Inshore, typically on coarse grounds, feeding on benthic invertebrates and small fish, using barbels to locate prey by taste-buds. Breeds May-July; eggs planktonic, 0.81-0.91 mm, segmented yolk and 1 oil globule; hatch at 2.8 mm, with yolk sac projecting beyond head. To Senegal. Very similar **Plain Red Mullet** *M. barbatus*, Ⓑ 30 cm, offshore shelf and uppermost slope (100-300 m), on finer grounds, has barbels not longer than P, and is reddish without other markings. *M. s. ponticus*, from the Black Sea, has a shorter mouth, and does not reach back to below eye. **West African Goat-fish** *Pseudopeneus prayensis*, Ⓒ 55 cm, has small spine on upper edge of opercle, more sloping snout, teeth on both jaws, and lateral stripes. Indo-Pacific **Golden Banded Goat-fish** *Upeneus moluccensis*, Ⓓ 25 cm, with teeth in both jaws, no opercular spine, P 16, yellow lateral band and dark markings on upper C, is a Suez Canal immigrant to eastern Mediterranean; *U. asymmetricus*, 14 cm, P 14, with lower C also marked and brown lateral stripe, has also penetrated through the canal into the Mediterranean.

RED BANDFISH *Cepola rubescens*. Very long, tapering body; one long D and A; C distinct; V thoracic as in other seaperches; D II/65-68; A 60; above and sides dark reddish, more yellowish below; D with red blotch. 70 cm. Shelf, burrowing in mud, but may swim above bottom; eats small crustaceans and arrow worms. Breeds spring-autumn (Mediterranean). To Senegal.

Great Barracuda

Striped Red Mullet

Plain Red Mullet

Red Bandfish

Thick-lipped
Grey Mullet
(right)

GREY MULLETS (Mugilidae)

Very common inshore and estuarine fishes, but
species can be difficult to identify and the family is of disputed
systematic position, sometimes classed with sand-smelts. Body silvery, moderately elongate, but broad, cylindrical, with flattened head
and small protractile mouth; no lateral line; D1 and D2 short-based,
widely separated; scales large, over head. May be seen from the shore,
browsing in large groups over rocks and hard substrates, using lips to
rasp off algae, small invertebrates and detritus, which is then digested via a muscular gizzard and long gut. Schools compact, moving near
surface, and grey mullet readily leap, notably over nets. Important
food fishes in Mediterranean and warmer coasts, both by fisheries and
fish culture. Eggs planktonic, usually about 1 mm.

THICK-LIPPED GREY MULLET *Chelon labrosus*. Commonest
species in cooler waters; upper lip prominent, with rows of
papillae along lower part; teeth tiny; adipose eyelid (thick, but
transparent in life) not over pupil; snout longer than upper jaw;
underside of lower jaw with narrow midline space; D1 and D2
short-based, well separated; D1 IV; D2 9-10; A III/8-9; V below rear
part of P; LL 45-46; above dark green to bluish, sides and below
silvery, with dark lines along scales. 90 cm, over 6 kg (a: 3.48 kg). Inshore and
lagoons. Breeds January-April (Biscay), December-March (Mediterranean).
Mature at over 30 cm, 4 yrs. To Senegal .

THIN-LIPPED GREY MULLET *Liza ramada*. As preceding, but
upper lip narrower than pupil diameter and only 1 row of small
teeth along lower edge; scales on upper body with only 1
groove; snout scaled to anterior nostrils; underside of lower
jaw with wide midline space; D2 8-9; A III/8-9; P tip short of D1
origin; black spot at P base. 60 cm (a: 2.38 kg). Often more estuarine habitat
than other mullets. Breeds October-December. Also to West Africa, *L. saliens*,
40 cm, has 2 grooves or more on upper scales; introduced into Caspian Sea.

GOLDEN GREY MULLET *Liza aurata*. Very similar to preceding,
but opercle and cheek with gold patches, and snout scaled only
to rear nostrils. 50 cm, 10 yrs. Breeds July-November (Mediterranean); fecundity to over 2 million eggs. To Senegal; introduced
to Caspian Sea and has penetrated Suez Canal to northern Red
Sea. Conversely, Indo-Pacific **Roving Grey Mullet** *L. carinata*,
30 cm, P tip to below origin of D1, now occurs in Levant Sea.

BOX-LIPPED GREY MULLET *Oedalechilus labeo*. Upper lip wide,
edged with hard processes; A III/11; grey or bluish above, sides
and below silvery; golden lines along sides. 25 cm. Inshore
marine, but not into brackish water (d).

FLAT-HEADED GREY MULLET *Mugil cephalus*. Eye, including
pupil, mostly covered by adipose eyelid; preorbital shorter
than upper jaw; large P axillary scale and dark blotch; A III/8; LL
36-45. 100 cm. Wide tolerance of salinity, from fully marine to
fresh water. Breeds July-October (Mediterranean). Farmed.
Similar Atlantic **Narrow-headed Grey Mullet** *M. capurii*, 45 cm, has A III/9.

Thick-lipped Grey Mullet

Thin-lipped Grey Mullet

head underside

Thick-lipped Grey Mullet (right)

Thin-lipped Grey Mullet

Golden Grey Mullet

Box-lipped Grey Mullet

Flat-headed Grey Mullet

WRASSES (Labridae)

Usually oblong, compressed bodies; prominent lips on protrusible mouth; jaw teeth conical, but molar-like teeth in pharynx; 1 D; C truncate to rounded. Inshore, usually on coarser grounds, feeding mostly on molluscs and crustaceans; active during day but sleep at night, often on side. Many hermaphroditic, females changing into males; eggs typically demersal. Some species are trapped for use in salmon farming as 'cleaners' to remove sea-lice from the salmon. The many species are often distinguishable by colour, but as this can be variable; counts of fin-rays and scales can confirm identification.

CUCKOO WRASSE *Labrus mixtus.* Slender body, long-snouted; females and immature males yellowish to red, with 3 dark blotches, edged white, on rear D base and C wrist; males with bluish head, body and fins yellowish with blue markings; jaws with 1 row of canines; scales behind eye 7-8; D XVI-XIX/11-14; A III/9-12; LL 45-48. 35 cm, 17 yrs. Shelf, over rocks and rough ground, feeding mostly on crustaceans; females may 'clean' other fish. Breeds May-July, eggs in nest on gravel made by both parents; mature at 16 cm, 2 yrs (f), 24 cm, 6-9 yrs (m) after sex change. To Senegal.

BROWN WRASSE *Labrus merula.* Both sexes dark blue, to green or brown; juveniles green, with paler spots or lateral band; scales behind eye 5-7; LL 40-48; D XVII-XIX/11-14; A III/8-12. 45 cm. Inshore rocks, feeding on invertebrates. Breeds February-May (western Mediterranean).

GREEN WRASSE *Labrus viridis.* As preceding, but head longer than depth of body; both sexes green, paler below, often with white band along side to C. 47 cm. Inshore, over rocks or seagrass. Breeds February to June (western Mediterranean).

BALLAN WRASSE *Labrus bergylta.* Stout, larger wrasse, often caught by anglers; both sexes variable in colour, often green or brownish with many small white spots, sometimes dark bars or lateral white band; short-based soft dorsal, D XVIII-XXI/9-13; A III/8-12; LL 41-47, scales behind eye 4-6. 60 cm (a: 4.35 kg). Inshore over rocks and weed, feeding on molluscs and other invertebrates; juveniles may clean other species. Breeds April-August; eggs in nest of weed bound by mucus threads on rocks or gravel, built by female, size about 39×17 cm; eggs typically 1.0 mm; hatch at 3.8 mm; mature at 6-9 yrs, 16-18 cm (f), 28 cm (m), after sex change.

Cuckoo Wrasse
male

Cuckoo Wrasse
female

Brown Wrasse

Green Wrasse

Ballan Wrasse

ROCK COOK *Centrolabrus exoletus.* Ⓐ Head and mouth small, with small conical teeth in single row; typically greenish-brown, paler below, with blue flecks, and lower head striped blue, yellow and pink; C with 2 dark and pale vertical bars; D XVIII-XX/5-7; A IV-V/6-8; LL 33-37. 15 cm, 8 yrs. Inshore weed beds and over rocks. Breeds May-July. Also to south-eastern Greenland. **Trout Wrasse** *C. trutta,* Ⓑ 16 cm, has D XV-XVII/8-9, and dark midline spot on C base. Rock Cook and following 2 species now fished for use as 'cleaners' of fish-lice from farmed salmon.

GOLDSINNY *Ctenolabrus rupestris.* Brown to orange-red, dark blotch on first rays of D and another, smaller but intense spot on upper C wrist just before C base; small teeth in several rows; D XVI-XIX/7-10; A III/6-9; LL 35-39, 3-4 scales behind eye. 18 cm, 15 yrs. Inshore rocky areas. Midwater spawning, April-August (British Isles), January-July (Mediterranean); eggs planktonic, 0.72-1.01 mm, yolk unsegmented and lacking oil globule. Off-shore *Lappanella fasciata,* 14 cm, more elongate, with 2 rows of teeth, also red-dish with dark spot on upper C wrist, has dark spot on rear half of D and another on C near edge; A III/8-11.

CORKWING WRASSE *Crenilabrus melops.* Oval body outline; coloration variable, mottled green or greeny-brown, often with blue and orange lines on lower head and belly; dark curved blotch behind eye and dark spot before C base, just below LL; mouth with single row of small teeth; LL 31-37, 1 scale behind eye, interorbit naked, opercle more or less scaled, 4½-5½ rows between LL and D base. 28 cm, 9 yrs. Inshore weedbeds and intertidal rock pools, feeding chiefly on molluscs. Breeds May-July (British Isles), March-June (western Mediterranean); nests of algae in intertidal crevices; eggs 0.7-0.85 mm, hatch at 2.5-3.0 mm; mature at 10 cm, 2-3 yrs (f).

PEACOCK WRASSE *Crenilabrus tinca.* Similar C spot to Cork-wing Wrasse, but longer snout, dark stripe from eye to upper lip, and dark blotch above P; females and juveniles brownish, with bands along sides; males green to bluish or yellowish, with rows of blue-red dots along sides, and upper head dark bluish. 35 cm. Inshore sea-grass beds and rocks, feeding on invertebrates. Breeds March-July (western Mediterranean).

BAILLON'S WRASSE *Crenilabrus bailloni.* Ⓐ Spot below C midline somewhat larger, and dark spot in middle of D (XIV-XV); P base with curved blue mark; young and females brownish, with 3 darker bands along sides; males green to reddish, head striped orange; opercle scaled. 22 cm. Inshore, on rocks and sea-grass. To Mauritania. *Lappanella fasciata,* Ⓑ 14 cm, from deep rocky areas, has similar dorsal spot but D XVI-XVIII, front and rear canine teeth, and dark spot on upper edge of C peduncle.

AXILLARY WRASSE *Crenilabrus mediterraneus.* C wrist with dark blotch mostly above LL, and prominent dark mark on P base; females and young brownish, mottled; males reddish-brown to blue, with lines of pale to bluish dots along upper body and blue or greenish stripes on head. 18 cm. Inshore, in sea-grass mead-ows. Breeds May-August (north-west Mediterranean).

BLACK-TAILED WRASSE *Crenilabrus melanocercus.* Very small-mouthed wrasse immediately recognized by black C, with yellow line across base and paler distal edge; young and females pinky-brown to yellow, males with blue and brown markings, and blue dots on upper body. 14 cm. Inshore, on rocks and sea-grass, feeding on invertebrates and also clean-ing. Breeds April-July (western Mediterranean), but no nest.

Rock Cook

Goldsinny

Corkwing Wrasse

Peacock Wrasse

Baillon's Wrasse

Axillary Wrasse

Black-tailed Wrasse

OCELLATED WRASSE *Crenilabrus ocellatus*. Another form with a small, dark C base spot just below LL; large spot on scale-less rear corner of opercle edged red; females and young yellow-brown, often with 2 brown stripes from snout along side; males orange to green, with greeny or bluish highlights. 12 cm. Inshore rocks and sea-grass, feeding on invertebrates. Breeds May-July (north-western Mediterranean), building nest.

DODERLEIN'S WRASSE *Crenilabrus doderleini*. Small dark spot above LL on C base; reddish to brown body with broad lateral dark band above white band. 10 cm. Inshore sea-grass meadows. Breeds May-July (north-western Mediterranean).

A ▪
B ▪

GREY WRASSE *Crenilabrus cinereus*. Ⓐ Large dark spot on C wrist below LL, and dark spot on first D rays; otherwise variable, grey, reddish, greenish. 15 cm. Inshore and estuaries, in silty areas with sea-grass, feeding on invertebrates. Breeds March-April (north-western Mediterranean). In Mediterranean, *C. c. cinereus* has many (25) snout pores; and Black Sea and French Mediterranean *C. c. staitii* has fewer than 10 snout pores. Another wrasse with a dark spot on first D rays, West African **Pejeperro** *Pseudolepidaplois scrofa*, Ⓑ 65 cm, has no C spot, large canines with fused bases, LL 45, 7 scales behind eye, pinkish to purple coloration with abdominal dark bar, and reaches Madeira.

FIVE-SPOTTED WRASSE *Crenilabrus roissali*. Mottled, green to brown, more or less barred; usually C base with small dark midline spot and D with about 5 dark areas; males have orange-pink lips; opercle with darker scaleless area. 17 cm. Sublittoral, on weed and rocks. Breeds April-July (north-western Mediterranean).

LONG-NOSED WRASSE *Symphodus rostratus*. Body somewhat slim, and snout long, total head length exceeding body depth; green to reddish-brown, with pale band along head and body. 13 cm. Inshore, on sea-grass meadows and rocky ground. Breeds March-July (north-western Mediterranean).

SCALE-RAYED WRASSE *Acantholabrus palloni*. Somewhat elongate; coloration variable, brown, greenish or reddish-brown, dark spot before upper end of C base, sometimes another on D at junction of spinous and soft parts; mouth with 2 rows of conical teeth; LL 39-45, 3-5 scales behind eye, interorbit scaled, and scales onto D, A and C; D XIX-XXI/7-10; A IV-VI/5-8. 25 cm. Shelf, over rocks and sand, more offshore in Mediterranean. To West Africa.

Scale-rayed
Wrasse

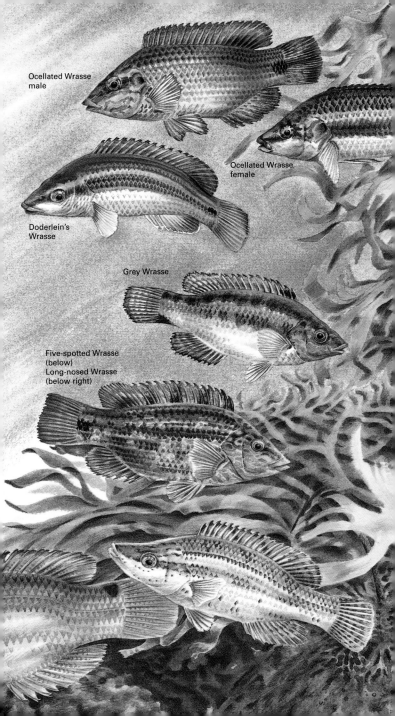

Ocellated Wrasse male

Ocellated Wrasse female

Doderlein's Wrasse

Grey Wrasse

Five-spotted Wrasse (below)
Long-nosed Wrasse (below right)

A
B

SEA-PEACOCK *Thalassoma pavo*. Ⓐ Compressed, uniform body depth; young and females greenish-brown, with 5 vertical bluish bars and many narrow dark lines, and dark blotch on middle of D base; males brighter, with red-edged blue band behind P; 1 row of narrow conical teeth; larger males with elongate C tips; D VIII/12-13; LL 26-31. 25 cm. Inshore, on rocky ground and sea-grass. Breeds June-July (southern Mediterranean). Another wrasse with elongate C tips in larger fish, tropical Atlantic *Bodianus speciosus*, Ⓑ 50 cm, D XI-XIV/10, LL 35-50, reddish, with broad dark bar below middle of D and black upper and lower C rays, reaches Morocco and Madeira.

RAINBOW WRASSE *Coris julis*. Long, slender, often colourful wrasse; immature and females with whitish band from snout to C and pale dots above LL; males with broad orange or rosy zigzagged band against pale green to blue sides, and dark horizontal bar below anterior end; D first few rays also elongate, with reddish-orange and black markings; usually 2 rows of canine teeth; D VIII-X/11-12; A III/11-12; scales tiny, LL 73-80. 25 cm. Inshore rocky areas and weed beds, feeding on invertebrates; young sometimes clean other fish. Some females change into males; breeds April-August (Mediterranean), eggs planktonic. To West Africa.

CLEAVER WRASSE *Xyrichthys novacula*. Head and body deep, compressed; snout very steep; young and females reddish to brown, with many vertical blue lines on head and body; males red or green above, bright pinkish-green below; mouth with stout canine teeth; D IX-X/11-12; A III/11-13; C truncated; LL 24-29, interrupted opposite rear end of D; most of head naked. 30 cm. Inshore on sand or mud and sea-grass, and can bury themselves in substrate; feed on small invertebrates. Midwater spawning in July-August (Mediterranean); eggs planktonic, hatching in a day at 1.6 mm. Mature at to 14 cm (f), and from 12 cm after sex change (m). Also tropical Atlantic.

Cleaver Wrasse
female

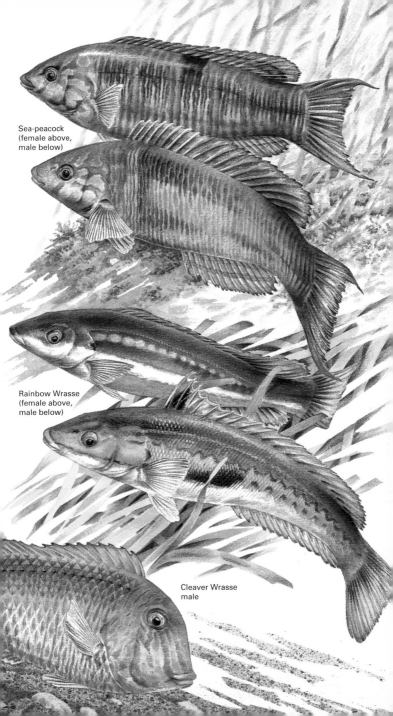

Sea-peacock
(female above,
male below)

Rainbow Wrasse
(female above,
male below)

Cleaver Wrasse
male

PARROT FISHES TO PONY FISHES (Tropical Families)

PARROT FISH *Sparisoma cretense* (**Scaridae**). Deep, compressed, robust body; reddish (females) to brownish (males), with lines of white dots along sides, females also with dark blotch about rear corner of opercle and yellow spot on upper C wrist; jaws with tooth-plates, edges indented in young; 1 D, VIII-IX/10; A III/9; LL interrupted on rear body, 18-19/5-7, scales large and cycloid; C convex. 50 cm. Inshore, over rocky and sandy areas, feeding chiefly on coralline algae, bitten off and milled by strong tooth-plates in pharynx. Breeds August-October (central Mediterranean).

MONROVIAN SURGEON-FISH *Acanthurus monroviae* (**Acanthuridae**). Body oval, deep, compressed; mouth small, with incisor-like teeth; 1 D, IX/24-27; LL about 130; tail wrist with retractile bony lancet on each side; C concave; brown, with pale area around lancet. 42 cm. Inshore, browsing on algae and other sessile organisms. From West Africa.

Dusky Rabbit-fish

A
B

DUSKY RABBIT-FISH *Siganus luridus* (**Siganidae**). Ⓐ Oval compressed body; mouth small, with single row of incisor-like teeth; small spine over eye; 1 D, XIV/10, first spine small, horizontal, pointing forwards; C slightly concave; greenish to brown, C barred. 30 cm. Inshore, in small schools, usually feeding on red algae. Breeds June-August. Indian Ocean and Red Sea migrant through Suez Canal, now well established in eastern Mediterranean. Mild ciguatoxicity reported, and fin spines (with poison glands) may inflict painful wounds; cultivated and local fisheries. **Marbled Rabbit-Fish** *S. rivulatus*, Ⓑ 40 cm, with dark spots and wavy golden lines on sides, C forked and no spine over eye, is another Red Sea colonist in the same area.

Parrot Fish

Pony Fish

PONY FISH *Leiognathus klunzingeri* (**Leiognathidae**). Deep, laterally compressed, with somewhat rugged head, downwardly protrusible mouth and slimy skin; single D and A with high anterior tips; D VII/15-16, A III/15-16, spinous rays lockable; C forked; scales cycloid; greyish above, sides with pink areas, silvery below; D and A bases dark-edged. 11 cm. Inshore schools, feeding on benthic invertebrates. Red Sea immigrant via Suez Canal, now well established in southern Mediterranean.

217

WEEVERS (Trachinidae)

Wedge-like fishes with poison glands along the spines of the short-based black D1 and along a spine at the upper corner of the opercle. Weevers bury themselves up to their eyes in sand, and use poison spines for defence, spreading D1 and opercles when handled. They are often taken by shrimpers and may be trodden underfoot when paddling in sandy shallows. The poison causes localized swelling and discomfort, rarely death in humans. Eggs and larval stages planktonic.

LESSER WEEVER *Echiichthys vipera.* Commonest weever of temperate Atlantic; upper rim of eye socket lacking spines; P rounded; C truncated; D2 21-24; LL about 60; sandy to light brown above, sometimes with thin dark lines along sides; paler below. 15 cm. Inshore sand, feeding chiefly on crustaceans and fish. Breeds June-August; eggs 1.0-1.37 mm, unsegmented yolk and 6-30 oil globules; hatch at 3.27 mm. Also to Azores.

GREATER WEEVER *Trachinus draco.* Larger species, upper rim of eye socket with 2 small spines; P with more angular outline; C more or less slightly concave rear edge; body depth at least 5.5 times in SL; D2 29-32; LL about 80; above greenish-brown, sides paler, with blue and yellow oblique lines. 40 cm (a: 1.67 kg). More offshore in northern waters (30-100 m). Breeds June-August; eggs 0.96-1.11 mm, with single oil globule.

Lesser Weever

Greater Weever

SPOTTED WEEVER *Trachinus araneus.* As preceding, but deeper-bodied (depth more than one-fifth SL) and sides with dark blotches; D2 26-29; LL 75-80. 40 cm. Also to West Africa.

STREAKED WEEVER *Trachinus radiatus.* Also deep-bodied, but sides with numerous short, dark, curved or ring-like markings; D2 24-27; LL about 70. 42 cm. To West Africa.

STARGAZER *Uranoscopus scaber* (**Uranoscopidae**). So called because of the broad head with upturned eyes. Moderately elongate body, stout anteriorly; strong spine above P, equipped with poison glands; mouth very oblique, with tentacle protruded from inside tip of lower jaw; 2 D, D1 short, III-IV, D2 13-15; LL 76-90; above brownish, with darker spots, paler below; D1 black; mouth tentacle grey. 35 cm (a: 0.94 kg). Shelf and upper slope, burying to the eyes in sand and mud; feeds mostly on fish, these probably lured by worm-like mouth tentacle and then stunned by shock from electric organ behind each eye. Breeds April-August, eggs planktonic.

Spotted Weever

Streaked Weever

Stargazer

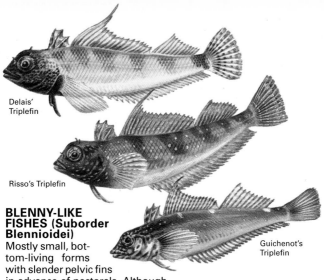

Delais' Triplefin

Risso's Triplefin

Guichenot's Triplefin

BLENNY-LIKE FISHES (Suborder Blennioidei)

Mostly small, bottom-living forms with slender pelvic fins in advance of pectorals. Although included here, Yarrell's Blenny, Gunnel and wolf-fishes may be classed with eelpouts and Viviparous Blenny (*see* page 136).

A ▨
B ▨
C ▨

DELAIS' TRIPLEFIN *Tripterygion delaisi* (**Tripterygiidae**). Ⓐ Unusual in having 3 Ds, contiguous, D1 III, D2 XVI-XVIII, with first rays elongated in males; D3 11-14; elongate, tapering body, scaled, with steep snout and large eye; A long, II/24-28; V 3, origin anterior to P; greyish with wide dark bars, darkest on tail wrist and C base; males in territories yellowish, with black head. 9 cm. Inshore, on rocky ground, typically in shaded situations but also more open areas, in 3-10 m. Breeds April-July (Mediterranean), with demersal eggs guarded by male. Two subspecies, Atlantic *T. d. delaisi* (courtship in midwater) and Mediterranean *T. d. xanthosoma* (courtship on substrate). Also **Risso's Triplefin** *T. tripteronotus*, Ⓑ 8 cm, with dark tail wrist bar not extending onto C base, and territorial males reddish; and **Guichenot's Triplefin** *T. melanurus*, Ⓒ 5.5 cm, always red and head finely mottled dark in non-territorial individuals.

A ▨
B ■

SILVER KLIPFISH *Clinitrachus argentatus* (**Clinidae**). Ⓐ Small, elongated, scaled body; 1 long D, deeply notched after first 3 rays, XXVIII-XXXI/3-4; V 1-2 long rays, origin before P; C rounded; green to brown, with alternate silvery and dark irregular lateral bars. 10 cm. Inshore shallows, benthic, among seaweed, feeding on invertebrates. Breeds April-June, eggs demersal, in clump with cavity occupied by guarding male. Another clinid recorded from Europe is a single specimen of the West Indian **Eelgrass Blenny** *Stathmonotus stahli*, Ⓑ to 3.8 cm, with 8 fleshy flaps on head, found in the gullet of a Fifteen-Spined Stickleback in the Conwy estuary, North Wales.

Silver Klipfish

BLENNIES (Blenniidae)

Small benthic fishes, typically of rocky shores, with prominent steep foreheads and tapering scaleless bodies; 1 long D; V origin before P, of a few long rays and used in moving over substrate. Territories are zealously guarded, often centring on a piddock hole bored in rock. Blennies have powerful jaw muscles and larger individuals can bite off whole barnacles from rock surfaces, smaller fish merely browsing on barnacle legs (and barnacle penises). Eggs demersal, in clump guarded by male.

MONTAGU'S BLENNY *Coryphoblennius galerita.* Nape with broad-based transverse triangular flap, fringed with tiny filaments; lower jaw with lateral canine tooth; gill membranes linked by transverse fold across underside; D XIII/16-17; brownish-green with bluish-white spots, especially in male, and with orange head flap. 8 cm. Intertidal rocks, typically in pools near high water, sometimes emerse at night; feeds on invertebrates and algae. Breeds May-August. To West Africa.

BUTTERFLY BLENNY *Blennius ocellaris.* Paired tentacles above eye, and tentacle on nostril and side of nape; anterior part of D much higher than rest, with conspicuous white-edged dark bluish spot; gill membranes not united by transverse fold across underside; D XI/14-15; brownish, with several dark, somewhat irregular dark bars. 20 cm. Shelf, on coarse grounds, but not intertidal. Breeds April-July, eggs in layer within mollusc shells and other hollow objects (once recorded inside the femur from an ox); eggs 1.12-1.20 mm, pink to brown; hatch at about 4.0 mm.

Montagu's Blenny

Butterfly Blenny

Tompot Blenny

TOMPOT BLENNY *Parablennius gattorugine.* A Largest European blenny. Paired branched tentacles above eyes; also tentacle on nostril; lower jaw with canines; gill membranes linked by transverse fold across underside; D XIII/18-19, edge only slightly concave in middle; P 14; brownish or green with several dark bars. 30 cm. Inshore rock faces and coarse substrates, sometimes intertidal at LWST on Atlantic coasts. Breeds May-July (western Ireland); eggs 1.6 mm; hatch at 4.9 mm. Similarly banded Atlantic **Red Tompot** *P. ruber,* B 9 cm, has branched rear LL, dark spot between first D rays, and more bushy eye tentacle.

HORNED BLENNY *Parablennius tentacularis.* D XII/20-21, outline only concave in middle; eye tentacles slender with rear protuberances, long in males; nape lacking small tentacles; both jaws with canine teeth; P 14; brownish, with several bars and dark spot on first rays of D. 16 cm. Inshore, on rocks with sand. Breeds March-July. To Senegal.

RED-SPECKLED BLENNY *Parablennius sanguinolentus.* As preceding, but P 13; greyish-blue, with dark dots in patches and oblique streaks; breeding males brown to purplish. 20 cm. Shallows, among weed-covered rocks, to 5 m, feeding chiefly on algae. Breeds May-July.

HAIRY-HORNED BLENNY *Parablennius pilicornis.* As preceding, D XII/21, but eye tentacles are a bunch of short filaments; P 14; greenish, with dark brown spots and mottling. 11 cm. Inshore, typically on rock faces under wave action, to 15 m. Tropical Atlantic.

ZVONIMIR'S BLENNY *Parablennius zvonimiri.* A D XII/18, its outline deeply indented; P 14; nape with small filaments; brown, with several white or yellowish spots along base of D, and dark blotch at C origin. 8 cm. Inshore, to about 5 m, in shady conditions, feeding on epiphytic plant material. Breeds May-July. Also with many small filaments on nape is *Scartella cristata,* B 10 cm, no canine teeth in upper jaw, inhabiting surf zone on rocky shores. *Petroscirtes ancylodon,* with nape filaments, is a Suez immigrant to eastern Mediterranean.

MYSTERY BLENNY *Parablennius incognitus.* As preceding, but D XII/17, and nape lacking filaments; greenish, with several bars, typically doubled or bifid. 7 cm. Inshore, among seaweed on rock faces, feeding on amphipods and weed. Breeds May-August.

Horned
Blenny

Red-speckled
Blenny

Hairy-horned
Blenny

Zvonimir's
Blenny

STRIPED BLENNY *Parablennius rouxi.* D XII/21-22, its outline virtually straight; both jaws with canines; P 14; pale with dark brown stripe from eye to C base; breeding males have longer, orange eye tentacles and greenish spot on first rays of D. 8 cm. Inshore, on rocky and coralline bottoms, to about 40 m, feeding on small crustaceans and epiphytic algae. Breeds May-July.

SPHINX BLENNY *Aidablennius sphinx.* D XII/16, anterior rays higher in males and outline notched in middle; eye tentacle long, branched at tip, orange in breeding male; gill membranes linked by transverse fold across underside; P 14; greyish to brownish-green with several olive-green bars, edged pale blue; blue spot, edged red, behind eye. 8 cm. Shallows, on exposed and weed-grown rock platforms, feeding on invertebrates and seaweed. Breeds April-July.

SHANNY *Lipophrys pholis.* The common blenny of temperate Atlantic rocky shores, often found out of water at low tide. No eye tentacles; nostril with many short tentacles; D XII/18-19, moderately notched; gill membranes linked by transverse fold across underside of head; P 13; olive to brownish-green, with several dark bars; dark spot between first 2 rays of D; breeding males almost black with white upper lip and D rays. 16 cm, 10 yrs. Inshore on rock faces and intertidal region, in higher pools and crevices, especially on exposed shores, feeding on barnacles and other invertebrates, and on green seaweed. Breeds April-August; eggs in layer under stones or in crevices, 1.18-1.6 mm, hatch at 4.0-5.0 mm; young in pools with large dark Ps. At Madeira as much larger *L. bufo*, 30 cm.

PEACOCK BLENNY *Lipophrys pavo.* A more colourful shanny, but minute eye tentacle and median convex crest on nape and interorbit; D XII/22, not notched; P 14; olive-green, with pale blue lines and spots; blue-edged dark spot behind eye; breeding male dark, with orange crest. 14 cm. Inshore and intertidal, in crevices on boulders and rock faces; also in brackish water on soft substrates. Breeds May-July. Present in Suez Canal.

FRESHWATER BLENNY *Lipophrys fluviatilis.* The only blenny in European fresh waters. As preceding, but D XII/17-18, tiny eye tentacle present, simple or tufted, and no blue-edged spot behind eye. 15 cm. In rivers and lakes, on stones as well as muddy bottoms with weed; feeds on insect larvae, fish eggs and fry. Spawns March-August; eggs under stone.

Freshwater Blenny

224

Striped Blenny

Sphinx Blenny

Shanny

Peacock Blenny
(male above and
female right)

Black-headed
Blenny

BASILISK BLENNY *Lipophrys basiliscus.* Also with nape crest and straight D edge, but no eye tentacles and nostril lacking processes; D XII/24-25; olive to paler green, with close-set dark bars delimited by pale blue lines. 20 cm. Inshore, among sea-grass. Some females may become male.

BLACK-HEADED BLENNY *Lipophrys nigriceps.* No eye tentacles or head crest, and nostril tentacles few in number; D XII/15; P 12; red with white dots; head pale with red spots; breeding males have dark nape and yellowish cheeks. 4.5 cm. Sublittoral, to 6 m, in shady overhangs and grottoes, often with similarly coloured Triplefin *T. melanurus* (distinguishable by 3 Ds); feeds on small invertebrates and weed. Breeds May-June.

ADRIATIC BLENNY *Lipophrys adriaticus.* As preceding, but D with shallow notch, dark banding, confluent to produce several large pale blotches along upper body; below white or yellowish; dark spot on first rays of D. 5 cm. Shallows, on sheltered rock faces. Breeds May-June; eggs in narrow crevices.

CANEVA'S BLENNY *Lipophrys canevae.* D XIII/15, with obvious notch at middle; no eye tentacles; nostril with only a few small processes; P 12; brown with white reticulation and streaks; breeding males dark, especially top of head, with sides of head yellow to reddish. 8 cm. Inshore rock faces, to about 2 m, feeding especially on algae. Breeds April-August. *L. sabry*, D XIII/17, 6 dark bands across back, is known from Benghazi.

DALMATIAN BLENNY *Lipophrys dalmatinus.* As preceding, but D XII/16, only slightly notched; pale green, with several dark bars, becoming broken towards C; breeding males yellowish with dark nape. 4 cm. Inshore, among filamentous algae on rock platforms, to about 2 m, and into brackish water. Breeds May-July.

GURNARD BLENNY *Lipophrys trigloides.* D XII/16-17, outline notched in middle; nostril with numerous small tentacles, but no nape crest or eye tentacles; head with numerous pores; P 13; greenish to grey, with several dark bars, males becoming dark brown. 13 cm. Inshore, somewhat lethargic, in rock crevices at surf level. Breeds February to May. To Senegal.

BANANA BLENNY *Hypleurochilus bananensis.* Prominent tufted eye and nostril tentacles; nape warty but no crest; both jaws with prominent canine tooth; gill membranes not linked across underside; D XII/15, with notch in middle; brown with several dark bars. 8 cm. Inshore. Also West Africa.

226

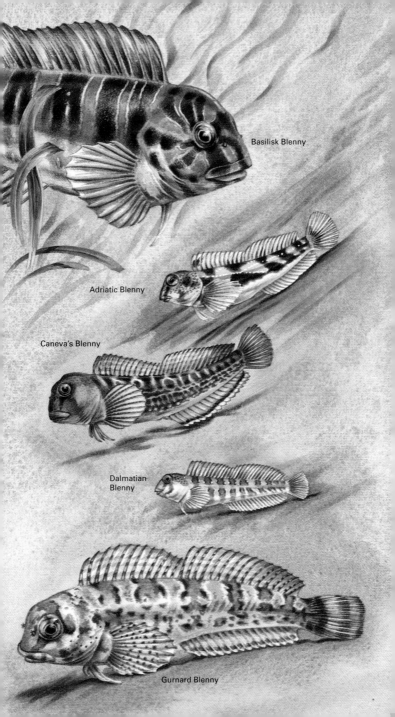

Basilisk Blenny

Adriatic Blenny

Caneva's Blenny

Dalmatian Blenny

Gurnard Blenny

Snake Blenny

Yarrell's
Blenny

YARRELL'S BLENNY *Chirolophis ascanii* (**Stichaeidae**). Elongate compressed body, with tiny scales; head with fringed tentacle above eye and other smaller processes; 1 long D, L-LIV, all rays spinous, and first ray with skin tentacle; V small, shorter than D height; brown to reddish, with dark bars or blotches. 25 cm. Shelf (to at least 175 m), on coarse ground and among algae, rarely in lower intertidal zone; feeds on molluscs, worms, and sessile organisms. Breeds October-December (North Sea); eggs pale, 2.3-2.8 mm, in flattened clump under stones; hatch at about 10 mm, in 5-6 weeks at 10-12°C. Also western Atlantic (Newfoundland).

A ▮
B ▨

SNAKE BLENNY *Lumpenus lampretaeformis* (**Lumpenidae**). Ⓐ Eel-like but a blenny; head without skin tentacles or processes; 1 long D, LXVIII-LXXVI, all rays spinous and first 2 free from fin membrane; P lower rays shorter than upper; V slender, as long as D height; yellowish-brown, with darker blotches or oblique bars. 49 cm, over 4 yrs. Shelf, on soft substrates and perhaps burrows; eats small crustaceans, molluscs and starfish. Breeds December-January. Also western Atlantic to New England. **Spotted Snake Blenny** *Leptoclinus maculatus*, Ⓑ 20 cm, of polar seas at 100-300 m, has lower P rays longer than upper, somewhat stouter body and truncate C.

GUNNEL *Pholis gunnellus* (**Pholidae**). Common on cold-temperate rocky shores; elongate, with small rounded C and minute V; 1 long D, LXXV-LXXXII, all spinous; reddish-brown, with usually about a dozen small, white-edged black spots along D base; below yellowish-orange; body often dotted with tiny black specks, an encysted stage of a parasitic trematode worm whose final host is a seabird. 25 cm. Inshore (to 40 m) and intertidal, under stones and flapping vigorously when disturbed; eats small invertebrates (mainly worms and crustaceans) and fish eggs. Breeds November-March (North Sea); eggs 1.71-2.17 mm, under stones, in ball-like clumps, embraced by either parent; hatch at 8.96-9.0 mm. Also western Atlantic.

Spotted
Snake Blenny

Gunnel

WOLF-FISHES (Anarhichadidae)
Also termed cat-fishes, but more like giant blennies; canine and molar teeth large, used to crush molluscs, crabs and sea-urchins.

WOLF-FISH *Anarhichas lupus.* Ⓐ Commonest wolf-fish in temperate waters; D 69-79; yellowish to greyish, with thin dark bars. 125 cm (a: 23.58 kg). Offshore, usually 100-300 m. Breeds December-February, with large yellowish eggs (5.5-6.0 mm) in balls. Also western Atlantic. Two more northerly species are: **Spotted Cat** *A. minor,* Ⓑ 144 cm (a: 23.35 kg), many distinct dark brown spots over body and D; and **Jelly Cat** *A. denticulatus,* Ⓒ 138 cm (a: 17 kg), uniform dark or with indistinct blotches, may occur in midwater.

Wolf-fish

Spotted Cat

SANDEELS (Ammodytidae)
Small, very elongate silvery fishes with protruding pointed chin, 1 long D, no V and forked C; form large schools that swim rapidly in midwater but suddenly dive down into sand or fine gravel. Eggs demersal, with papillose capsule, on substrate, but young planktonic. Important intermediaries in marine food webs, feeding mostly on plankton, and in turn eaten by larger fish and seabirds, especially puffins. Sandeel stocks are now depleted by North Sea industrial fisheries.

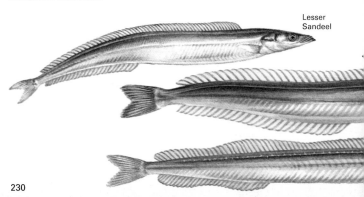

Lesser Sandeel

A
B

LESSER SANDEEL *Ammodytes tobianus*. Ⓐ Most commonly encountered in shallows, and may be dug out of sand at low water. Upper jaw protrusible; palate lacking teeth in midline; scales on belly in regular oblique rows; base of C lobes with small areas of scales; D 49-58; body with numerous oblique skin ridges. 20 cm, 7 yrs. Inshore. Breeds February-April and September-November; eggs about 0.75 mm, pale yellow with large oil globule; sexually mature at 1-2 yrs, above 8 cm. Very similar **Raitt's Sandeel** *A. marinus*, Ⓑ 25 cm, 9 yrs, has D 56-63, belly scales more randomly arranged, and no scales on base of each C lobe; typically offshore and breeds November-February; eggs 0.87-1.2 mm. Main species of industrial fishery.

A
B

GREATER SANDEEL *Hyperoplus lanceolatus*. Ⓐ Upper jaw not protrusible; single bifid tooth-like structure at front of palate; belly scales regular; D 53-60; body with skin ridges; dark spot on side of snout; above greenish, especially in young. 40 cm. Inshore, to about 60 m, feeding on plankton and small fish. Breeds March-August. Also with non-protrusible upper jaw, **Corbin's Sandeel** *H. immaculatus*, Ⓑ 35 cm, lacks obvious snout spot but has dark chin, D 59-62, and is darker; more offshore.

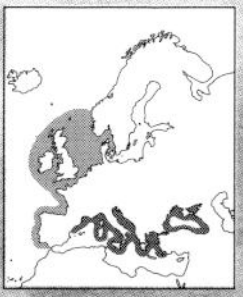

A
B

SMOOTH SANDEEL *Gymnammodytes semisquamatus*. Ⓐ No skin ridges and scales only on rear part of body; no teeth on palate; D and A with wavy outline; LL canal with short side branches, especially below; longitudinal fold below P ends opposite P tip. 28 cm. Over shell-gravel, typically offshore. Breeds March-September. **Mediterranean Smooth Sandeel** *G. cicerellus*, Ⓑ 17 cm, has longer fold under P, extending beyond tip of fin.

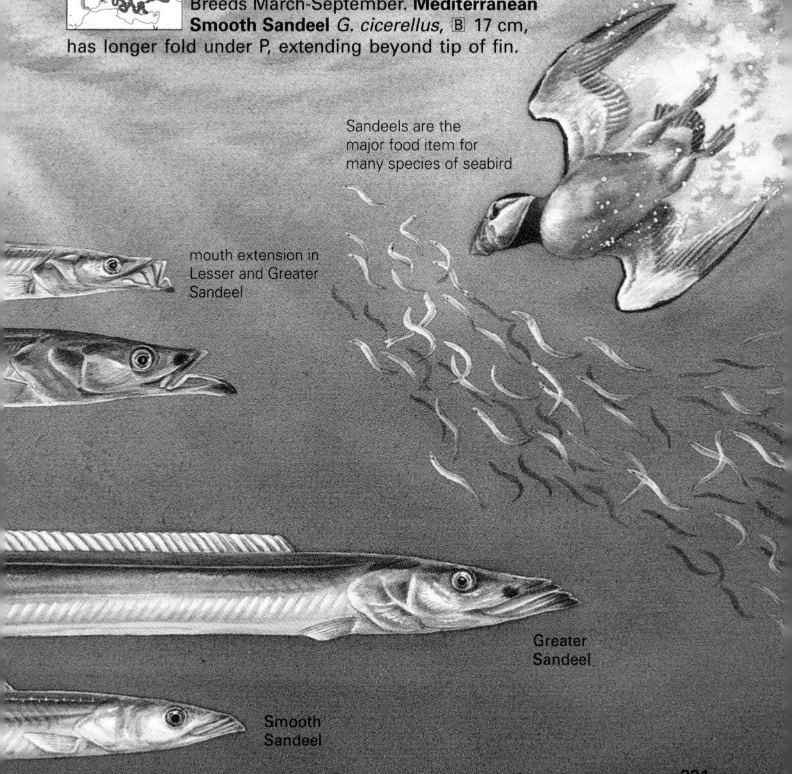

Sandeels are the major food item for many species of seabird

mouth extension in Lesser and Greater Sandeel

Greater Sandeel

Smooth Sandeel

GOBIES (Gobiidae)

In temperate and warmer areas, gobies and their relatives (**suborder Gobioidei**) are the most numerous in species of any group of higher teleost fishes. Typically small, bottom-living, with cylindrical body and head, and round cheeks; 2 Ds; Vs usually fused in simple round or oval sucker, with transverse anterior membrane; no body lateral-line canal. Eggs pear-shaped, with attachment filaments at one end, demersal, in patch on underside of hard substrate, guarded by male. Smaller species are often very abundant, and reputedly difficult to identify. Important characteristics for grouping gobies are the patterns of sensory papillae rows on the head and the extent of head lateral-line canals. For species identification, adult coloration is often useful, as are meristic features, such as the vertebral counts given below (these include the urostyle).

Gobies with transverse cheek rows but no longitudinal series around lower border of eye:

BLACK GOBY *Gobius niger.* D1 VI, rays elongated; nape scaled to varying extent; upper opercle with scales but cheek naked; D2 I/12-13 (11-13); LL 35-41 (32-42); vertebrae 28 (27-29); P with uppermost rays free from membrane; pale brown with lateral blotches, males darker; D1 and D2 with dark spot in upper anterior corner. 15 cm, 5 yrs. Inshore, on sand or mud, and seagrass, into estuaries and lagoons; feeds on benthic invertebrates and small fish. Breeds April-May (Channel), May-August (Baltic), March-May (Naples); fecundity to 2,000; eggs spindle-shaped, with blunt apex; 1.5 × 0.45 mm, under stones and shells. To Mauritania, and through Suez Canal. **Roule's Goby** *G. roulei*, 8 cm, lacks nape scales.

A
B

ROCK GOBY *Gobius paganellus.* Ⓐ Nape completely scaled, cheek sometimes scaled in upper rear corner; anterior nostril with branched tentacle; P free rays well developed; LL 50-55 (46-59); D2 I/13-14 (12-15); fawn with mottling and blotches, to deep purply-brown in breeding male; D1 upper edge white to orange. 12 cm, 10 yrs. Inshore rocks and rock pools on sheltered, weedy shores. Breeds April-June (Isle of Man), January-June (Naples); fecundity to 9,000; eggs 2.2-2.6 mm (1.84-3.0 mm) long, in patches under stones and other objects; hatch at 3.6-4.8 mm; sexually mature at 2-3 yrs. To Senegal, and reported from Gulf of Aqaba, Red Sea, perhaps as Suez Canal migrant. Similar **Bellotti's Goby** *G. ater*, Ⓑ 7.1 cm, has LL 38-40.

GIANT GOBY *Gobius cobitis.* At 27 cm (10 yrs), the largest Mediterranean-Atlantic goby. Anterior nostril with tentacle, more or less divided; pelvic-disc anterior membrane with large lateral lobes; LL 59-67; D2 I/13-14; free P rays present; brownish-olive 'pepper and salt', with dark blotches below lateral midline above A, especially in small fish; breeding males dark, Ds, A and C edged white. Inshore, to about 10 m, and in hightide pools, often brackish, in Atlantic localities. Breeds March-May (Naples); fecundity to 12,000; eggs 3.6-5.45 × 1.23-1.54 mm, under stones; sexually mature at 2-3 yrs. Also Gulf of Suez, presumably via Suez Canal.

A
B

RED-MOUTHED GOBY *Gobius cruentatus.* Ⓐ Pelvic disc with anterior membrane very shallow and rear edge of disc concave; scales on cheek as well as opercle; P free rays; anterior nostril with single process; D2 I/14; P 20-21; LL 52-58; reddish-brown with darker blotches; lips and cheeks with red stripes; sensory papillae rows black. 18 cm. Inshore. Another larger goby with reduced pelvic disc, the **Slender Goby** *G. geniporus*, Ⓑ 16 cm, lacks cheek scales and red mouth stripes, and is much slimmer, with P 17-19 and LL 50-55.

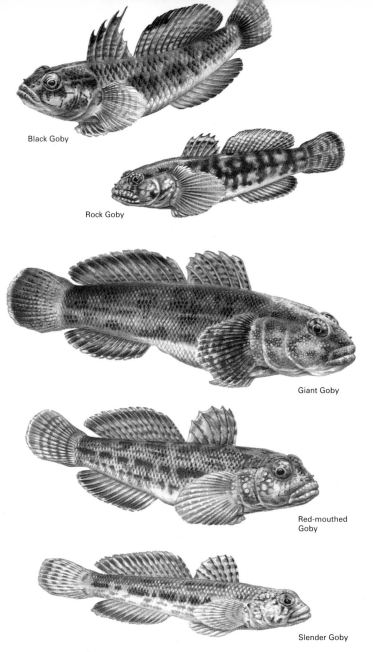

Black Goby

Rock Goby

Giant Goby

Red-mouthed
Goby

Slender Goby

BUCCHICH'S GOBY *Gobius bucchichii*. Pelvic disc complete; cheek naked; P free rays; anterior nostril with simple process; LL 50-56; fawn, with longitudinal series of small dark spots, and dark blotch on upper P base. 10 cm. Inshore soft deposits, typically hiding among snakelock anemones; usually feeds on amphipods, molluscs and algae; breeds June-August (Black Sea); eggs 1.05-1.50 × 0.5-0.57 mm; hatch at 2.17 mm in 6 days at 21-22°C; sexually mature by 1 yr.

COUCH'S GOBY *Gobius couchi*. Ⓐ Recognized as a new species of British fish only in the 1970s. Pelvic disc complete; P free rays; cheek naked; LL 40-41 (35-45); anterior nostril with flap; D2 I/13 (12-14); P 16-17 (15-18); fawn, with golden dots and mottling, 5 lateral midline blotches below D2; P base with dark, pale-edged mark deeper than long. 9.0 cm, 6 yrs. Inshore and intertidal at LWST on sheltered shores. Breeds spring (Helford). Other gobies with a dark P mark, more or less reduced pelvic disc, and naked cheek are in some systematic confusion; they include: **Golden Goby** *G. auratus*, Ⓑ 10 cm, with deeply cleft disc, often longitudinal golden lines on body, P 19-20 (18-20), P mark deeper than long; **Steven's Goby** *G. gasteveni*, Ⓒ 12 cm, 4 blotches under D2, P 19-21 (18-22), base with upper dark blotch longer than deep, anterior nostril with short tentacle; **Sarato's Goby** *G. fallax*, Ⓓ 9 cm, longitudinal series of dark spots on body, LL 39-48, Canaries and Mediterranean; and *G. luteus*, 6.5 cm, canary yellow, P 19 (18-19), LL 43-45.

STRIPED GOBY *Gobius vittatus*. Immediately distinguished by broad, dark stripe from snout to C base. Pelvic disc with only vestigial anterior membrane and rear edge deeply cleft; P free rays little developed; cheek naked; C slightly concave. 5.8 cm. Offshore, to 85 m, on coralline grounds.

MADEIRAN GOBY *Mauligobius maderensis*. Endemic to Madeira and Canaries. Anterior nostril with long tentacle; cheek scaled; P free rays well developed; pelvic-disc anterior membrane with lateral lobes; LL 53-55 (48-57); D2 I/13 (13-14); dark, with about a dozen dark bars; Ds with pale spots near bases. 15 cm. Intertidal rock pools.

LEOPARD-SPOTTED GOBY *Thorogobius ephippiatus*. Ⓐ Vividly marked with large orange and red blotches, but rediscovered along European coasts only by scuba-diving. Anterior nostril lacking tentacle; nape and head naked; P without free rays; LL 36-38 (33-42); D2 I/11 (10-12); D1 with rear dark spot. 13 cm, 9 yrs. Inshore, typically sublittoral (6-12 m), in or near crevices of rock faces, very rarely in deep shore pools at LWST; feeds on crustaceans, worms, molluscs and algae. Breeds May-July; fecundity to 12,000; sexually mature at 3-4 yrs. Related **Large-Scaled Goby** *T. macrolepis*, Ⓑ 6.5 cm, has pale-spotted head, LL 27-28, and reduced V disc.

Leopard-spotted Goby

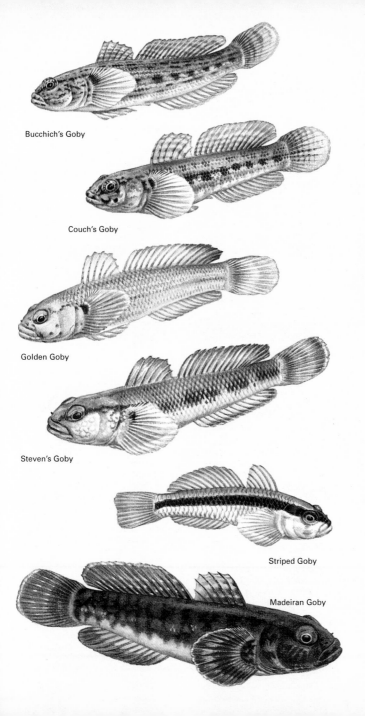

Bucchich's Goby

Couch's Goby

Golden Goby

Steven's Goby

Striped Goby

Madeiran Goby

GRASS GOBY *Zosterisessor ophiocephalus* Anterior nostril lacking process; nape scaled but cheek naked; LL 59-64 (53-68); D2 I/14-15 (13-16); P free rays rudimentary; greenish, with irregular dark bars and small dark spot at C base and upper P origin. 24.5 cm, 5 yrs. Brackish estuaries and lagoons, in sea-grass beds, with burrows among roots, feeding on small fish and shrimps. Breeds February-May (Venezia), April-July (Black Sea); fecundity to 45,000; eggs 2.6 × 0.8 mm; sexually mature at 2-3 yrs. Some local fisheries.

PAPUAN GOBY *Oxyurichthys papuensis.* Colourful Indo-Pacific immigrant via Suez Canal, now well established in Levant Sea. Eye with flap on upper edge; nape scaled, with low median ridge, but cheek naked; no P free rays; C pointed; LL 75-80; D2 I/12; grey-blue, with yellow midline band; head streaked purple and yellow, nape ridge orange. 11.1 cm. Muddy grounds in 35-45 m.

Grass Goby

Papuan Goby

There are many small Mediterranean gobies whose distribution needs further recording. Those associated with inshore rocky ground include **Zebra Goby** *Zebrus zebrus*, 5.5 cm, long anterior nostril tentacle, LL 32-34 (29-38), D2 I/11, vertebrae 27, several dark bars; among other species, none of the following have anterior nostril tentacle or free P rays: **Miller's Goby** *Millerigobius macrocephalus*, LL 28-32, D2 I/10-11, vertebrae 27-28, variable bars; elongated **Banded Goby** *Chromogobius quadrivittatus*, 6.6 cm, head with dark mottling, followed by pale transverse band across rear nape, and dark bars on body, LL 56-72, vertebrae 28; **Kolombatovic's Goby** *C. zebratus*, 5.3 cm, similar but LL 41-52; **Koch's Goby** *Didogobius kochi*, 5.65 cm, elongated, brownish, P black bar, C black and pointed, LL 33-37, D2 I/12, Gran Canaria; **Ben Tuvia's Goby** *D. bentuvii*, eyes reduced, LL 65-70, fawn, from muddy sand, off Israel; **Nebula Goby** *D. schlieweni*, black with white spots, among pebbles in shallows, Adriatic; and **Splechtna's Goby** *D. splechtnai*, with 4 dark bars, from submarine caves at Ibiza. **Steinitz's Goby** *Gammogobius steinitzi*, 3.8 cm, has several broad dark bands, D2 base with small dark spots, and 27 vertebrae. Some very small Mediterranean or Canaries species with V fins almost separate (no disc), upper and lower scales at C base greatly enlarged, with long cteni, and 28 vertebrae, are: **Balearic Goby** *Odondebuenia balearica*, 3.2 cm, reddish, with blue bars in males; **Canary Goby** *Vanneaugobius canariensis*, V with central dark blotch; and **Pruvot's Goby** *V. pruvoti*, 3.7 cm, offshore, D1 with dark blotch.

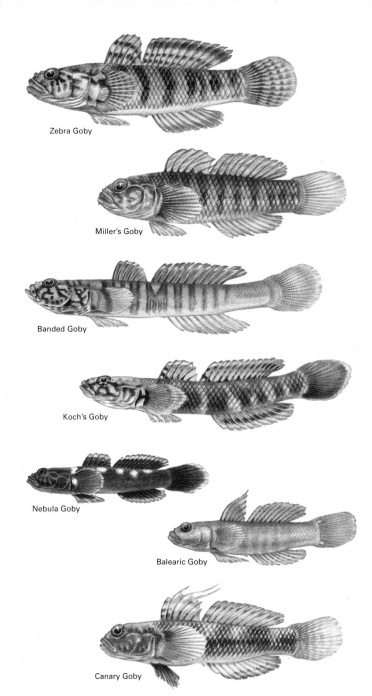

Zebra Goby

Miller's Goby

Banded Goby

Koch's Goby

Nebula Goby

Balearic Goby

Canary Goby

MARTENS' GOBY *Padogobius martensii*. An entirely freshwater goby, of northern Adriatic catchments. Nape and head naked; no anterior nostril process; no head lateral-line canals; no free P rays; LL 29-44; D2 I/10 (9-11); vertebrae 28-29; dark bars. 8.6 cm (m), 7.5 cm (f). Freshwater, under flat stones (both sexes highly territorial) in pebbly streams with moderate flow, from 400 m to sea-level, and at lake edges. Breeds May-July.

ARNO GOBY *Padogobius nigricans*. As Martens' Goby, but head lateral-line canal present; LL 40-50; D2 I/11-12; vertebrae 29-30. 12.5 cm. Freshwater, under stones but only territorial in breeding season (May-June).

A ▮
B ▨

MONKEY GOBY *Neogobius fluviatilis*. Ⓐ One of several fresh- and brackish-water, relatively large goby species endemic to Black (Pontic) and Caspian Sea basins. No anterior nostril process or free P rays; nape completely scaled; V disc anterior membrane lacking large lateral lobes; LL 55-61 (52-65); D2 I/15-16 (14-17); vertebrae 33 (32-34); sandy, breeding males black. 20 cm, 4 yrs. Brackish and fresh waters, on sand and mud, feeding especially on amphipods. Breeds April-September (Black Sea); sexually mature at 1-2 yrs. Other Black Sea species include **Round Goby** *N. melanostomus*, Ⓑ 22 cm, with black spot on D1 and LL 49-55 (45-57); now introduced into Baltic. Local commercial fisheries and canning.

TUBE-NOSED GOBY *Proterorhinus marmoratus*. As preceding, but anterior nostrils tubular, projecting beyond upper lip; LL 45-48 (42-50); D2 I/15-16; vertebrae 32 (30-33); brownish to yellowish-green, with several broad oblique dark bars, breeding males dark. 11 cm. Brackish and fresh waters, under stone and weed, feeding on crustaceans and insects. Breeds late spring-summer; eggs 2.5 × 1.3 mm, under stones and shells; sexually mature at 1 yr. Both Tube-nosed and Round Gobies now occur in Great Lakes Basin of North America, probably introduced in ballast water of ships.

KNOUT GOBY *Mesogobius batrachocephalus*. Related to other Ponto-Caspian species, but largest European goby, at 34.5 cm (4 yrs); LL 75-82; D2 I/17-18 (16-19); vertebrae 34-36; yellowish-grey, with dark blotches and streaks on Ds, P and C. Inshore and lagoons, rarely fresh water, feeding chiefly on fish. Breeds February-May (Varna); eggs very large, 5.2 × 2.6 mm, on or between stones; sexually mature at 3 yrs.

TADPOLE GOBY *Benthophilus stellatus*. Representing a very distinct group of smaller Ponto-Caspian endemics. Head broad and flattened, body thin, tapering, with 3 longitudinal series of spiny plates and no scales; no head lateral-line canals; D1 reduced, III-IV; D2 I/7-8; vertebrae 28; dark bars, from above forming three circular dark markings. 13.5 cm (m), 11 cm (f). Brackish and fresh waters, on finer deposits and shell debris, feeding on invertebrates and small fish. Breeds May-June (Sea of Azov), with low fecundity (700-2,500). There are other, mostly Caspian, *Benthophilus* species. Related *Benthophiloides brauneri*, 7.2 cm, with 3 broad dark bands and D1 VI, lacks both scales and plates when adult; Black and Caspian basins.

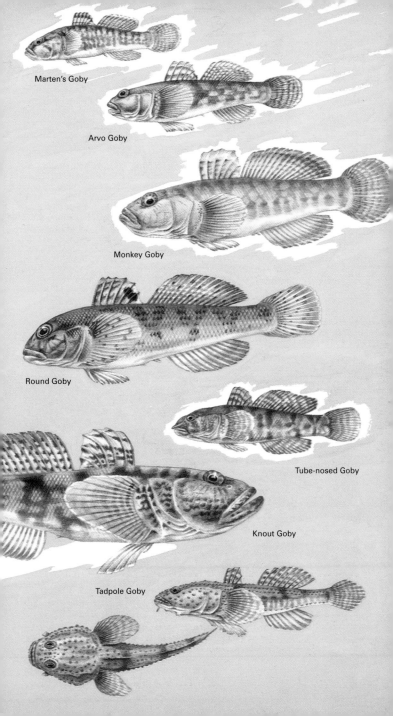

Marten's Goby

Arvo Goby

Monkey Goby

Round Goby

Tube-nosed Goby

Knout Goby

Tadpole Goby

Gobies with longitudinal row of sensory papillae around lower border of eye, with or without transverse rows from this, and with other transverse rows on cheek; anterior nostril never has tentacle, P rays never free from membrane, and V disc complete:

A ■
B ▨

SAND GOBY *Pomatoschistus minutus.* Ⓐ Abundant in coastal waters. Slender, with long tail wrist; breast scaled; V disc anterior membrane fringed with minute papillae; branchiostegal membrane attached only to anterior half of isthmus; scales on rear nape; LL 55-75; D2 I/10-12; P 18-21; vertebrae 33 (32-34); sandy, with rusty flecks; breeding males have D1 with dark blue spot nearer rear edge, 4 dark bars on body, dark V and A, but pale breast. 9.5 cm; Inshore sand and muddy sand, eating worms and small crustaceans. Breeds February-May; repeat spawning, fecundity to 3,000 per batch at 6.0 cm; eggs 0.9-1.4 × 0.7-0.8 mm, in patches under empty bivalve shells or stones, hatch at 3.0 mm. Offshore **Norwegian Goby** *P. norvegicus,* Ⓑ 6.5 cm, is paler, with P 17 (16-18), vertebrae 32 (31-33), but males have more bars and dark breast; and **Lozano's Goby** *P. lozanoi,* 8 cm, more speckled, P 18-21, vertebrae 32 (30-33), occurs in Atlantic estuaries and inshore; precise identification of Sand Goby forms is based on head papillae patterns.

A ■
B ■

MARBLED GOBY *Pomatoschistus marmoratus.* Ⓐ As Sand Goby, but nape naked, branchiostegal membrane attached to all isthmus, and LL 40-46 (37-48), D2 I/9 (8-10); vertebrae 33 (31-34); males with dark breast. 6.5 cm. Inshore sand and brackish or hypersaline waters. Breeds spring and summer (Mediterranean); eggs 1.0 × 0.6 mm. This species has colonized Suez Canal south to Lake Timsah; conversely, sand-dwelling Red Sea **Egyptian Goby** *Silhouettea aegyptia,* Ⓑ 4.4 cm, with VC 26 and many short vertical marks on body, has reached Mediterranean Sinai coast.

COMMON GOBY *Pomatoschistus microps.* One of the commonest small fishes of eastern Atlantic estuaries. Back naked to rear of D1; breast lacking scales; V disc anterior membrane lacking minute papillae; branchiostegal membrane attached to all isthmus; LL 39-52; D2 I/8-9 (8-11); P 17-19 (15-20); vertebrae 31 (30-32); greyish to fawn; males with at least several dark bars, and orange-tinged dark breast and underside of head; D1 dark blue spot nearer base. 6.4 cm; 2 yrs. Inshore, estuaries, and brackish pools and lagoons; feeds on small crustaceans and worms. Breeds April-August; fecundity to 3,400 at 4.65 cm; eggs 0.7-1.2 × 0.65-0.8 mm, hatch at 3.0-3.2 mm.

PAINTED GOBY *Pomatoschistus pictus* As preceding, but LL 34-43; vertebrae 30 (30-31); fawn with large pale saddles and four doubled spots along lateral midline; Ds with large black spots and rosy bands. 5.7 cm, 2.5 yrs. Inshore, on gravel and sand, sometimes in shore pools; breeds March-July (Irish Sea); eggs 0.8 × 0.65 mm, under scallop valves and other objects; hatch at 2.7-3.0 mm.

A ■
B ■

TORTONESE'S GOBY *Pomatoschistus tortonesei.* Ⓐ As preceding but LL 32-34 (30-36); D2 I/7 (6-8); vertebrae 31 (30-31); fawn, males with ill-defined dark bars, dark V and breast, yellowish; females with 3 bars and bright yellow underside of head. 3.7 cm. Lagoons, on sand near sea-grass. **Bath's Goby** *P. bathi,* Ⓑ 3.2 cm, D2 I/8 (7-9), with short bars in both sexes, is not yellow and has dark median band along underside of head in female.

QUAGGA GOBY *Pomatoschistus quagga.* As preceding, but C truncated or slightly concave; LL 35-40; D2 I/9; vertebrae 33; yellowish, with 3-4 intense dark bars. 4.6 cm. Inshore, into mid-water. Also Mediterranean, with concave C and barred in both sexes, reddish **Kner's Goby** *P. knerii,* has LL 41-44 (38-46), D2 I/10 (9-11), vertebrae 31, and large dark C blotch.

Sand Goby

Marbled Goby

Common Goby
male

Common Goby female

Painted Goby

Tortonese's Goby

Quagga Goby

CANESTRINI'S GOBY *Pomatoschistus canestrinii.* Back to D2 and breast lacking scales; branchiostegal membrane attached to isthmus; C rounded; LL 36-42; D2 I/8-9; vertebrae 30; fawn to greyish, with many tiny black spots; males with 4 bars and spot on rear D1. 6.7 cm. Brackish estuaries and lagoons. Breeds March-July; sexually mature by 1 yr.

A
B

CAUCASIAN GOBY *Knipowitschia caucasica.* A Small, very abundant euryhaline gobies with paired anterior interorbital pores of head lateral-line system; head and back to at least D1/2 space naked; LL 33-35 (31-38); D2 I/8; P 15-17 (15-18); vertebrae 31 (30-32); greyish to fawn; males with about 4 dark bars, D1 spot, and dark breast, V and A; females with black chin spot and dark band across D1. Fresh to hypersaline waters, in shallow lagoons, lakes and estuaries, on weedy substrate, eating small crustaceans and midge larvae. Breeds March-July (Varna), fecundity low (220-500) but eggs relatively large, 1.65-2.4 × 0.58-0.85 mm, on underside of bivalve shells, stones and plant roots or stems; hatch at 3.0-3.8 mm, and mature at 2.0-2.2 cm. Local forms in Balkan rivers. **Lagoon Goby** *K. panizzae,* is from the Adriatic, very similar in form and biology to Caucasian Goby, but lacking scales before middle of D2, vertebrae typically 30 (29-30) and male with shorter first dark bar. 4 cm. Brackish estuaries and lagoons. Breeds March-August (Venezia). Also Black Sea and Caspian *K. longecaudata,* B 4 cm, in fresh and slightly brackish waters, has short dark bars in both sexes and vertebral counts of 32-33 (32-34).

A
B

ORSINI'S GOBY *Knipowitschia punctatissima.* A Restricted to northern Italy. Larger and stockier than Caucasian Goby, but similar sensory papillae patterns; no head canals; body naked except for patch of scales behind P; D1 VII; D2 I/8 (7-8); vertebrae 31; males with several dark bars, females with chin spot. 5.5 cm, 2-3 yrs. Freshwater, typically in springs with constant water temperature and slow current. Breeds spring and early summer; fecundity to 300; eggs 2 mm long; hatch at 3-4 mm. Related **Thessaly Goby** *K. thessala,* B 4.4 cm, with head canals, and D1 VI (V-VII), also has scale patch behind P and some scales along lateral midline of tail; males with numerous thin dark bars; streams of the Pinios river system, eastern Greece. With limited, entirely freshwater distribution, both species are vulnerable to habitat destruction.

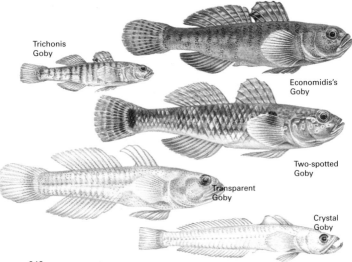

Trichonis Goby

Economidis's Goby

Two-spotted Goby

Transparent Goby

Crystal Goby

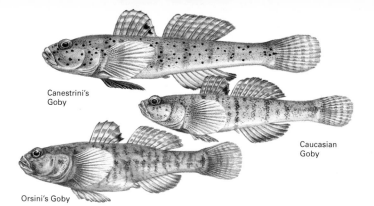

Canestrini's
Goby

Caucasian
Goby

Orsini's Goby

ECONOMIDIS'S GOBY *Economidichthys pygmaeus*. A West Balkan endemic genus, with pitted raised area around anus (*perianal organ*), unique among fishes; no head canals; pelvic disc anterior membrane reduced; back to middle D2 and belly naked; LL 30-38; D1 VI (V-VI); D2 I/8-9 (8-11); vertebrae 29-30 (28-31); dark or with short transverse lateral blotches or bars, never more than half body depth. 5.2 cm. Freshwater, rivers and streams, in flowing and stagnant shallows with abundant vegetation and detritus.

TRICHONIS GOBY *Economidichthys trichonis*. Europe's smallest freshwater fish, 3.0 cm, females mature at 1.8 cm; perianal organ small; body naked, except for patch of scales below D1 and series along lateral midline to C; D2 I/10-11 (9-12); P 15 (13-16); vertebrae 30 (30-31); pale, with long vertical stripes in both sexes, some over two-thirds body depth. Freshwater, known only from Lake Trichonis, western Greece; small schools near surface, over open areas of gravel or stones, at mouths of tributaries.

TWO-SPOTTED GOBY *Gobiusculus flavescens*. Midwater, with eyes more lateral; D1 VII; nape naked; LL 35-40; D2 I/9-10; vertebrae 32 (32-33); reddish, with large, yellow-edged black spot on C base; males with similar spot on lateral midline below D1. 6 cm, 2 yrs. Inshore, in schools above weed, and in weedy shore pools, feeding mostly on plankton. Breeds April-August, eggs 0.7-0.8 × 0.6 mm, often lining inner surface of oarweed holdfast.

A ▪
B ▨

TRANSPARENT GOBY *Aphia minuta*. Ⓐ Comparable to postlarval gobies which have grown but never become demersal. Transparent, compressed body, with lateral eyes; males with large canines; LL 19-25 (18-25), easily lost; nape naked; D1 V (IV-VII); D2 I, 12 (11-13); pigmented only along D, A and C bases and on head. 5.8 cm (m), 5.3 cm (f); 1 yr. Marine and estuarine, midwater, feeding on zooplankton. Breeds June-August (Oslofjord), May (Adriatic), dying after single breeding season. Similar Mediterranean **Ferrer's Goby** *Pseudaphya ferreri*, Ⓑ 3.5 cm, also transparent, has large black spot on C base, D2 I/7-10, and occurs in schools over sandy beaches.

CRYSTAL GOBY *Crystallogobius linearis*. Also transparent and 'annual', aberrant compressed gobies, lacking scales and with great sexual dimorphism in body form; males with curved lower jaw, large fangs, deep V disc, and D1 only II-III; females lack D1, V disc vestigial and jaws toothless; D2 long, I/18-20. 4.7 cm (m), 3.9 cm (f); 1 yr. Midwater, more offshore, to 400 m, also plankton-feeding. Breeds May-August (Oslofjord), males on substrate, guarding eggs in empty worm tubes.

Gobies with only longitudinal rows or groups of sensory papillae on cheek; scales large (LL 25-35):

FOUR-SPOTTED GOBY *Deltentosteus quadrimaculatus.* Ⓐ Head canals expanded, with many secondary pores; D1 VI, second ray elongated; D2 I/8-9; LL 33-35; vertebrae 33; nape scaled; fawn, with 4 black spots along lateral midline and D1 with black streak along front edge and rear dark spot; V and A dark. 8 cm. Inshore, sand and muddy grounds, to 90 m. Breeds in spring (Mediterranean). Related Mediterranean **Toothed Goby** *D. colonianus,* Ⓑ 7 cm, has longer jaw (angle below rear eye) and D2 I/10-11.

JEFFREY'S GOBY *Buenia jeffreysii.* Small, typically offshore goby, with large eyes; nape naked; LL 25-30; D1 VI, second ray elongated in males; D2 I/8-10; vertebrae 30; 4 lateral dark spots, broad pale saddles across back. 6 cm. Shelf to upper slope, on coarse to muddy grounds. *B. affinis* is a similar Mediterranean species.

FRIES' GOBY *Lesueurigobius friesii.* Relatively larger goby, with scaled nape; LL 28-29; D2 I/13-16; A I/12-15; P 18-19; vertebrae 27; D1 rays, especially I, elongate; C pointed; fawn, with many small yellow spots over body and fins. 10 cm, 11 yrs. Shelf, burrowing in muddy ground, often with Dublin Prawn. Breeds May-August, eggs 1.8-1.9 × 0.9-1.0 mm, in burrows; sexually mature at 2 yrs. Similar **Sanzo's Goby** *L. sanzoi,* has A I/16-17; P 22; yellowish with at least several dark bars. 9.5 cm. Offshore shelf, Alboran Sea to Mauretania.

LESUEUR'S GOBY *Lesueurigobius sueri.* Similar pointed C, but nape naked; LL 26-28; D2 I/13-14; A I/13-14; P 17-20; head and body with yellow and blue bands. 5 cm. Shelf. *L. heterofasciatus,* 4.4 cm, off Morocco and Madeira, also with naked nape, has narrow dark bars.

DIMINUTIVE GOBY *Lebetus scorpioides.* Ⓐ Tiny species, pelvic disc lacking anterior membrane and rear edge concave; LL 25-29; D2 I/9-10; A I/7-8; P 17-21; vertebrae 27-29; both sexes with pale band across tail, otherwise adult male (once called *L. orca*) yellowish to grey, D1 enlarged, dusky yellow, P, V and A dark; female with pale brown with purplish-brown bars, and dark spot on D1. 3.9 cm. Offshore shelf, to 375 m, chiefly on coralline grounds. Breeds February-October; fecundity less than 300 (a). Similar **Guillet's Goby** *L. guilleti,* Ⓑ 2.4 cm, has D2 I/7-9, A I/5-6, P 16-17 (15-17), vertebrae 25-26. Mediterranean **Grotto Goby** *Speleogobius trigloides,* Ⓒ 2.26 cm, inshore, on boulders and in caves, also with pale band across tail, has scales on nape, D2 I/7 (6- 7), A I/5 (5-7), LL 26-30, vertebrae 29.

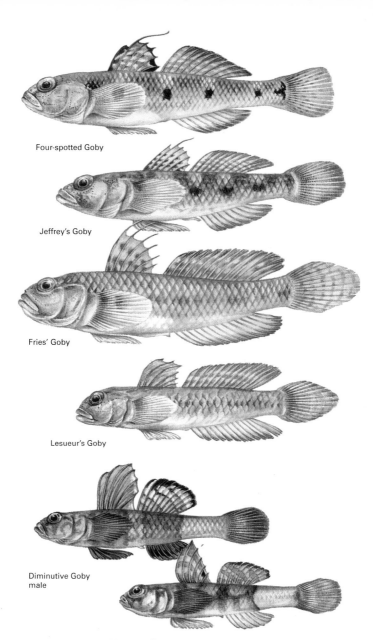

Four-spotted Goby

Jeffrey's Goby

Fries' Goby

Lesueur's Goby

Diminutive Goby
male

Diminutive Goby
female

DRAGONETS (Suborder Callionymoidei: Callionymidae)

Small coastal fishes with cylindrical bodies; flattened head, prominent snout and horizontal mouth; rear cheek with large spine; 2 Ds, D1 short-based. Bottom-living; eggs planktonic.

COMMON DRAGONET *Callionymus lyra*. Cheek spine with 4 points, lowest pointing forwards; opercle opens dorsally; D1 IV; D2 9 (8-10), only last ray branched; pale brownish; males with blue spots and lines, and D2 yellow with bright blue longitudinal bands but no distinct rows of dark spots; females and immature males with lateral blotches and 3 brown saddles, once thought to be different species ('sordid dragonet') from colourful male ('gemmeous dragonet'). 30 cm (m), 25 cm (f). Shelf, typically inshore, young occasionally in sandy shore pools; eats benthic invertebrates. Breeds February-April (January-August), with pairs rising off sea-bed to spawn; eggs 0.8-1 mm, lacking oil globule but with segmented yolk and reticulated capsule; hatch at about 2.0 mm.

BARRED DRAGONET *Callionymus fasciatus*. Cheek with 4 spines, lowest pointing forwards; D1 IV; D2 I/10 (9-10); reddish; male D2 with oblique bands of brown spots, A with horizontal dark band. 12 cm (m), 8 cm (f). Inshore sands.

RETICULATED DRAGONET *Callionymus reticulatus*. Cheek spine with only 3 well-developed points, none forward pointing; D2 10; above brownish with bluish spots, and 4 orange-red saddles; male Ds with vertical to very oblique rows of dark spots, separated by dark-edged bluish lines and dots. 11 cm (m), 6.5 cm (f). Inshore. Breeds April-September (western Channel). To Mauritania.

SPOTTED DRAGONET *Callionymus maculatus*. Cheek spine with 4 points, lowest pointing forwards; D2 9 (8-10); Ds dark-spotted in both sexes; 4 horizontal rows of dark spots in males, 2 rows in females. 16 cm (m), 10 cm (f). More offshore, shelf to upper slope. Breeds April-November (western Channel); eggs 0.66-0.79 mm. To Senegal.

A
B

FESTIVE DRAGONET *Callionymus pusillus*. A Cheek spine with 4 or 5 points, lowest pointing forwards; D1 IV; D2 6-7, high but shorter-based than A, 9 (8-10); brownish, male with blue spots and lines, D2 striped blue. 14 cm (m), 10 cm (f). Sandy shallows. Breeds May-August (Mediterranean). With several small points along upper edge of cheek spine, **Haifa Dragonet** *C. filamentosus*, B 18 cm, has D1 first ray (separate from rest) and elongated long middle C rays in males, and is an Indo-Pacific immigrant via Suez Canal to Levant Sea.

RISSO'S DRAGONET *Callionymus risso*. Cheek spine with 3 well developed points, forwardly directed point rudimentary; D1 III, D2 8 (7-8), A 9 (8-9); yellowish-grey; male D1 with rear black spot, uniformly dark in females and juveniles. 8 cm. Shelf. Breeds April-September (Mediterranean).

Common Dragonet
courtship display

Barred Dragonet

Reticulated
Dragonet

Spotted
Dragonet

Festive
Dragonet

Risso's
Dragonet

MANDARIN FISH *Synchiropus phaeton.* Representing a highly colourful group of coral fishes. Cheek spine with 2 upward points; opercular opening lateral; D1 IV; D2 8-9, rays branched; above reddish or orange, blotched olive, silvery below; D1 with dark spot. 18 cm (m), 12 cm (f). Offshore shelf and upper slope, on sand or mud. Breeds June-September (Mediterranean). To West Africa.

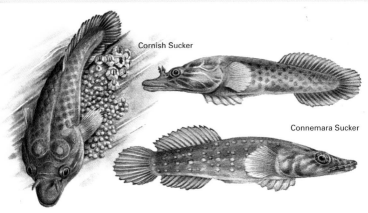

Cornish Sucker

Connemara Sucker

CLINGFISHES (Suborder Gobiesocoidei)

Small benthic fishes (in a single family, **Gobiesocidae**) with flattened heads and spatulate snout, clinging strongly to any flat surface by means of their complex abdominal sucker, which incorporates pelvic fins and parts from the pectoral skeletal girdle. 1 D set far back; C rounded. Eggs demersal, guarded by male.

A
B

CORNISH SUCKER *Lepadogaster lepadogaster purpurea.* Ⓐ D long-based, 17-21, both D and A united to C; anterior nostril with long tentacle; P 20-23; reddish, with paired blue spots in dorsal view of back. 7.5 cm. Intertidal and sublittoral, under stones on sheltered, weed-covered shores, from midtide to ELWST. Breeds May-August; eggs golden-yellow, flattened oval, 1.8-1.9 × 1.5-1.56 mm × 1.0 mm high, in patches under stones; hatch at 5.1 mm in about 13 days. *L. l. lepadogaster,* Ⓑ 6.5 cm, D 16-19, in Adriatic and eastern Mediterranean. **Zebra Clingfish** *L. zebra,* 5.4 cm, as preceding, but body with vertical bars, D 15-18, only Canaries and Madeira.

CONNEMARA SUCKER *Lepadogaster candollei.* As preceding but D and A not joined to C; anterior nostril tentacle very short; D 13-16; P 26-29; males reddish, with red spots on head; females greenish-yellow. 7.5 cm. Sublittoral, in weedbeds, and sometimes intertidal at extreme low waters of spring tides. Breeds April-July.

BLUNT-NOSED SUCKER *Gouania wildenowii.* D and A united with C, but very low; D 14-19; A 13-20; P 18-21; pale yellow, grey, sometimes with red spots. 5 cm.

Mandarin Fish

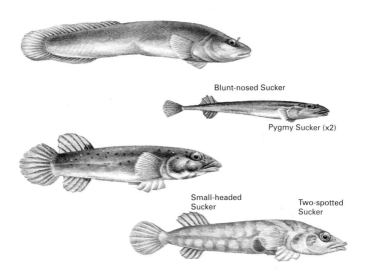

Blunt-nosed Sucker

Pygmy Sucker (x2)

Small-headed Sucker

Two-spotted Sucker

PYGMY SUCKER *Opeatogenys gracilis.* One of the smallest European marine fishes, at 2.1 cm. Elongate, with tiny D, 3, and A, 4; spine on lower edge of opercle; P 16; reddish, with white spots.

A
B

SMALL-HEADED SUCKER *Apletodon dentatus.* D (5-6) and A (5-7) relatively short-based, not joined to C; P 21-24; jaws with lateral canine teeth; olive-green, males with dark blotch on D and A. 4 cm. Inshore weedbeds and under stones at low water of spring tides. Breeds May-July, eggs often on inner surface of hollow *Saccorhiza* holdfasts, accompanied by male. *A. d. bacescui,* 3.6 cm, with slightly shorter head, in Black Sea. By contrast, **Pellegrin's Sucker** *A. pellegrini,* B 3.2 cm, from southern Africa to Canaries and Madeira, has a longer head (more than two-fifths standard length), and D, A and C with reddish lines.

TWO-SPOTTED SUCKER *Diplecogaster bimaculatus.* Similar to preceding, but no enlarged canine teeth; D 5-7; A 4-6; P 21-25; C 9-10; reddish, males with large nape spots. 4 cm. Shelf, offshore, on coarser and shelly grounds. Breeds May-August, eggs 1.37-1.54 × 1.08-1.24 × 0.62-0.7 mm usually on underside of bivalve shells; hatch at 2.97-4.26 mm. *D. b. pectoralis,* 2.2 cm, P 25-26, C 11-12, occurs around Cape Verdes, Canaries and Azores; and *D. b. euxinica,* 4 cm, P 21-26, C 12-14, in Black Sea.

TUNAS (TUNNIES) AND MACKERELS
(Suborder Scombroidei: Scombridae)

Fast midwater species, streamlined for efficient and incessant swimming, with spindle-shaped body, narrow tail wrist, with tiny D and A finlets, and lunate C, of high aspect ratio; 2 Ds, depressible into grooves on back; P set high, sickle-shaped; eye faired into surface of head; and upper jaw not protrusible. Sustained swimming relies on abundant red muscle, seen in tuna steaks, and gills ventilated by ram-jet effect; larger forms may have body temperature raised to 10°C above surrounding water. Eggs planktonic, young minute on hatching. Typically of warm seas, many of economic importance, and much exploited. Vigorous and popular quarry for big-game fishing.

YELLOW-FINNED TUNA *Thunnus albacares.* As Blue-finned Tuna but D2 and A greatly elongated, much longer than height of D1, P tip to below origin of D2; D2 and finlets bright yellow, and belly with thin dark lines and dots. 200 cm (a: 176.35 kg). Epipelagic. Breeds June-July (May-September); fecundity to about 8 million. With small Blue-finned Tuna, the source for much tinned tuna.

BIG-EYED TUNA *Thunnus obesus.* D2, A and P not elongated, P to below origin of D2; A finlets yellow, edged black; C edge not white. 239 cm (a: 170.32 kg). Epipelagic, and deeper, to 250 m. Probably breeds all year in tropical seas. Similar market to that for Blue-finned Tuna.

Big-eyed Tuna

BLUE-FINNED TUNA *Thunnus thynnus.* Despite being the fastest fish (burst swimming may reach about 90 kph), blue-finned tuna are among the most intensively pursued by man. Body with small scales behind well-developed corselet of larger scales; tongue with 2 longitudinal ridges; teeth slim, conical; P 31-35, short, not to opposite D1/D2 junction; Ds hardly separated, D1 XII-XVI; D2 anterior part not much longer than D1; D finlets 7-9, A finlets 6-8; process between Vs shorter than V rays; tail wrist with larger lateral midline keel and smaller keel above and below; above dark blue, sides with yellow band in life, below silvery-white, lacking dark stripes and spots; D2 reddish-brown. 300 cm, 710 kg, 15 yrs (a: 679 kg). Oceanic, epipelagic, undertaking long migrations, transoceanic and adults into northern waters in summer, feeding on fish, squid and crustaceans, and attacking fish schools in packs. Breeds June-August (Mediterranean and Gulf of Cadiz); fecundity to 30 million; eggs 1.0-1.12 mm, with yellow oil globule, homogeneous yolk and finely reticulated capsule; hatch at 3 mm in about 2 days; sexually mature at 80-105 cm, 2-4 yrs. The most valuable of tunas, especially as raw *sashimi* in Japan (where a 238 kg individual fetched £54,000 in 1996), and heavy commercial fishing, using purse-seines and long-lines, as well as trap-nets along migration routes, together with other factors, has greatly depleted stocks throughout world.

Blue-finned Tuna

Yellow-finned Tuna

251

LITTLE TUNA *Euthynnus alletteratus.* Similar to larger tunnies, but no scales behind corselet; D2 much lower than D1, P 26-27, short; dark blue above, with close-set striping; silvery below, with several pale-edged dark spots usually conspicuous near P and V. 100 cm (a: 15.95 kg). Epipelagic and over shelf. Breeds April-November.

SKIPJACK TUNA *Katsuwonus pelamis.* Also known as Oceanic Bonito. Slightly larger than Little Tuna, with 4-6 dark bands along body below lateral midline; P 24-28, short; only LL scales behind corselet. 108 cm, 35 kg (a: 19 kg). Epipelagic. Breeds April-September (Morocco); fecundity to 1.5 million. Tropical seas, and of great commercial importance in Pacific, where 20 km gill nets much criticized by marine conservationists.

BONITO *Sarda sarda.* Slimmer and smaller than Plain Bonito, D1 arising over P base, XX-XXIII; P short, 23-26; body scaled behind corselet; LL wavy; above steel-blue, with at least several long bands above lateral midline. 91 cm (a: 8.3 kg). Typically inshore. Breeds May-July (Mediterranean).

Albacore

Plain Bonito

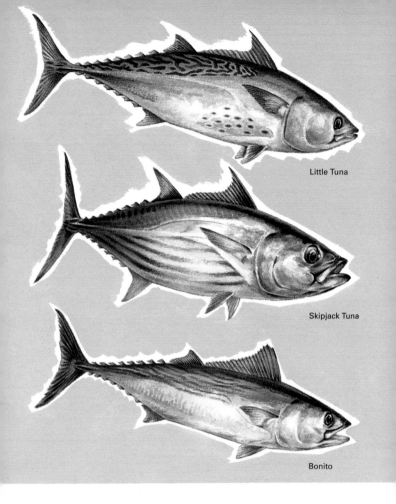

Little Tuna

Skipjack Tuna

Bonito

ALBACORE *Thunnus alalunga*. Smaller tuna, differing from preceding in D2 and A similar in height to D1, but P greatly elongate, tip to opposite D2 and A finlets; D2 yellow, A finlets dark, C white-edged. 127 cm. (a: 40 kg). Epipelagic. Breeds in summer (Mediterranean); eggs 0.84-0.98 mm, as Blue-finned Tuna. Fisheries include summer Biscay trolling (traditionally with ribbons or maize leaves as lure), or angling with double rods on pilchard bait. Another source of tinned tuna.

PLAIN BONITO *Orcynopsis unicolor*. Deeper-bodied, with D1 arising over opercle; P 21-23, short; patches of scales behind corselet; blue-black above, with traces of mottling, and no conspicuous spots or bands; D1 mostly black. 130 cm, 13.1 kg. Shelf, midwater. Breeds July-September (Mediterranean). To Senegal.

253

A
B
C

CHUB OR SPANISH MACKEREL *Scomber japonicus*. Ⓐ Similar to Mackerel but body below midline with dark lines or spots, D1 only VIII-X, and swimbladder present. 50 cm (a: 2.17 kg). Also with many dark lines *down* lower flank. Indo-Pacific **Narrow-barred Spanish Mackerel** *Scomberomorus commerson*, Ⓑ 220 cm (a: 44.9 kg), with long D1 (XV-XVIII), large, compressed teeth, and median C keel as well as smaller keels, and **Indian Mackerel** *Rastrelliger kanagurta*, 35 cm, with narrow dark lines *along* body, spot below P, and very obvious gill rakers, can transit Suez Canal. **Wahoo** *Acanthocybium solandri*, Ⓒ 211 cm (a: 70.53 kg), similar to preceding but snout as long as rest of head, is cosmopolitan in tropical oceans, but known in European waters only from an old museum specimen at Palermo.

MACKEREL *Scomber scombrus*. An important commercial species fished by drift nets as food fish or for industrial use, but also an easy catch by individual trolling in summer. Body with small scales, and no distinct corselet; D1 short, XI-XIII, well separated from smaller D2; 5D and A finlets; tail wrist with 2 small keels on each side; internally, no swimbladder; greeny or darker blue, with many dark wavy lines above lateral midline; below silvery-white, without markings. 50 cm, 1.8 kg, probably 20 yrs (a: 1.2 kg). Shelf, in schools near surface in warmer months but forming more compact aggregations near sea-bed in winter, from inshore areas to deeper water near edge of shelf; eats neritic crustaceans and small fish. Batch-spawning April-May (March-August) (Celtic Sea), June-July (North Sea), schools tending to disperse inshore afterwards; eggs planktonic (to 90,000 per spawning), 1.0-1.38 mm, with unsegmented yolk and pale greenish black-pigmented oil globule, hatching at 3.3-3.9 mm after 2-6 days; metamorphosed by 21 mm; juveniles more offshore, joining major schools at about 30 cm, 2 yrs, when sexually mature. To Cape Verdes and also western Atlantic.

Chub Mackerel

Frigate Mackerel

FRIGATE MACKEREL *Auxis rochei.* Mackerel-like in short D1, over P, only IX-XI and well separated from much smaller D2, but tunny-like corselet scales present, extending far back along lateral-line to opposite finlets, and no other scales; process between Vs as long as V; at least a dozen short dark bars above LL to rear of D1 base. 50 cm (a: 1.35 kg). Inshore, in large schools. Breeds November-August.

Mackerel

255

BILLFISHES (Istiophoridae)

Large fishes of warm oceans, the ultimate catch in big-game angling, with snout elongated into a spear, round in section; D1 long-based, much larger than small D2; no D finlets, but A in 2 parts; tail wrist with paired keels; C lunate. Eggs planktonic.

ATLANTIC SAILFISH *Istiophorus albicans*. D1 enormous, XLII-XLIV; pelvic fins very elongated, tip to near A origin; above bluish-black, sides and below silvery; D1 dark blue, with black spots. 300 cm (a: 61.4 kg). Epipelagic and over shelf, feeding on fish, squid and crustaceans. Breeds all year (tropical Atlantic). Differs from larger Indo-Pacific *I. platypterus* in longer P and C of juveniles.

BLUE MARLIN *Makaira nigricans*. D1 smaller, but anterior tip pointed; rest of D1 very low; V long, but tip distant from A; steep nape; bluish or darker above, silvery below; D1 with blue lines. 400 cm (a: 636 kg). Epipelagic; feeds on pelagic fish and squid. Breeds mostly July-September (eastern Atlantic).

A ▨
B ▨
C ▧
D ■

MEDITERRANEAN MARLIN

Tetrapterus belone. Ⓐ Similar to preceding, but anterior tip of D1 rounded and body more compressed; dark blue above, sharply defined from silvery underside. 240 cm, 70 kg (a: 41.2 kg). Epipelagic. Fished commercially. Other marlins entering Mediterranean or straying north are: **White Marlin** *T. albidus*, Ⓑ 300 cm (a: 82.5 kg) (once to Morecambe Bay), with anus at A origin and D1 as high as body depth; and **Round-scaled Marlin** *T. georgei*, Ⓒ 200 cm, with anus somewhat before A origin and D1 higher than body depth. The Atlantic **Long-billed Spearfish** *T. pfluegeri*, Ⓓ 250 cm (a: 43 kg), has rough scales on body, and distance from anus to A origin is more than half A height.

SWORDFISH *Xiphias gladius* (**Xiphiidae**). Long, flattened 'sword' from snout; D1 high but short-based, XXI-XXX, well separated from tiny D2 (3 rays) in adults; V absent; 1 keel on each side of C wrist; dark brown above, sides and below paler. 450 cm, 650 kg (a: 536.15 kg). Epipelagic, to 800 m, feeding on fish and squid. Breeds January-October (eastern Atlantic), June-September (Mediterranean); eggs 1.6-1.87 mm, with oil globule; hatch at 4.5 mm in about 2.5 days, young fish have relatively longer lower jaw and continuous D. Commercial fisheries, including harpooning, for food as well as game-fishing.

Swordfish

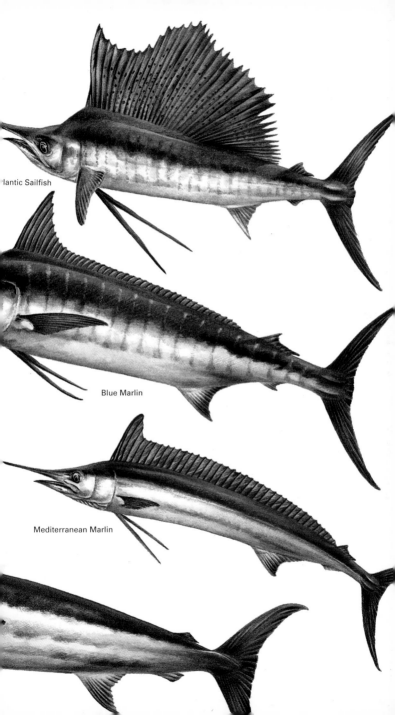

lantic Sailfish

Blue Marlin

Mediterranean Marlin

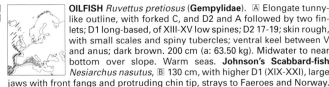

Silver Scabbard-fish

SCABBARD-FISHES (Trichiuridae) and SNAKE-MACKERELS (Gempylidae)

Large, very elongate, compressed fishes, with long jaws and strong front canines; D long-based, from head to tail, notched between spinous and branched rays or with continuous outline; V minute or absent. Active predatory fishes. Eggs planktonic. Commercial fisheries.

SILVER SCABBARD-FISH *Lepidopus caudatus* (**Trichiuridae**). Head with nape crest; D continuous, without notch, IX/90-107; A anterior rays reduced, only rear part evident as fin; V I/2, merely a tiny spine seen in larger fish; C small, deeply forked; no scales; silvery, fins edged dark. 205 cm. Offshore shelf and upper slope, feeding on fish and squid. To Senegal; also southern hemisphere.

ESPADA *Aphanopus carbo*. As Silver Scabbard-fish but jet black; D notched XXXVIII-XLII/53-57; V absent in adult. 110 cm. Mesopelagic to bottom over slope. Worldwide. Long-line fisheries especially off Madeira. **Frostfish** *Benthodesmus elongatus*, 130 cm, is more elongated, silvery, with notched D, XLIV-XLVI/104-109, V I/1.

HAIRTAIL *Trichiurus lepturus*. Body tapering to tail tip, C absent; D without notch, III/134-139; A not evident externally; silvery, with dark-edged fins. 150 cm (a: 3.2 kg). Shelf to upper slope, in schools. Breeds July-August (Mediterranean). Warm seas.

A ▮
B ▨

OILFISH *Ruvettus pretiosus* (**Gempylidae**). Ⓐ Elongate tunnylike outline, with forked C, and D2 and A followed by two finlets; D1 long-based, of XIII-XV low spines; D2 17-19; skin rough, with small scales and spiny tubercles; ventral keel between V and anus; dark brown. 200 cm (a: 63.50 kg). Midwater to near bottom over slope. Warm seas. **Johnson's Scabbard-fish** *Nesiarchus nasutus*, Ⓑ 130 cm, with higher D1 (XIX-XXI), large jaws with front fangs and protruding chin tip, strays to Faeroes and Norway.

LUVAR *Luvarus imperialis*. (**Luvaridae**) Traditionally grouped with tunas but probably closer to percoids. Tuna-like falcate C and narrow-keeled tail wrist, but front deep, elliptical, with high rounded forehead; single D and A low, fewer rays evident in adults (D, 12-14; A, 13-14); teeth lost; V minute. Blue above, sides pink, silvery below; D dark, other fins reddish; young have black spots. 188 cm. Oceanic, occasionally over shelf, feeding on plankton. Breeds spring-summer (Mediterranean); fecundity to near 50 million. Warm temperate seas.

Espada

Luvar

Oilfish

FLATFISHES (ORDER PLEURONECTIFORMES)

The most distinctive group of teleosts, swimming on one side of the greatly flattened body. This is actually compressed from side to side, not from top to bottom as in rays. Flatfish swimming on the left side (right side upwards) are *dextral*, while those swimming with left side upwards are *sinistral*. The orientation is normally characteristic for the species, but 'reversed' individuals may occur. The upper 'eyed' side is pigmented, the 'blind' underside is pale and may differ in other features. Abnormally, the underside may be pigmented, or the upper side show pale patches. Both eyes are on the upper side of the head, the eye originating on the blind side shifting around the edge of the head during development of the young fish before it becomes bottom-living. Body typically oval in outline, fringed by very long-based D, arising on head, and A. Eggs and larval stages planktonic. Important fisheries for many species.

SPOTTED FLOUNDER *Citharus linguatula* (**Citharidae**). Left side up; V base narrow, l/5; D 64-72; A 44-48; LL 35-39; brownish, with dark spot at end of D and A bases at tail wrist. 25 cm. Shelf. To West Africa.

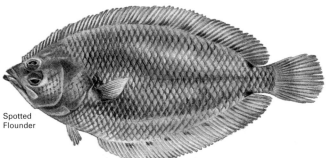

Spotted
Flounder

A ▣
B ▨

TURBOT *Psetta maxima*. Ⓐ Perhaps the best tasting of all sea fish and a valuable commercial species, both in fisheries and farming. Body outline circular; upper side at least with many bony tubercles; D 57-80, A 43-58; V of both sides long-based; brownish to sandy, variable, C with dark dots to edge. 90 cm. Inshore shelf, to 80 m, on sand and gravel, young in shallows; feeds on fish (especially sprats and sandeels). Breeds April-August; fecundity several million; eggs 0.91-1.2 mm, with black-pigmented pale yellow oil globule; hatch at 2.14-2.8 mm in 7-9 days; long planktonic life (4-6 months), metamorphosing at 20-30 mm; sexually mature at 30 cm (m), 35-45 cm (f). Black Sea *P. m. maeotica* Ⓑ has bony tubercles on both sides, upper ones very large (eye diameter). Hybrids between Turbot and Brill have bony tubercles but these are much less evident; other characteristics intermediate.

BRILL *Scophthalmus rhombus*. Commercial landings, but less esteemed than Turbot; body scaled (cycloid, LL 115-125), and no bony tubercles; outline more oval; D 73-83, front rays branched and free at tips; A 56-62; brown or greyish, with many dark dots but C not heavily spotted. 75 cm. Shelf, feeding on fish. Breeds April-August; eggs 1.24-1.5 mm, with oil globule and black pigment on yolk; hatch at 3.8-4 mm after 14 days; metamorphosing at 20-35 mm.

Turbot

Brill

LEFT-EYED FLOUNDERS (Bothidae)
Left side up; mouth large; rear rim of cheek free.

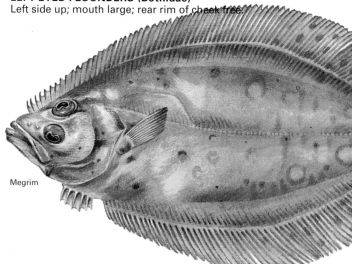

Megrim

A
B

 MEGRIM *Lepidorhombus whiffiagonis*. A Outline more oval; lower eye somewhat more anterior to upper eye; D (85-94) and A (64-74) end with only slight extension under tail wrist; yellowish to browny-grey, with indistinct markings. 61 cm. Offshore shelf, on muddy grounds, feeding chiefly on shrimps and fish. Breeds March-May; eggs 1.02-1.22 mm, oil globule with black pigment; hatch at 4 mm in 5-6 days; metamorphoses at about 19 mm. To Mauritania. **Four-Spot Megrim** *L. boscii*, B 40 cm, from offshore shelf and upper slope, has eye diameter longer than snout length, and D and A with dark spots on rear part.

 NORWEGIAN TOPKNOT *Phrynorhombus norvegicus*. Similar shape to Megrim, but eyes very close together; D (76-84) and A (58-68) end with distinct lobe under tail wrist; brown, with many dark spots over upper side and fins. 12 cm. Shelf, on rough ground. Breeds March-June (Channel); eggs 0.72-0.92 mm.

 ECKSTROM'S TOPKNOT *Phrynorhombus regius*. Body deeper, about half standard length; head outline notched at D origin; D 70-80; A 60-68; LL 72-80; brownish, with dark blotches, including 4 larger, rounded spots. 20 cm. Shelf. Breeds April-June; eggs 0.9-0.99 mm.

 TOPKNOT *Zeugopterus punctatus*. Deep outline, mouth almost • vertical to head; D (85-102) and A (67-80) end with distinct lobe under tail wrist; D begins on snout, behind upper lip; upper P longer than lower P; Vs joined to A; upper scales ctenoid; brown with dark blotches, especially spot after lateral-line curve, and dark bands from eyes. 25 cm. Inshore rocky grounds, able to cling to flat surfaces by suction from underside; eats small fish and crustaceans. Breeds February-May (Channel); eggs 0.92-1.07 mm, with pinkish oil globule; hatch at 2.5-2.94 mm.

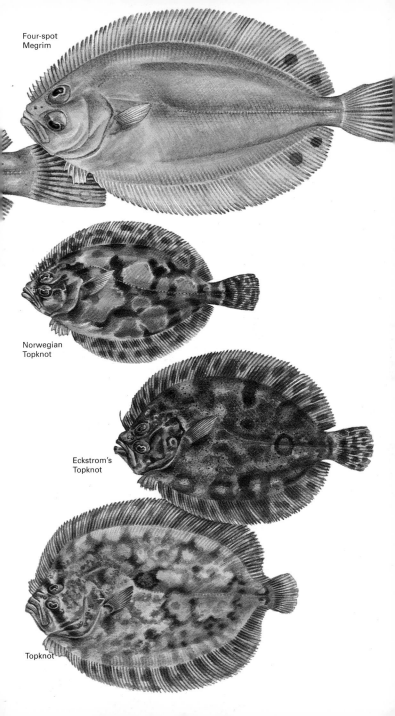

Four-spot
Megrim

Norwegian
Topknot

Eckstrom's
Topknot

Topknot

SCALDFISH *Arnoglossus laterna.* Body outline oval; eyes adjacent, separated by ridge; V on underside (right) shorter-based than upper (left); D 82-98; A 63-74; LL 51-56; brownish or greyish, with variable darker markings. 20 cm. Shelf, typically inshore, on sand or muddy grounds. Breeds April-June (Celtic Sea), June-August (North Sea); eggs 0.6-0.76 mm, with oil globule; hatch at about 2.5 mm, metamorphosing at 16-30 mm. To Mauritania.

IMPERIAL SCALDFISH *Arnoglossus imperialis.* As Scaldfish, but D 95-106; A 74-82; LL 51-66; D anterior rays more or less elongated, especially in males; grey or brownish, V with dark spot, conspicuous in males. 25 cm. Offshore shelf, to 350 m. To West Africa.

A
B
C

THOR'S SCALDFISH *Arnoglossus thori.* Ⓐ Somewhat deeper outline; D with second ray elongate, fringed dark; D 81-93; A 61-69; LL 49-56; grey or brownish, with dark spots; larger dark blotch behind LL curve and near C base. 18 cm. Inshore shelf, typically on coarse grounds. Breeds April-July (Biscay). Also **Kessler's Scaldfish** *A. kessleri*, Ⓑ 10 cm, A 51-57, and **Rueppell's Scaldfish** *A. rueppelli*, Ⓒ 15 cm, D 110-118, A 86-94, elongate.

WIDE-EYED FLOUNDER *Bothus podas.* Deep outline, eyes separated by concave area and very distant in males; D 85-95; A 63-73; LL 75-86; anterior end of lateral-line forked behind eye; pale brown with dark spots. 45 cm. Inshore shallows. To West Africa. Dark brown or violet *B. p. maderensis*, from Madeira and Canaries, has LL 88-91.

female

Wide-eyed
Flounder

male

Scaldfish

Imperial Scaldfish

Thor's Scaldfish

RIGHT-EYED FLOUNDERS (Pleuronectidae)

Right side up; V bases equal; rear edge of cheek free; lateral-line on both sides. Very familiar species of great economic importance.

PLAICE *Pleuronectes platessa*. The best-known, and most important flatfish in British fisheries, immediately identified by reddish or orange spots on brown upper side, with underside white; LL 88-115, almost straight; several bony knobs between eyes; mouth small, angle opposite front edge of eye; D 65-79; A 48-59. 100 cm. Shelf, typically inshore, to over 100 m, on sandy or muddy grounds; young in shallows, larger fish in progressively deeper water; feeds, chiefly from March-October (North Sea), on crustaceans, worms and bivalves, the last especially for larger plaice which may also eat small fish. After migrating to spawning grounds, breeds December-March (southern North Sea, in 20-50 m), February-April (Irish Sea), as late as June (Murman coast); spawning occurs above sea-bed, with female across upper side of male; fecundity 16,000-345,000 in females of 22-61.5 cm; eggs 1.65-2.17 mm, yellow, without oil globule, hatching at 6.0-7.5 mm in 21-12 days at 5-10°C; eye shifts at 35-45 days, reaching final position in young of 13-14 mm. Maturity in northern North Sea at 33-39 cm, 5-6 yrs (m), 41-43 cm, 6-7 yrs (f), but in western Channel, at only 23.5-25 cm, 3 yrs (m), 16 cm, 4 yrs (f). Hybrids with Flounder and Dab in Baltic and southern North Sea.

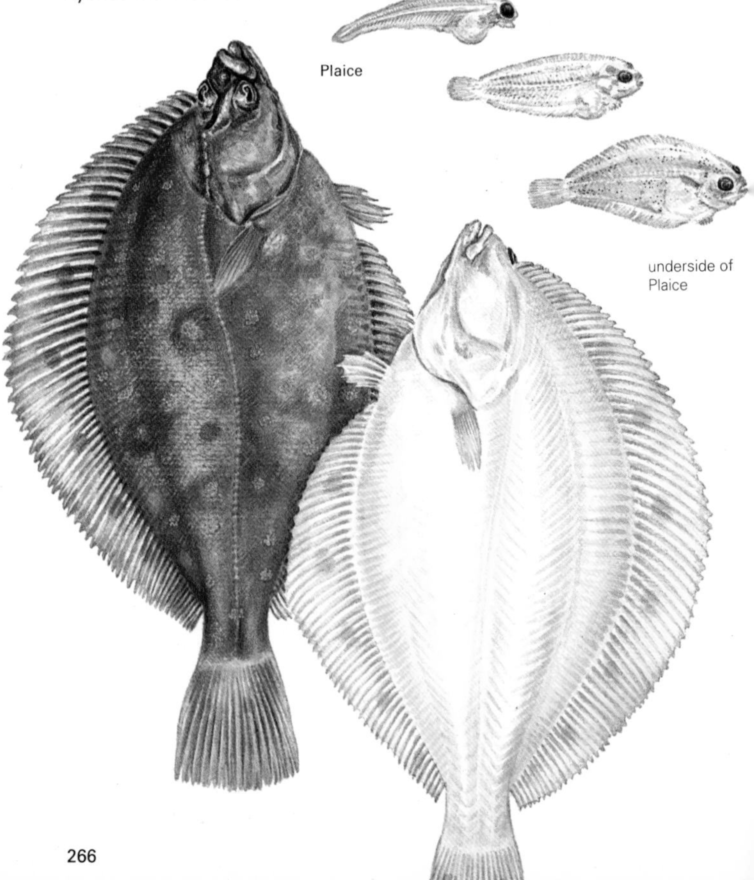

Plaice

underside of Plaice

DAB *Limanda limanda.* Widely fished, very abundant smaller flatfish; upper side with ctenoid scales, and rough texture; LL strongly curved over P; D 65-81; A 50-64; LL 73-90; sandy to brownish. 40 cm. Usually inshore, on sand; feeds on benthic invertebrates, especially crustaceans, and small fish. Breeds February-April (western Channel), April-June (northern North Sea); eggs 0.65-1.2 mm, lacking oil-globule; hatch in 6-15 days at 4-10°C, at 2.5-2.7 mm, metamorphosing by 16 mm.

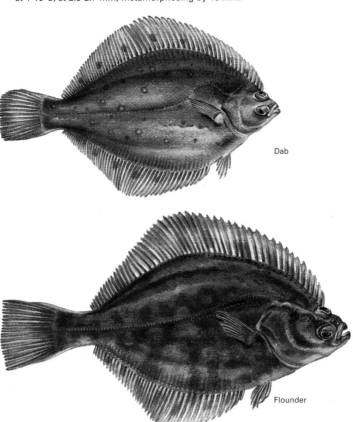

Dab

Flounder

FLOUNDER *Platichthys flesus.* Commercial fisheries in Baltic and adjoining waters, but a game flatfish for anglers anywhere; usually right side up but more frequently reversed than other species; series of spiny scales along D and A bases and flanking lateral-line (little curved); D 52-67; A 36-46; brown to greenish, often dark, sometimes speckled orange; underside very white. 50 cm, 3.5 kg; 6 yrs (a: 1.2 kg). Inshore shelf and estuaries, ascending rivers, and feeding on aquatic stages of insects. Breeds in sea January-April, and more fecund than related species (to 2 million); eggs 0.8-1.13 mm, without oil globule; hatch at 2.3-3.3 mm, metamorphosing at 10-13 mm. In sea, mature at 11 cm (m), 17 cm (f); in fresh water, may reach almost 38 cm, 5 yrs before return to sea and maturation. Hybrids with Plaice common in Baltic.

LEMON SOLE *Microstomus kitt.* An important commercial fish, especially in northern North Sea; similar to Dab but lateral-line less curved; head very small; upper side smooth; D 85-97; A 69-76; LL 110-125; brownish with irregular markings. 45 cm. Shelf, typically more offshore gravel, feeding chiefly on polychaete worms. Breeds April-July (western British Isles), May-August (Faeroes and Iceland); eggs 1.13-1.45 mm, without oil globule but black pigment on yolk; hatch at 3.5-5.5 mm.

 WITCH *Glyptocephalus cynoglossus.* More elongate body, depth at least two-fifths standard length; mouth small; lateral-line straight; D 95-120; A 85-102; LL 110-140; brown to greyish brown; D, A and P edges darker. 60 cm. Offshore shelf and uppermost slope, on muddy grounds, eating benthic invertebrates. Breeds March-May (Irish Sea); eggs 1.07-1.25 mm, without oil globule; hatch at about 4 mm. Also western Atlantic.

 LONG ROUGH DAB *Hippoglossoides platessoides.* Mouth large, angle of jaws below eye; upper surface rough; C with central rays longest; LL only slightly curved; D 76-101; A 60-79; LL 85- 97; brown. 50 cm. Shelf, more offshore in warmer areas, on finer deposits, eating chiefly brittle stars, urchins and crustaceans. Breeds March-April (Irish Sea); eggs 1.38-2.64 mm, with wide space between yolk and capsule; hatch at 4-6 mm; mature at 10-12.5 cm. Eastern Atlantic to Iceland as *H. p. limandoides*; in western Atlantic to Cape Cod as *H. p. platessoides*.

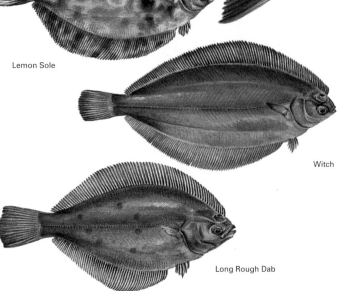

Lemon Sole

Witch

Long Rough Dab

Greenland
Halibut

Halibut

 GREENLAND HALIBUT *Reinhardtius hippoglossoides*. Similar in body form to Halibut but upper (left) eye on edge of head, and underside also dark brown or black like upper surface; jaws larger, angle below rear edge of eye; D 92-102; A 71-76; LL about 110. 100 cm. Over edge of shelf and slope, to 2,000 m, in midwater with normal orientation of body, hunting fish. Breeds April-July. Arctic basin. Long-line fisheries.

 HALIBUT *Hippoglossus hippoglossus*. Robust, long-bodied, the largest flatfish, valuable but easily overfished; mouth large, angle below eye; upper surface smooth; lateral-line curved over P; D 98-110; A 73-85; LL about 160; dark green to almost black, smaller fish with pale markings. 245 cm, 316 kg, 60 yrs (a: 115.78 kg). Shelf and slope, to 1,500 m, in cold water (2.5-8.0°C); highly predatory, probably hunting above bottom, feeding on fish, especially redfish. Breeds over slope (300-700 m), December-March (Norway and Faeroes); fecundity to several million; eggs planktonic but relatively large, 3.06-3.8 mm, hatch at 6.5-7.0 mm in 13-20 days at 4.7-7.0°C. Around Faeroes, mature at 3-8 yrs, 50-80 cm (m), 6-10 yrs, 100-130 cm (f). Also Greenland and western Atlantic.

SOLES (Soleidae)

Right side up; outline elliptical, snout rounded and mouth curved, on lower edge of head; eyes small; rear edge of cheek merged with opercle. Fisheries for larger species.

COMMON SOLE *Solea solea*. D and A united to C by membrane; upper P rear margin rounded, little larger than P of underside; D 69-97; A 53-79; LL 116-165; greyish to brown, with darker blotches; upper P with black spot; C with dark rear edge. 70 cm. Shelf, on sand and mud, nocturnal, eating benthic invertebrates. Breeds February-June (south-western British Isles), April-August (North Sea); eggs 1.0-1.6 mm, with many tiny oil globules and segmented yolk surface; hatch at 2.5-3.7 mm in 2-14 days at 7-19°C, bottom-living from 9-11 mm. To Senegal, and into Suez Canal (as nominal *S. aegyptia*). Commercial fisheries.

A ▪
B ▤
C ▥
D ▨
E ▧

SAND SOLE *Solea lascaris*. Ⓐ Similar to Common Sole, but anterior nostril of underside enlarged, rosette-shaped, as wide as eyes on upper side; brownish with many small dark spots; P dark spot edged white and yellow. 40 cm. Inshore sandy ground. Breeds late April-August (western Channel); eggs 1.28-1.38 mm, segmented yolk, and around 50 small oil globules; hatch at about 3.5 mm. Also West and southern Africa. Other soles include **Senegal Sole** *S. senegalensis*, Ⓑ 60 cm, greyish-brown with many small blue dots, P of upper side black with yellowish rays; **Klein's Sole** *S. kleinii*, Ⓒ 40 cm, brownish with white spots; P with dark blotch near root, white-edged distally; **Snouted Sole** *S. nasuta*, Ⓓ 20 cm, dark brown with many ill-defined black blotches, P with dark spot in middle of fin; and **Adriatic Sole** *S. impar*, Ⓔ 25 cm, dark brownish with blue spots, P spot white-edged (latter 2 soles may both be forms of Sand Sole).

PORTUGUESE SOLE *Synaptura lusitanica*. Elongate oval, with tapering rear; D and A united with C; D 79-83; A 57- 67; LL 100-123; greyish-brown, with dark blotches, especially along lateral midline. 35 cm. Inshore, on sand and mud. To West Africa.

WEDGE SOLE *Dicologlossa cuneata*. Similar tapering body to Portuguese Sole, but D and A connected by merely low membrane to C; LL on head in S-shaped pattern; D 77-90; A 62-78; LL 114-126; greyish to darker brown; P with dark spot in distal part of fin. 30 cm. Inshore shelf to upper slope in south. Breeds May-September (Biscay). To West and southern Africa.

SIX-EYED SOLE *Dicologlossa hexophthalma*. As Wedge Sole, but immediately recognized by 3 pairs of dark eye-spots and associated dark bands on upper side; D 61-72; A 52-56; LL 90-92. 20 cm. Inshore. To West Africa.

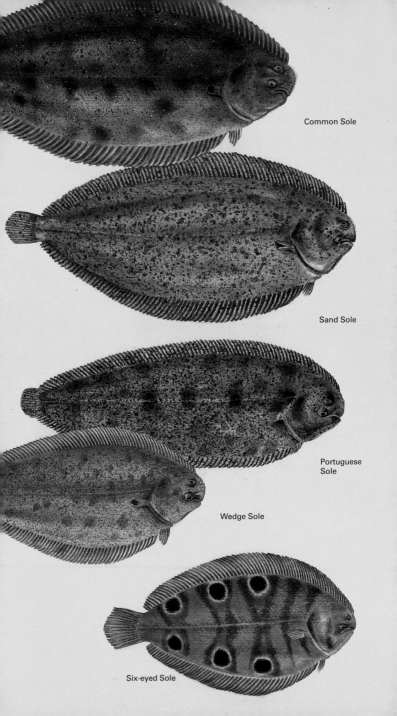

Common Sole

Sand Sole

Portuguese Sole

Wedge Sole

Six-eyed Sole

Solenette

Bastard Sole

Thick-backed Sole

A
B
C

SOLENETTE *Buglossidium luteum*. Ⓐ Tapering outline, eyes small; P of underside much smaller than upper P, latter without black spot; anterior nostril of underside not enlarged; D and A connected by membrane with C; sandy to brownish, D and C with usually every 5th-6th (4th or 7th) ray dark. 15 cm. Shelf and uppermost slope, typically 10-40 m, feeding on small invertebrates. Breeds April-August (western Channel); eggs 0.64-0.94 mm, with 12-15 evenly sized and spaced oil globules; hatch at 1.83-2.29 mm in 5-6 days, metamorphosing by 10 mm. **Deepwater Sole** *Bathysolea profundicola*, Ⓑ 21 cm, with similar reduction of underside P, is reddish brown with dark mouth; from slope to 1,300 m; to West Africa. A West African sole, *Microchirus boscanion*, Ⓒ 11 cm, also has dark rays at intervals along D and A, but these fins are not connected to C.

BASTARD SOLE *Microchirus azevia*. Long, oval outline, eyes small; LL with S-shaped part on head; P of underside much smaller than upper P; anterior nostril of underside not enlarged; D and A not connected to C; D 71-86; A 58-68; LL 107-128; greyish to brown, several eye-spots in smaller fish. 40 cm. Shelf. To Senegal; isolated record from western Channel.

THICK-BACKED SOLE *Microchirus variegatus*. As Bastard Sole, but several dark bars across brownish upper side, with corresponding dark patches on D and A; D 63-77; A 51-64; LL 70-92. 20 cm. Offshore shelf and upper slope. Breeds February-July (western Channel); eggs 1.28-1.42 mm, with about 50 evenly sized and spaced tiny oil globules; hatch at 2.4-2.88 mm.

Four-eyed Sole

Whiskered Sole

Spotted Tongue-sole

FOUR-EYED SOLE *Microchirus ocellatus*. As Thick-backed Sole, but easily identified by large dark area on anterior lateral-line, and 2 large spots adjoining both D and A; LL 66-75. 20 cm. Shelf, on softer deposits, especially sea-grass beds. To Mauritania.

WHISKERED SOLE *Monochirus hispidus*. Oval; anterior nostril on upper side tubular, reaching back to pupil of lower eye; underside lacking P; D 50-58; A 40-45; LL 52-54; greyish to brownish, with indistinct bands and spots. 20 cm. Shelf, on sand and mud. To West Africa.

A ▢
B ▨
C ▪
D ▨

TONGUE SOLES (Cynoglossidae)

SPOTTED TONGUE-SOLE *Symphurus nigrescens*. Ⓐ Left side up; body more elongate than true soles; D and A united with C; V separate from A; P minute; mouth terminal, somewhat curved; D 83-94; A 71-78; no lateral-line; brownish-grey, with or without dark spots or bars. 12 cm. Shelf and slope, on sand or muddy grounds. Breeds May-October (Mediterranean). To West Africa. Other southern species are: **Long Tongue-sole** *S. ligulatus*, Ⓑ 10 cm, more elongate, D 100-110; A 90-98; **Nigerian Tongue-sole** *Cynoglossus browni*, Ⓒ 40 cm, has snout rounded, with very inferior, strongly curved mouth, two lateral- lines (upper near D base), D 115-125, no P, and V united by membrane to A, has been recorded once from southern North Sea; and **Red Sea Tongue-sole** *C. sinusarabici*, Ⓓ 15 cm, with only one lateral line and D 99-101, a Suez Canal immigrant.

TETRAODONTIFORMS (ORDER TETRAODONTIFORMES)

Essentially warm-water, with relatively short, deep or stout bodies showing a range of unusual forms - filefish, triggerfish, pufferfish, cofferfish and sunfish. All tend to use fins for propulsion rather than body movements.

A ▪
B ▥
C ▨
D ▤

GREY TRIGGERFISH *Balistes capriscus* (**Balistidae**). Ⓐ Compressed rhomboidal body, with scales (LL 52-62); mouth small, with distinct incisor-like teeth; 2 Ds, short D1, spine II serving to lock first spine erect; V reduced to spine; greenish to bluish, fins lined or spotted pale blue. 40 cm (a: 6.15 kg). Inshore, rocky areas, or under floating objects, feeding on crustaceans and molluscs. Spawn in summer in nest-pit excavated by female; demersal eggs guarded by male. Warm Atlantic. Also tropical **Spotted Triggerfish** *B. punctatus*, Ⓑ 45 cm, spotted brown or blue, from Madeira; and **Queen Triggerfish** *B. vetula*, 50 cm (a: 5.44 kg), with 2 long blue stripes across cheek, from Azores. **Filefishes** (**Monacanthidae**), with visible D1 of 1 large serrated spine, are *Stephanolepis diaspros*, Ⓒ 25 cm, Red Sea immigrant to eastern Mediterranean, and, from tropical Atlantic, *S. hispidus*, Ⓓ 17 cm, at Madeira, and *Aluterus monoceros*, 50 cm, straying to southern Biscay.

A ▪
B ▨

PUFFERFISH *Lagocephalus lagocephalus* (**Tetraodontidae**). Ⓐ Body plump, capable of inflation with air or water; two lateral lines, separate to C; mouth small, but with large tooth-plates; two nostrils on each side of snout; scales absent but bony spines on belly; one short-based D, 14-15; grey to bluish above, white below; small fish with dark bars. 60 cm (a: 3.17 kg). Over shelf and pelagic, eating crustaceans and squid. Warm seas. *L. spadiceus*, Ⓑ 30 cm, with spines also on back, which is dark green, and D 12, is a Suez Canal migrant in eastern Mediterranean.

A ▪
B ▨
C ▧
D ▥
E ▤

BENNETT'S PUFFERFISH *Ephippion guttiferum*. Ⓐ As Pufferfish but upper lateral-line curves down to join lower above A; back with bony plates; 1 nostril on each side of snout; D 9-11; brown with white spots, paler below. 50 cm (a: 4.3 kg). Inshore shelf, on muddy ground; feeds on benthic invertebrates. To West Africa, once from Biscay. Infrequent warm Atlantic puffers are: *Sphoeroides spengleri*, Ⓑ 30 cm, with 2 nostrils on each side of snout, 1 lateral line, row of large black spots along lower part of head and body; **Smooth Pufferfish** *S. pachygaster*, Ⓒ 24 cm, similar but with smooth skin and no spots; and *Canthigaster rostrata*, 10 cm, back ridged, no lateral line, brownish with small white dots and blue lines from eye. Two **Porcupine Fishes** (**Diodontidae**), with prominent spines and single fused tooth-plate in upper and lower jaws, also straying from tropical Atlantic, are: *Chilomycterus atringa*, Ⓓ 50 cm, with stout upright spines, horizontal back profile, brown with black spots and dark blotch on flank; and *Diodon hystrix*, Ⓔ 90 cm, with slender spines, erect when body is inflated. A recent Suez immigrant, **Trunkfish** *Tetrasomus gibbosus* (**Ostraciidae**), encased in a coffer of bony plates, has toxic flesh.

Pufferfish inflated

Grey
Triggerfish

Pufferfish

Bennett's Pufferfish

A ▓
B ▨

OCEAN SUNFISH *Mola mola* (**Molidae**). Ⓐ Enormous oceanic fishes, the heaviest teleost, at 300 cm and 1.5 tonnes. Deep, compressed bodies, ending abruptly after high D and A with a vertical 'false' C, actually derived from D and A parts; skin very thick, reputedly proof against a .22-calibre bullet, and overlies a fibrous connective tissue up to 2.5 cm thick; small mouth with tooth-plates; lateral-line absent; brownish-grey, silvery. Sluggish swimmers and drifters; epipelagic and down to 350 m, feed on invertebrates and possibly seaweed. Exceptionally fecund (300 million eggs at 150 cm); 3 stages in development of young, last formerly regarded as distinct genus. Another sunfish of similar shape, *Masturus lanceolatus*, 300 cm, silvery-blue with silver spots, with middle of 'C' somewhat elongated, is reported from the Azores. **Truncated Sunfish** *Ranzania laevis*, Ⓑ is a smaller sunfish, body much longer, and mouth almost vertical, slit-like; hexagonal bony plates over body; dark blue above, with silvery bars. 80 cm. Oceanic, epipelagic, often in schools; very spiny developmental stage. Warm seas.

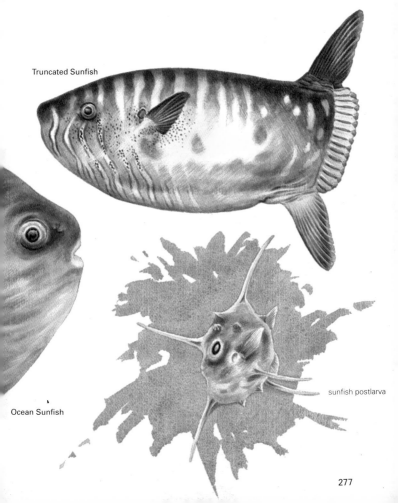

Truncated Sunfish

Ocean Sunfish

sunfish postlarva

Glossary

Abdomen In fish, the body between pectoral fins and anus; pelvic fins situated well behind the level of the pectorals are said to be abdominal.

Abyssal Deep-sea, beyond the foot of the continental slope (>2000 m).

Adipose fin Small fin lacking rays between the dorsal and caudal fins.

Anadromy Migration from the sea into fresh water (*see also* catadromy).

Arctic Relating to waters whose mean summer maximum temperature is <10°C; the north Atlantic European boundaries are north-east Iceland and North Cape, Norway.

Barbels Elongate processes from the head and jaws associated with sensory functions.

Base For a median fin, measured from the root of the first to that of the last ray; in general, the root of a fin.

Bathymetric Relating to water depth.

Bathypelagic Living in the deep-sea water column below 2,000 m.

Benthic Bottom-living.

Benthopelagic Living immediately above the bed of the deep sea.

Bifid Divided into two parts.

Bioluminescence Light produced by living organisms.

Boreal Marine distribution from North Cape, Norway, to the Celtic Sea; essentially the cold-temperate waters of the eastern Atlantic.

Branchiostegal rays Bony rays below the gill cover, supporting a branchiostegal membrane as a continuation of the gill cover under the head to enclose the lower opening of the gill chamber.

Breast Underside of the body in front of the pelvic fins.

Buccal Pertaining to the mouth.

Calcified Impregnated with calcium carbonate, not bone (calcium phosphate).

Cartilaginous Skeleton of cartilage, a softer supporting tissue than bone.

Catadromy Migration from fresh water to the sea (*see also* anadromy).

Caudal Pertaining to the tail region (post-anal body), or the tail fin.

Caudal peduncle That part of the body between the bases of the dorsal and anal fins and the base of the caudal fin.

Celtic Sea Sea area south of Ireland and west of the English Channel.

Circumpolar Around the shores of the Arctic Ocean.

Claspers Intromittent organs of male cartilaginous fishes.

Cloaca Common opening for anus, urinary and reproductive organs, found in cartilaginous fish but not in teleosts.

Compressed Flattened from side to side, in contrast to dorso-ventral flattening.

Corselet Areas of retained or modified scales on the anterior body of tunas.

Ctenoid Scales whose free rear edges are fringed with tiny spines (cteni).

Cusp The pointed part of a tooth.

Cycloid Scales whose free edges are smooth.

Deep-sea Beyond edge of continental shelf and below uppermost 200 m of ocean water column.

Demersal Occurring on or in conjunction with the sea bed.

Denticles Small tooth-like structures, notably in the skin of cartilaginous fishes.

Depressed Flattened dorso-ventrally in contrast to lateral compression.

Dextral Flatfish swimming on left side, right side up (*see also* sinistral).

Dimorphism Two forms of a species, typically the two sexes.

Disc Flattened body and pectoral fins of a skate or ray.

Dorsal Upper side of body.

Dorsal fin Median fin or fins along back.

Dorsolateral Between midlines of back and side.

Dorsoventral Between lateral midline and that of underside.

Endemic Confined to a particular region.

Epipelagic Living in the uppermost 200 m of the sea beyond the limits of the continental shelf.

Euryhaline Able to tolerate a wide range of salinities.

Falcate/falciform Shaped like a scythe.

Fecundity The number of eggs or offspring in a spawning or brood.

Filament A thin process from the skin.

Finlets Small fins located behind the dorsal and anal fins, with fin-rays.

Fusiform Shaped like a spindle.

Gape Mouth width.

Gill arch Skeletal support for the gills.

Gill rakers Horny processes fringing the inner edges of the gill arches.

Gonad A reproductive organ – testis or ovary – producing sex cells (gametes).

Hypersaline Salinity greater than that of seawater.

Imbricate Overlapping like the tiles on a roof.

Incisor A chisel-like tooth.

Infraorbital Below the eye (also suborbital).

Interorbital Between the eyes.

Isthmus The underside of head between branchiostegal membranes.

Jaw angle The joint between upper and lower jaws; its position relative to the eye may be used in descriptions.

Jugular Pelvic fins arising in advance of the vertical of the pectoral fin root.

Juvenile The life stage between metamorphosis and sexual maturity.

Keels Ridges along enlarged scales or along the caudal peduncle.

Larvae Young fish newly hatched and retaining the yolk-sac.

Longitudinal Along the body.

Low-Arctic The region or a distribution around the southern boundary of the Arctic basin.

Lunate Shaped like a half moon.

Lusitanian Distribution in the warm temperate eastern Atlantic, from the Celtic Sea to the Straits of Gibraltar.

Maxilla The rear bone of the upper jaw.

Medial Towards the midline of the body.

Meristic Relating to countable serial features, such as fin rays, scales in lateral series and vertebrae.

Mesopelagic Referring to the oceanic water-column from 200 to 1,000 m.

Metamorphosis The change from post-larval to juvenile form.

Molariform Referring to a flattened tooth.

Nacreous Pearl-like.

Naked No scales.

Nape The rear dorsal area of the head.

Nekton Swimming animals of the water column.

Neritic Relating to a water-column habitat.

Nictitating membrane A membrane which can be drawn across the eye in cartilaginous fishes.

Oceanic Waters beyond the continental shelf.

Opercle The gill cover.

Origin The point of origin of a fin is the position of the root of the first ray in the case of a median fin, or the position of the fin-base of the caudal and paired fins.

Otolith An ear-stone, a crystalline calcareous structure within the inner ear.

Oviparous Egg-laying.

Ovipositor A tube through which eggs are deposited.

Ovoviviparity Livebearing, but with the young nourished mostly from yolk already in the egg at fertilization.

Pectoral Relating to the anterior paired fins, corresponding to the forelimbs of land vertebrates.

Pelagic Occurring in the ocean water column.

Pelvic Relating to the rear paired fins, equivalent to the hindlimbs of land vertebrates.

Peritoneum The lining of the abdominal cavity.

Pharyngeal teeth Teeth on the rear gill arches.

Photophores Organs emitting light.

Postlarva A young fish with yolk sac absorbed but prior to metamorphosis.

Predorsal Relating to the back between the origin of the dorsal fin and the rear boundary of the head.

Preopercle The rear edge of the cheek, before the opercle.

Prolarva See larva.

Protandry Hermaphroditism in which the male phase functions before that of the female.

Protogyny Hermaphroditism in which the female phase precedes that of the male.

Pyloric caeca Blind tubes at the start of the intestine in teleosts.

Rays Bony structures supporting the fins.

Relicts Species' populations isolated after contraction of the original area of distribution.

Salinity The dissolved mineral content of water.

Scale Small bony plate in the skin of a fish.

School A coordinated grouping of fish, the present term being used in preference to 'shoal'.

Shelf The shallow continental margin surrounding a land mass, down to about 200 m.

Sinistral Flatfish swimming on the right side, left side up (*see also* dextral).

Slope The steep slope from the outer edge of the continental shelf to the abyssal plain of the deep sea, from 200 to about 2,000 m.

Snout Front of head between anterior edge of eye and tip of upper jaw.

Soft ray An articulated (segmented) fin ray, usually branched (indicated by Arabic numerals).

Spatulate Shaped like a spoon.

Spinous ray A fin ray, usually stiff, without joints or branches (indicated by Roman numerals).

Spiracle A small aperture behind the eye in cartilaginous fishes derived from a gill slit.

Standard length Fish length from the tip of the snout to the base of the caudal fin.

Subhorizontal Almost horizontal.

Sublittoral Relating to the sea immediately below extreme low water of tides.

Suborbital Below the eye (also infraorbital).

Subspecies A regional population of a species, intergrading with others.

Subterminal Slightly below the tip of the head.

Symbiotic Living with another organism in mutual benefit.

Tail wrist The body constriction immediately before the base of the caudal fin.

Thoracic Describing pelvic fins situated below the vertical of the pectoral fin root.

Tongue The projection from the floor of the mouth in fish, representing a median junction of gill arches and not comparable to the mobile mammalian tongue.

Total length Fish length from the tip of the snout to the tip of the caudal fin.

Transverse Across the long axis of the body.

Truncate With a straight vertical edge.

Tubercles Small protuberances.

Ventral Referring to the underside of the body.

Viviparity Livebearing, with the embryos nourished before birth via a placenta-like structure.

Vomer A bone in the midline of the anterior roof of the mouth which may carry teeth.

Watercolumn The water mass between bottom and surface.

West Balkanian The endemic fauna of fresh waters along the western Balkan Peninsula from Greece to Slovenia.

Wings The enlarged pectoral fins of skates and rays.

Yolk sac A sac containing the nutritive yolk for developing or larval fish.

Further Reading

There are innumerable books and articles on all aspects of fish identification and biology. The following provides a lead in to further reading about the fish and topics in this book.

Classification
The standard text is J. S. Nelson's *Fishes of the World* (Wiley, 3rd ed., 1994).

Biology
A comprehensive summary of form and function is given by Q. Bone, N. B. Marshall & J. H. S. Blaxter, *Biology of Fishes* (Blackie, 2nd ed., 1995) while ecology is treated by R. J. Wootton *Ecology of Teleost Fishes* (Chapman & Hall, 1990). A long series of technical volumes on *Fish Physiology* is published by Academic Press.

Marine Fish
The essential source for identification is *The Fishes of the North Atlantic and Mediterranean*, edited by P. J. P. Whitehead, M. L. Bauchot, J. C. Hureau, J. Nielsen & E. Tortonese (3 vols, UNESCO, 1984-86), with detailed synonymy in J. C. Hureau & T. Monod (eds), *Check List of the Fishes of the Eastern North Atlantic and Mediterranean* (2 vols, revised impression, UNESCO, 1979).

For British species, the major accounts are A. C. Wheeler's *Fishes of Great Britain and North-west Europe* (Macmillan, 1969), and F. S. Russell's *The Eggs and Planktonic Stages of British Marine Fishes* (Academic Press, 1976).

For adjoining waters, there is A. P. Andriashev's *Fishes of the Northern Seas of the USSR* (Israel Program for Scientific Translations, 1964), while temperate western Atlantic species are included in J. & G. Lythgoe's *Fishes of the Sea* (Blandford, 1991).

For the Black Sea fauna, see A. N. Svetovidov's *Fishes of the Black Sea* (1964).

Tropical species of the eastern Atlantic are listed in J. C. Quero, J. C. Hureau, C. Karrer, A. Post & L. Saldanha (eds), *Check List of the Fishes of the Eastern Tropical Atlantic* (3 vols, Lisbon: JNICT and UNESCO, 1990) and commercial species identified in W. Fischer, G. Bianchi & W. B. Scott (eds), *FAO Species Identification Sheets: Eastern Central Atlantic* (vols 1-5 and 7, 1981).

For Indo-Pacific tropical species and possible Suez Canal immigrants, E. Lieske and R. Myers provide a comprehensive pocket guide to *Coral Reef Fishes* (HarperCollins, 1994).

Freshwater Fish
The basic reference for Europe is the German text by W. Ladiges & D. Vogt, *Die Süsswasserfische Europas bis zum Ural und Kaspischen Meer* (2nd ed., Paul Parey, 1979).

A series of nine volumes, *The Freshwater Fishes of Europe*, to be published in English by AULA-Verlag, Wiesbaden, so far comprises J. Holčik (ed.), *Petromyzontiformes* (1/I, 1986) and *General Introduction to Fishes. Acipenseriformes* (1/II, 1989), H. Hoestlandt (ed.), *Clupeidae, Anguillidae* (2, 1991), and J. Holčik, *Endangered Fishes of Europe* (9, 1987).

For the British Isles, there is the New Naturalist *Freshwater Fishes of the British Isles* by P S. Maitland & R. N. Campbell (HarperCollins, 1992).

A selection of species from the vast freshwater fish fauna of what used to be the USSR is included in the present guide; the basic reference for this is still L. S. Berg's *Freshwater Fishes of the USSR and Adjacent Countries* (3 vols, Israel Program for Scientific Translations, 1965).

The systematics of freshwater fish in southern Europe needs much investigation; many are illustrated by A. J. Crivelli, *The Freshwater Fish endemic to the northern Mediterranean Region* (Tour du Valat, 1996). Two important monographs are I. Doadrio, B. Elvira & Y. Bernat, *Peces Continentales Españoles* (ICONA, Madrid, 1991) and G. Gandolfi, S. Zerunian, P. Torricelli & A. Marconato, *I Pesci delle Acque Interne Italiane* (Istituto Poligrafico e Zecca, Roma, 1991).

Further references, books and articles dealing with more specialized topics, local faunas, or particular groups of fish, can be found through abstracting periodicals such as the *Zoological Record*, *Biological Abstracts* and *Aquatic Science and Fisheries Abstracts*. These and other sources may be accessible via computer networks and Web sites.

Index

287